NAUGHT IS LIKE UNTO HIM

DIVINE TRANSCENDENCE IN ISLAMIC THOUGHT

Hakim Ibn Adam

Centre for Studies in Matter, Mind, and Meaning

threerosespublishing.com

ISBN: 978-1-9990656-5-2

AUTHOR'S NOTE

This is a publication of the "Centre for Studies in Matter, Mind, and Meaning", a division of Three Roses Publishing. The Centre's mission is to produce scholarly work that integrates scientific inquiry, philosophical analysis, and spiritual reflection.

CONTENTS

DEDICATION

To the Mystery that remains when reason's work is done.

PREFACE

This study emerges from years of engagement with the rich intellectual heritage of Islam, seeking to understand how Muslim thinkers across centuries have approached the Quranic declaration that "naught is like unto Him" (laysa kamithlihi shay'un). In undertaking this work, I have been guided by a profound respect for the traditional sources and methodologies that have shaped Islamic thought, while attempting to provide a systematic analysis of patterns that have long been present within this tradition.

It is crucial to state at the outset what this work does and does not claim to do. This is not an attempt to introduce new theological concepts or to impose foreign frameworks upon Islamic thought. Rather, it is an effort to articulate systematically certain patterns of theological and mystical expression that have appeared consistently throughout Islamic intellectual history. What may appear as theoretical innovation is, in fact, careful observation and analysis of methods that classical scholars employed—often intuitively—when grappling with the ultimate mystery of divine transcendence. The great masters of Islamic thought, from the earliest exegetes to the philosophical theologians to the mystical writers, have consistently faced the challenge of expressing the inexpressible: how to speak meaningfully about the Divine while preserving the truth that nothing resembles Him. In their varied responses to this challenge, certain recurring patterns emerge—patterns that this study seeks to identify and examine.

In preparing this work, I have endeavored to ground every significant claim in the primary sources of Islamic tradition. The reader will find citations from the Quran and its major classical commentaries (tafsīr), authenticated hadith collections and their scholarly expositions, the works of major theologians (mutakallimūn) from all major schools, classical philosophical texts from the falāsifa tradition, the writings of recognized Sufi masters and their authenticated teachings, and the responses of orthodox scholars to various theological positions. Where I have identified patterns of complementary opposition or apparent paradox in theological expression, these observations arise from the texts themselves rather than from any predetermined theoretical framework. The terminology I employ seeks to describe phenomena clearly present in the sources rather than to impose external categories that might distort the tradition's own self-understanding.

Any study of Islamic intellectual history must necessarily be selective, given the vast ocean of scholarship produced over fourteen centuries. I acknowledge that my selection of sources reflects certain emphases. The study focuses on figures and texts that explicitly engaged with the philosophical and mystical dimensions of divine transcendence, giving attention to thinkers who developed sophisticated theoretical frameworks for understanding divine incomparability, while including voices from diverse schools and periods to demonstrate the persistence of certain patterns across different contexts. This selectivity is not intended to marginalize other important voices or to suggest that the patterns identified represent the only valid approaches within Islamic thought. Rather, it reflects the specific focus of this study on how Muslim thinkers have navigated the apparent tensions that arise when finite human language and concepts encounter infinite divine reality.

Some readers may be concerned that systematic analysis of paradoxical patterns in Islamic thought constitutes unwarranted innovation (bid'a). This concern deserves a serious response. The Islamic tradition has always distinguished between praiseworthy systematization that clarifies and preserves traditional teachings and blameworthy innovation that introduces foreign elements. This study firmly situates itself within the former category. Consider the precedent of Imam al-Ghazali, who systematized Sufi teachings within an orthodox framework, or the Ash'arite theologians who developed sophisticated methodologies to defend traditional beliefs. These scholars were not innovating in the sense of introducing new beliefs; they were providing a systematic articulation of truths already present within the tradition. This study follows their methodological precedent, seeking to make explicit what has long been implicit in how the tradition has functioned.

Throughout this work, I have been mindful of the traditional safeguards that Islamic scholarship has developed. These include maintaining the absolute distinction between Creator and creation that lies at the heart of Islamic monotheism, preserving the authority of revelation over human speculation so that reason serves rather than displaces scriptural guidance, respecting the limits of human reason when approaching divine mystery and acknowledging that some realities exceed rational comprehension, and acknowledging the diversity of legitimate interpretive approaches within orthodox bounds without requiring uniformity where the tradition itself permits diversity. At the same time, I believe that a systematic understanding of how classical Islamic thinkers approached divine transcendence offers valuable resources for contemporary challenges. These include interfaith dialogue that requires a sophisticated understanding of one's own tradition before meaningful engagement with others becomes possible, philosophical challenges that demand intellectually rigorous responses rather than mere assertion or defensive posturing, the need to articulate Islamic teachings in contemporary academic contexts where traditional forms of discourse may not communicate effectively, and the spiritual needs of Muslims seeking a deeper understanding of their intellectual heritage beyond simplified presentations.

This study, like all human endeavors to understand the Divine, remains fundamentally limited. The patterns identified here are offered not as an exhaustive truth but as one systematic attempt to understand how Islamic tradition has preserved the central mystery of divine transcendence. Other scholars may identify different patterns or offer alternative systematizations. Such diversity of approach has always been a strength of the Islamic intellectual tradition, with multiple valid perspectives enriching rather than fragmenting the whole. I submit this work with full recognition that the ultimate reality of which it speaks—the Divine who is "naught is like unto Him"—infinitely exceeds all attempts at systematic understanding. If this study helps readers appreciate the sophistication with which Islamic thinkers have approached this ultimate mystery and if it provides resources for continued faithful engagement with these questions, it will have achieved its purpose.

Finally, I invoke the traditional scholarly prayer that has concluded works of Islamic learning for centuries: whatever is correct in this work comes from Allah's guidance through the inherited wisdom of Islamic tradition; whatever errors remain are from my own limitations. I seek refuge in Allah from speaking about Him without knowledge, and I ask His forgiveness for any shortcomings in this attempt to understand how His servants have approached His transcendent reality. May this work serve those who seek to know their Lord better through understanding how the scholars and saints of Islam have articulated the principle that nothing whatsoever resembles Him.

INTRODUCTION

In the forty-second surah of the Quran, within a passage describing the divine creative power, appears a brief declaration that has profoundly shaped Islamic thought for over fourteen centuries: "laysa kamithlihi shay'un"—"naught is like unto Him" (42:11). These words encapsulate one of Islam's most fundamental theological principles while simultaneously presenting one of its greatest intellectual challenges. How can human beings, bound by finite language and limited understanding, speak meaningfully about a Reality that admits no comparison? How can theological discourse proceed when its very Subject transcends all categories of thought and expression?

This question is not merely theoretical. It touches the heart of Islamic worship, theology, philosophy, and mystical experience. From the earliest Quranic exegetes to contemporary Muslim thinkers, the challenge of preserving divine incomparability while enabling authentic religious understanding has generated a remarkably rich tradition of theological reflection. This study examines that tradition, seeking to identify and analyze the recurring patterns through which Muslim scholars have navigated this fundamental tension.

The Quranic assertion of divine incomparability appears in Surah al-Shura (42:11) within a verse of profound theological density: "The Creator of the heavens and the earth. He has made for you from yourselves, mates, and among the cattle, mates; He multiplies you thereby. Naught is like unto Him, and He is the All-Hearing, the All-Seeing." The Arabic construction "laysa kamithlihi shay'un" employs a double emphasis that intensifies the negation. The particle "laysa" categorically negates, while "ka-mithli-hi" (like-His-likeness) creates a comparative structure that is then absolutely denied by "shay'un" (anything). Early grammarians and exegetes noted that this construction goes beyond simple negation to establish absolute incomparability.

Al-Tabari (d. 310/923), in his monumental Quranic commentary, reports multiple early authorities who understood this verse as establishing a fundamental principle ('asl) for all theological discourse. Ibn 'Abbas, the Prophet's cousin and renowned interpreter of the Quran, is reported to have said: "This verse is the foundation of tawhid (divine unity)—it negates from Allah all resemblance to His creation." The verse's immediate context is significant. It follows an affirmation of divine creative power and precedes the attribution of divine names (All-Hearing, All-Seeing). This placement suggests a methodological principle: even as we affirm divine attributes and actions, we must maintain consciousness of divine incomparability. The classical exegete al-Zamakhshari (d. 538/1144) observed that the verse "establishes the rule (qa'ida) by which all other divine descriptions must be understood."

Yet this very principle creates what we might call the fundamental challenge of Islamic theology. If nothing resembles Allah, how can any human language—drawn inevitably from created experience—meaningfully refer to Him? If He is All-Hearing and All-Seeing, but not as creatures hear and see, what content remains in these descriptions? The Quran itself employs numerous divine names and attributes, uses anthropomorphic language, and describes divine actions. How are these to be understood in light of absolute divine incomparability? The history of Islamic thought can be read, in large part, as a series of increasingly sophisticated responses to this fundamental challenge. Each major school and figure has contributed distinctive insights while grappling with the same underlying question: how to preserve divine transcendence without rendering religious discourse meaningless.

The Companions and Successors (Sahaba and Tabi'in) established interpretive principles that would guide later reflection during the early period. When asked about apparently anthropomorphic verses, they often responded with formulations that affirmed the scriptural language while denying crude literalism. Imam Malik's (d. 179/795) famous response regarding divine "establishment on the Throne" (istiwa') became paradigmatic: "The establishment is known, the 'how' is unknown, believing in it is obligatory, and asking about it is innovation." This early approach established several enduring principles. Scriptural language about God must be accepted as authoritative. The mode or manner (kayfiyya) of divine attributes transcends human understanding and cannot be subjected to speculative inquiry. Faith requires accepting mystery alongside meaning, refusing to dissolve the former into the latter. Speculative questioning beyond appropriate bounds can lead to error and innovation. These principles would shape all subsequent theological development.

As Islamic theology (kalam) developed into a systematic discipline, different schools emerged with distinctive approaches to divine incomparability. The Mu'tazilites emphasized rational demonstration of divine unity, interpreting all apparently anthropomorphic language metaphorically to preserve God's absolute transcendence and justice. Their commitment to "divine justice and unity" led them to develop sophisticated philosophical arguments, though later critics argued they had reduced divine transcendence to rational categories, subordinating revelation to reason. The Ash'arites developed the famous "bila kayf" (without asking how) methodology, affirming divine attributes while systematically negating any resemblance to created attributes. Al-Ash'ari (d. 324/936) and his followers sought to preserve both scriptural authority and divine transcendence through a methodology that acknowledged the limits of human understanding while refusing to reduce divine attributes to mere metaphors. The Maturidites developed nuanced positions that sought to balance rational theology with traditional affirmation, contributing sophisticated discussions about the relationship between divine essence and attributes that would influence centuries of subsequent thought and providing alternatives to both Mu'tazilite rationalism and strict traditionalist literalism.

Muslim philosophers (falasifa) brought Greek philosophical tools to bear on the question of divine incomparability with impressive sophistication. Al-Farabi (d. 339/950) and Ibn Sina (d. 428/1037) developed elaborate metaphysical systems demonstrating divine transcendence through the concept of "necessary existence," distinguishing God as the only being whose essence and existence are identical. Yet al-Ghazali (d. 505/1111) would later argue that their rational systems ultimately failed to preserve authentic divine transcendence, leading to his famous critique in "The Incoherence of the Philosophers" that challenged whether purely philosophical approaches could adequately grasp the living God of religious experience.

The Sufi tradition contributed perhaps the most profound insights into divine incomparability through direct spiritual experience. Figures like al-Junayd (d. 298/910), al-Hallaj (d. 309/922), and supremely Ibn 'Arabi (d. 638/1240) developed sophisticated frameworks for understanding how the Incomparable could be experienced by the finite. Their expressions often took forms that appeared paradoxical, speaking of union and separation, presence and absence, knowledge and unknowing as simultaneous realities. These apparent contradictions were not logical failures but attempts to express experiences that transcended ordinary categories of thought and language.

Perhaps most remarkably, Islamic tradition has generally not seen these various approaches as mutually exclusive. Major figures like al-Ghazali integrated Ash'arite theology, philosophical reasoning, and Sufi experience in comprehensive syntheses that drew strength from each approach. Later thinkers like Fakhr al-Din al-Razi (d. 606/1210) produced vast syntheses that drew from all available intellectual resources while maintaining fidelity to scriptural foundations. This capacity for integration rather than forcing choice between approaches demonstrates the tradition's remarkable intellectual sophistication and theological maturity.

This study undertakes a systematic examination of how Muslim thinkers across these various schools and approaches have addressed the challenge of divine incomparability. In surveying this vast tradition, certain recurring patterns emerge—patterns that suggest underlying commonalities in how finite human consciousness encounters and expresses the Infinite. The study identifies recurring patterns that appear across diverse schools and periods despite differences in terminology and emphasis. These include the use of complementary opposites in divine description, where apparently contradictory attributes are held simultaneously in creative tension; the preservation of mystery within affirmation, whereby positive statements about God are made while maintaining that ultimate divine reality exceeds all formulation; the transcendence of ordinary logical categories, recognizing that divine reality cannot be captured by either-or thinking; and the integration of rational and super-rational approaches, employing reason while acknowledging its necessary limits.

Rather than imposing external frameworks, this study analyzes the methods Muslim scholars themselves developed and employed, seeking to understand their internal logic and effectiveness. By examining how these methods functioned within their original contexts and how they were adapted across different schools and periods, we gain insight into the tradition's own self-understanding. Despite apparent differences between schools—Ash'arite versus Mu'tazilite, philosopher versus theologian, mystic versus jurist—this study reveals underlying continuities in how Muslim thinkers have preserved divine transcendence while enabling meaningful religious discourse. These continuities suggest that beneath surface disagreements lies a shared commitment to certain fundamental principles and methods. By understanding these traditional patterns, we gain resources for addressing contemporary challenges in theology, interfaith dialogue, and religious understanding that face Muslims navigating modern intellectual and spiritual contexts.

This study does not introduce new doctrines. All patterns identified are drawn from the tradition itself, with the contribution lying in systematic analysis and explicit articulation rather than doctrinal innovation. What may appear novel is simply the systematic identification of methods that classical scholars employed intuitively. While necessarily selective in its source material, this study seeks to appreciate insights from various Islamic intellectual traditions without suggesting that any one approach is exclusively valid or that patterns identified exhaust the tradition's richness. The patterns identified often involve maintaining productive tensions rather than achieving systematic resolution. This reflects the tradition's own recognition that divine incomparability exceeds human systematization, with mystery remaining essential to authentic theology.

In undertaking this analysis, several methodological principles have guided the work to ensure fidelity to sources and fairness in interpretation. Every significant claim is grounded in primary sources, with extensive citation allowing readers to verify interpretations and engage directly with classical texts. Thinkers and texts are understood within their historical contexts while recognizing trans-historical patterns that appear across different periods and regions. Each approach is presented in its strongest form, seeking to understand its internal logic before critical evaluation, avoiding the common error of critiquing caricatures rather than engaging genuine positions. While respecting the integrity of individual thinkers and their distinctive contributions, the study seeks to identify patterns that may not have been explicitly recognized by any single figure but emerge from comparative analysis across the tradition.

To make this study accessible while maintaining scholarly precision, certain conventions regarding transliteration and terminology require explanation. This study follows a simplified version of the International Journal of Middle East Studies (IJMES) transliteration system. Long vowels are indicated by ā for alif when long, with ' representing hamza and ' representing 'ayn. The definite article appears without indication of sun letters for simplicity, and common names and terms follow conventional English spellings, with Quran preferred to Qur'ān for accessibility to general readers.

Throughout this study, certain Arabic technical terms appear frequently, requiring familiarity for full comprehension. Among theological terms, tawhid refers to divine unity as the fundamental principle of Islamic monotheism. Tanzih denotes transcendence, declaring God free from creaturely attributes, while tashbih indicates immanence or affirming similarity when properly balanced with tanzih. Sifat are divine attributes, with dhat referring to divine essence. The phrase bila kayf means "without asking how," accepting divine descriptions without speculating on their mode.

Philosophical terminology includes wujud for existence or being, mahiyya for quiddity or essence, and wajib al-wujud for necessary existence as applied uniquely to God. Mumkin refers to the possible or contingent, encompassing all created being. Mystical terms prove particularly important for understanding Sufi contributions. Ma'rifa denotes gnosis or experiential knowledge of the Divine, distinguished from intellectual knowledge. Fana' refers to annihilation or ego-dissolution in spiritual experience, with baqa' indicating subsistence or continuing through divine reality after annihilation. Tajalli means divine self-disclosure, while wahdat al-wujud refers to unity of being or existence as articulated especially by Ibn 'Arabi and his followers.

Methodological terms locate discussions within specific disciplinary traditions. Kalam refers to Islamic theology as a systematic discipline employing rational argumentation. Falsafa denotes Islamic philosophy influenced by Greek philosophical traditions. Tasawwuf encompasses Islamic mysticism or Sufism as a comprehensive spiritual tradition. Ta'wil means interpretive explanation, often non-literal, especially of anthropomorphic verses. Tafsir refers to Quranic exegesis more broadly, including linguistic, historical, and theological commentary.

This introduction has sought to establish the scriptural foundation, historical development, and contemporary relevance of the question that animates this entire study: How have Muslim thinkers preserved and expressed the fundamental truth that "naught is like unto Him?" The chapters that follow examine this question through multiple lenses—theological, philosophical, mystical, and practical—revealing the remarkable sophistication and enduring relevance of Islamic reflection on divine transcendence across fourteen centuries of intellectual engagement with the ultimate mystery.

Chapter 1. "Naught is like unto Him" Scriptural Contexts and Classical Exegesis

The principle of divine incomparability finds its clearest Quranic articulation in the phrase "laysa kamithlihi shay'un" (naught is like unto Him), yet this declaration appears within a rich scriptural context that shapes its meaning and implications. This chapter examines how the Quran establishes divine incomparability not as an isolated theological assertion but as a comprehensive principle that pervades the entire scriptural discourse. Through careful analysis of the verse's immediate context, its relationship to other Quranic passages, and the earliest interpretive traditions, we can observe how Muslim scholars from the beginning recognized both the centrality and the complexity of maintaining divine transcendence within religious discourse.

The declaration "laysa kamithlihi shay'un" appears in Sūrat al-Shūrā (42:11), a Meccan sūra that addresses fundamental aspects of divine nature and revelation. The full verse presents a carefully constructed theological statement: "Fāṭir al-samāwāti wa-l-arḍ ja'ala lakum min anfusikum azwājan wa-min al-an'āmi azwājan yadhara'ukum fīhi laysa kamithlihi shay'un wa-huwa al-samī' al-baṣīr" (The Creator of the heavens and the earth. He has made for you from yourselves, mates, and among the cattle, mates; He multiplies you thereby. Naught is like unto Him, and He is the All-Hearing, the All-Seeing).

The verse's structure reveals sophisticated theological teaching through its careful arrangement, as al-Ṭabarī (d. 310/923) notes in his Jāmi' al-bayān.

The passage begins with divine creative action (Fāṭir), proceeds through created multiplicity—human and animal pairs—then declares absolute divine incomparability before concluding with divine attributes. According to al-Ṭabarī, this structure teaches that "the Creator's absolute distinction from creation must be understood precisely in the context of His creative power and His attributes." The progression is deliberate: the verse establishes God's role as Creator, demonstrates His power through the multiplication of created beings, asserts His radical difference from all creation, and then affirms His knowledge of creation through the attributes of hearing and seeing.

Al-Zamakhsharī (d. 538/1144) provides a detailed grammatical analysis in al-Kashshāf, observing that the emphatic construction "laysa kamithlihi" employs what grammarians term "ta'kīd al-nafy" (emphatic negation). The doubling of comparison in the phrase ka-mithli intensifies the negation beyond what a simpler construction would convey. As al-Zamakhsharī writes, "It is as if the verse says: 'There is nothing that resembles even a resemblance of Him.'" This linguistic observation proved significant for later theological discussions about the nature and degree of divine transcendence, as it suggested that the Quran employs the most forceful possible negation of similarity between Creator and creation.

The placement of this verse within Sūrat al-Shūrā carries additional significance. Ibn Kathīr (d. 774/1373) observes that this sūra, named "Consultation," addresses the relationship between divine sovereignty and human agency. The verse appears after discussions of revelation in verse 42:7 and before elaboration of divine attributes in verses 42:12-13, suggesting that proper understanding of divine incomparability is essential for comprehending both how God reveals Himself to humanity and how He acts in the world. This contextual placement indicates that divine transcendence is not merely an abstract theological principle but the foundation for understanding God's relationship with creation.

Early Arabic linguists paid meticulous attention to each element of the phrase, recognizing that divine incomparability required the most precise possible expression. Al-Farrā' (d. 207/822) in Ma'ānī al-Qur'ān analyzes the term "shay'" (thing), noting that when the Quran negates that any "shay'" resembles Allah, it employs the most comprehensive term possible. According to al-Farrā', "'Shay'' encompasses everything that exists or could exist, whether substance or accident, essence or attribute." This linguistic observation established that the Quranic negation of similarity is all-encompassing, excluding any possible comparison between God and anything in creation.

Ibn Qutayba (d. 276/889) in Ta'wīl Mushkil al-Qur'ān addresses what would become a central theological question: the apparent paradox created by the verse's conclusion. How can God be described as "All-Hearing, All-Seeing" when hearing and seeing are attributes humans know from creation? Ibn Qutayba's answer would prove foundational for later theological development: "These names point to divine perfections that transcend creaturely limitations, while the reality of divine hearing and seeing remains unlike any created instance." This formulation acknowledges that the same terms apply to God and creation while maintaining that they signify entirely different realities in each case.

Classical exegetes consistently read this verse in connection with other Quranic passages that establish divine transcendence, recognizing that the principle of divine incomparability appears throughout the Quran in various formulations. Al-Qurṭubī (d. 671/1273) in his al-Jāmi' li-aḥkām al-Qur'ān identifies what he terms "the transcendence verses" (āyāt al-tanzīh), demonstrating how different Quranic passages reinforce and elaborate the central principle. Sūrat al-Ikhlāṣ (112:1-4) declares, "Say: He is Allah, One; Allah, the Eternal Refuge; He neither begets nor is begotten; And there is none comparable to Him." Al-Qurṭubī notes that the phrase "lam yakun lahu kufuwan aḥad" (none comparable to Him) serves as a parallel to verse 42:11, establishing that divine incomparability appears in both Meccan and Medinan contexts, suggesting its fundamental importance to Quranic theology.

Similarly, Sūrat Maryam (19:65) poses a rhetorical question: "Lord of the heavens and earth and what is between them, so worship Him and be steadfast in His worship. Do you know any similar to Him (hal ta'lamu lahu samiyyan)?" The rhetorical question, according to al-Qurṭubī, "demands the answer 'no,' reinforcing through interrogative form what 42:11 states declaratively." This variation in expression demonstrates that the Quran employs multiple rhetorical strategies to emphasize divine transcendence. Another key passage appears in Sūrat al-An'ām (6:103): "Vision perceives Him not, but He perceives all vision." Al-Qurṭubī argues that this verse "specifies one aspect of divine incomparability—the transcendence of physical perception—while our verse establishes the general principle."

Through this network of verses, the Quran constructs a comprehensive doctrine of divine transcendence.

The juxtaposition of absolute negation ("naught is like unto Him") with affirmative attributes ("All-Hearing, All-Seeing") within a single verse created what early exegetes recognized as a fundamental interpretive challenge that would occupy Muslim theologians for centuries. Al-Māturīdī (d. 333/944) articulates this tension clearly in Ta'wīlāt ahl al-sunna, writing that "this verse establishes the method ('aṣl al-manhaj) for understanding all divine attributes. When we affirm that Allah hears and sees, we simultaneously affirm that His hearing and seeing share no essential similarity (mushābaha dhātiyya) with created hearing and seeing. The verse teaches us to hold both truths without compromise." This formulation would prove foundational for later theological development, as it established the principle that meaningful affirmation of divine attributes must be maintained alongside radical negation of any similarity to creaturely attributes.

The earliest preserved Quranic commentaries reveal diverse yet complementary approaches to understanding divine incomparability, establishing interpretive patterns that would persist throughout Islamic intellectual history. Muqātil ibn Sulaymān (d. 150/767), whose work represents one of the earliest complete commentaries, addresses the verse with notable brevity: "Laysa kamithlihi shay'un: Nothing from His creation resembles Him in His sovereignty (mulk), His power (qudra), or His knowledge ('ilm)." This early interpretation focuses on specific divine attributes rather than abstract essence, suggesting that early exegetes were concerned primarily with practical implications rather than philosophical speculation. The emphasis on sovereignty, power, and knowledge reflects concerns central to Quranic theology more broadly.

Preserved fragments of Sufyān al-Thawrī's (d. 161/778) commentary, as recorded by his students, reveal attention to the devotional implications of divine incomparability. Al-Thawrī stated, "When the servant truly understands 'laysa kamithlihi shay'un,' he ceases to compare his Lord to creation in his heart. This is the beginning of true worship ('ubūdiyya)." This approach explicitly links theological understanding to spiritual transformation, suggesting that correct comprehension of divine transcendence has direct consequences for the quality of one's worship and spiritual life. For al-Thawrī, the verse functions not merely as doctrinal information but as transformative knowledge that reshapes the believer's relationship with God.

Al-Ṭabarī's Jāmi' al-bayān provides the most extensive early treatment of the verse, collecting numerous interpretive traditions and demonstrating the methodological sophistication of early Islamic exegesis. His approach reveals how the first generations of Muslims engaged with divine incomparability through multiple complementary methods. Al-Ṭabarī cites several prophetic traditions related to divine transcendence, including the hadith "Allah was, and there was nothing with Him" (kāna Allāh wa-lam yakun shay'un ghayruh). He comments that "this hadith illuminates our verse—if nothing existed alongside Allah, then nothing can claim essential similarity to Him." The connection between divine preexistence and incomparability becomes explicit through this interpretive move: if God alone is eternal and uncreated, then creation by definition cannot share His essential nature.

Al-Ṭabarī presents debates among early linguists about whether "mithl" and "ka-mithl" differ in meaning, ultimately concluding that "the strongest position is that 'ka-mithlihi' intensifies the negation, removing even the possibility of analogical comparison (qiyās)." This linguistic conclusion carries significant theological implications, as it suggests that not only direct comparison but even analogical reasoning from creation to Creator is fundamentally limited. The emphatic grammatical construction reinforces the absolute nature of divine transcendence.

Addressing early theological debates, al-Ṭabarī tackles a question that would become increasingly prominent in later theological discussions: "Some have asked: If nothing resembles Allah, how can we know Him through His creation? The answer is that we know His existence and attributes through their effects (āthār), not through essential similarity (mushābaha dhātiyya)." This distinction between knowledge through effects and knowledge through similarity would become crucial for later theological method. It suggests that creation testifies to God's existence and attributes without implying any essential resemblance between Creator and created.

Analysis of these early commentaries reveals several consistent methodological approaches that characterized early Islamic engagement with divine transcendence. First, early exegetes demonstrated remarkable linguistic precision, paying careful attention to grammatical structures and word choice, recognizing that divine incomparability required exact expression. Second, they practiced intertextual reading, consistently interpreting verses in light of other Quranic passages to create a comprehensive framework for understanding transcendence. Third, they connected abstract theological principles to worship, ethics, and spiritual development, refusing to separate doctrine from practice. Fourth, they often acknowledged the limits of human understanding without attempting full rational resolution, preserving space for mystery within theological discourse.

The earliest Muslim community's approach to divine incomparability, preserved in numerous reports from the Companions and their Successors, reveals sophisticated understanding combined with practical wisdom. These reports demonstrate that from the beginning, Muslims grappled seriously with the implications of divine transcendence for theological language and religious practice. Ibn 'Abbās (d. 68/687), known as the "interpreter of the Quran" (turjumān al-Qur'ān), left numerous explanations that became foundational for later exegesis. Al-Ṭabarī reports with his chain of transmission that Ibn 'Abbās was asked about "laysa kamithlihi shay'un" and responded: "This means that nothing from the creation—neither in the heavens nor on earth—resembles Allah in His essence (dhāt), His attributes (ṣifāt), or His actions (af'āl). Yet He has named Himself with names and described Himself with attributes that He has permitted His servants to use, so they might know Him and call upon Him."

This interpretation establishes several key principles that would guide later theological development. It affirms comprehensive negation of similarity across all categories—essence, attributes, and actions. It maintains the distinction between divine and human attributes even when they share names. It grounds theological language in divine permission rather than human speculation, suggesting that humans may speak of God only in the ways He has authorized through revelation. The formulation acknowledges both the radical transcendence of God and the reality that He has made Himself knowable through revealed names and attributes.

'Alī ibn Abī Ṭālib (d. 40/661) offered a formulation that captures the paradox of divine transcendence and manifestation. Al-Qummī reports in his tafsīr that 'Alī said regarding this verse: "The Creator is known through creation, but not compared to it. He manifests Himself to intellects through what He has made, yet remains veiled from vision. This is the meaning of 'naught is like unto Him.'" This statement articulates a sophisticated understanding of how creation serves as a sign (āya) pointing to the Creator without implying resemblance. God becomes known through His effects while remaining incomparable to them—a formulation that would be elaborated by later philosophical theologians.

'Ā'isha bint Abī Bakr (d. 58/678) applied the principle of divine incomparability to the interpretation of apparently anthropomorphic verses, establishing a hermeneutical principle that would be widely adopted. When asked about such verses in light of divine incomparability, she reportedly stated: "His istiwa' is not like our sitting, His hand is not like our hands, His pleasure is not like our pleasure. 'Laysa kamithlihi shay'un' governs all such verses." This interpretive principle maintains the reality of what scripture affirms while systematically negating any creaturely mode. The same terms apply to God and creation, but their meanings differ fundamentally.

Among the Successors—the generation that followed the Companions—we find continued development of these themes. Al-Ḥasan al-Baṣrī (d. 110/728), this influential early figure, emphasized the spiritual and theological implications of divine incomparability. He stated, "Whoever truly understands 'laysa kamithlihi shay'un' will never fall into shirk (associationism), whether manifest or hidden. For shirk begins when the heart likens something to Allah in what is exclusively His." This formulation connects correct theological understanding directly to the preservation of pure monotheism, suggesting that misunderstanding divine transcendence opens the door to associationism in its various forms.

Sa'īd ibn Jubayr (d. 95/714), known for his theological precision, offered a methodological principle that would guide later theological discourse: "This verse is the scale (mīzān) by which all theological speech is measured. Whatever contradicts it is false, whatever accords with it may be true." This establishes divine incomparability as the fundamental criterion for evaluating theological claims, suggesting that any statement about God that implies similarity to creation must be rejected. Mujāhid ibn Jabr (d. 104/722) focused his interpretation on divine names, stating: "When Allah says He is All-Hearing, All-Seeing after saying 'naught is like unto Him,' He teaches us that His names are true while their reality in Him differs entirely from their reality in creation." This formulation addresses the central tension between affirmation and negation that would occupy later theologians.

Reports from the Companion and Successor era reveal sophisticated theological discussions that laid the groundwork for later systematic theology. Al-Dārimī preserves a report where students of Ibn 'Abbās debated whether divine attributes are identical to the divine essence or distinct from it—a question that would become central to later theological controversy. The conclusion reached was striking: "This question itself assumes categories applicable to creation. 'Laysa kamithlihi shay'un' means such categories do not apply to Allah." This response demonstrates remarkable sophistication, recognizing that the very terms of philosophical debate about divine attributes may themselves presuppose creaturely categories inapplicable to God.

Early authorities developed consistent approaches to apparently anthropomorphic texts in scripture, approaches that would be refined but not fundamentally altered by later generations. Umm Salama (d. 62/681) reportedly addressed the question of the divine "throne" (al-'arsh) by saying: "The throne is real, but 'laysa kamithlihi shay'un' means it is unlike any throne we know." This formulation became paradigmatic: affirm what scripture affirms, but negate any creaturely mode of existence. The throne is real but not comparable to created thrones; divine attributes are real but not comparable to created attributes.

'Umar ibn 'Abd al-'Azīz (d. 101/720) articulated what became a foundational principle about the limits of theological language: "Human language was created for human purposes. When applied to Allah, it points to truth but cannot contain it. This is why He says 'laysa kamithlihi shay'un'—to remind us of language's limits." This observation recognizes that theological language functions differently from ordinary descriptive language. Words applied to God perform a pointing or indicating function without exhaustively capturing divine reality. The recognition that language has limits when speaking of the infinite became a constant theme in Islamic theological reflection.

Several consistent patterns emerge from these early sources that would characterize Islamic theological discourse throughout its history. First, divine attributes are affirmed while their creaturely mode is systematically negated—affirmation with negation becomes the characteristic move of Islamic theology. Second, rather than elaborate philosophical speculation, early authorities focused on practical implications for worship and conduct, maintaining the connection between doctrine and practice. Third, anthropomorphic language in Quran and hadith was neither denied nor explained away but understood through the lens of divine incomparability, preserving scriptural language while preventing literalistic misunderstanding. Fourth, early Muslims comfortably acknowledged that divine reality exceeds human comprehension without seeing this as theological failure, preserving space for mystery within theological discourse.

These early interpretations established principles that would guide all subsequent Islamic thought on divine transcendence. Divine incomparability was recognized from the beginning as the fundamental principle governing all theological discourse. Scriptural language about God must be accepted and affirmed, while its precise mode remains mysterious and inaccessible to human understanding. The same terms apply to God and creation with entirely different meanings—a principle that allows meaningful theological language while preserving transcendence. Practical piety and theological precision must be maintained together, never separated into distinct spheres. Human reason has a legitimate role in theological reflection while recognizing its inherent limitations when approaching the Infinite.

Ibn Taymiyya (d. 728/1328) would later observe with characteristic directness: "The Companions and Successors laid down the method. All sound theology since then has been commentary on their understanding of 'laysa kamithlihi shay'un.'" While this may somewhat overstate the case, it captures an important truth about Islamic theological tradition. The fundamental principles for approaching divine transcendence were established in the earliest period, and later theological developments—however sophisticated and elaborate—represented variations on these founding themes rather than departures from them.

This examination of the scriptural contexts and earliest interpretations of "laysa kamithlihi shay'un" reveals that from the beginning, Muslims recognized both the centrality and the complexity of divine incomparability. The verse's Quranic context, with its careful balance of negation and affirmation, established patterns that would persist throughout Islamic intellectual history. The progression from divine creative action to created multiplicity to absolute transcendence to affirmed attributes within a single verse provided a template for how later thinkers would negotiate the relationship between God's radical difference from creation and His knowability through revelation.

Early exegetes and the first generations of Muslims developed sophisticated approaches that maintained scriptural fidelity while acknowledging the profound challenges of speaking about the Incomparable. They recognized that theological language functions in unique ways when applied to God, that affirmation must always be accompanied by negation, that mystery is inherent in theological discourse, and that doctrine cannot be separated from spiritual and ethical practice. These early interpretations did not resolve all tensions—indeed, they could not, given the nature of the subject matter—but rather established frameworks for productively engaging with them.

The patterns observed in these early sources—the conjunction of affirmation with negation, the preservation of mystery within meaning, the connection of theology to practice, the recognition of language's limits, the maintenance of scriptural authority alongside intellectual rigor—would be elaborated, refined, and systematized by later thinkers but never fundamentally altered. Ash'arite theologians, Mu'tazilite rationalists, philosophical synthesizers like al-Ghazālī, and mystical writers like Ibn 'Arabī would all develop their distinctive approaches to divine transcendence, but each would do so within the framework established by these early interpreters. In this way, the earliest Islamic sources established divine incomparability not as a problem to be solved but as the fundamental principle that governs all authentic theological discourse—a principle to be preserved, elaborated, and applied rather than overcome or transcended.

Chapter 2. Divine Names in Quran and Hadith

The Quranic revelation that "naught is like unto Him" exists in profound tension with the equally Quranic teaching that God possesses "the most beautiful names" (al-asmā' al-ḥusnā) by which He may be known and invoked. If divine reality truly transcends all comparison, how can names derived from human language—terms like "merciful," "powerful," or "wise"—meaningfully apply to Him? Furthermore, how can apparently contradictory names—the Giver and the Withholder, the Manifest and the Hidden—simultaneously characterize the divine essence without compromising divine unity? This chapter examines how the Quran and hadith literature present the divine names, how early Muslims enumerated and understood them, and how classical authorities recognized and addressed the interpretive challenges they pose.

The Islamic tradition of enumerating God's beautiful names originates in Quranic verses and prophetic traditions that have generated centuries of scholarly reflection and popular devotion. The Quran establishes the concept of divine names in several key passages that serve as the foundation for all subsequent theological reflection on this subject. In Sūrat al-A'rāf, God declares, "And to Allah belong the most beautiful names, so invoke Him by them. And leave those who practice deviation concerning His names" (7:180). This verse not only affirms the existence of divine names but commands believers to invoke God through them, while warning against those who distort or misuse these names. Similarly, Sūrat al-Isrā' instructs, "Say, 'Call upon Allah or call upon the Most Merciful (al-Raḥmān). Whichever you call, to Him belong the most beautiful names'" (17:110), suggesting a certain flexibility in how the divine names may be employed while maintaining that they all refer to the same divine reality.

Other Quranic passages reinforce this theme. Sūrat Ṭā Hā declares, "Allah—there is no deity except Him. To Him belong the most beautiful names" (20:8), directly connecting the divine names to the fundamental principle of monotheism. In Sūrat al-Ḥashr, after a series of divine names, the verse concludes, "He is Allah, the Creator, the Inventor, the Fashioner; to Him belong the most beautiful names" (59:24), demonstrating how the Quran itself employs multiple names to describe divine attributes and actions. These verses establish that the divine names are not human inventions or metaphorical approximations but authentic divine self-disclosures through which God has chosen to make Himself known to His creation.

Al-Ṭabarī, commenting on verse 7:180, notes a significant linguistic point: "The phrase 'al-asmā' al-ḥusnā' indicates not merely 'good' names but 'the most beautiful'—suggesting perfection in each attribute these names signify. Yet this very perfection must be understood through the principle 'laysa kamithlihi shay'un.'" This observation highlights the tension that runs throughout Islamic theology: the divine names indicate perfection, yet this perfection must be understood as categorically different from any created perfection. Al-Rāzī (d. 606/1210), in his monumental Quranic commentary Mafātīḥ al-Ghayb, observes a crucial grammatical distinction that would prove theologically significant. He writes, "Notice that Allah says the names are 'His' (lahu), not that they are 'Him' (huwa). This indicates that while the names truly belong to Allah and reveal authentic divine attributes, they remain distinct from the ineffable divine essence which transcends all naming." This subtle grammatical point suggests that the names provide genuine knowledge of God while the divine essence itself remains beyond complete comprehension.

The most influential prophetic tradition regarding divine names is the hadith reported by Abū Hurayra, preserved in both Ṣaḥīḥ al-Bukhārī and Ṣaḥīḥ Muslim: "Indeed, Allah has ninety-nine names, one hundred less one. Whoever enumerates them (aḥṣāhā) will enter Paradise." This brief statement generated extensive commentary and multiple attempts at enumeration that would occupy Muslim scholars for centuries. The hadith's promise of Paradise to those who "enumerate" the names prompted detailed discussions about what enumeration actually means. Al-Nawawī (d. 676/1277), in his commentary on Ṣaḥīḥ Muslim, clarifies an important point: "The hadith does not mean Allah has only ninety-nine names. Rather, it indicates that among His infinite names, ninety-nine have special significance for human spiritual development." This interpretation recognizes that the number ninety-nine represents a particular set of names with pedagogical and spiritual importance rather than an exhaustive catalog of divine names.

Ibn Ḥajar al-'Asqalānī (d. 852/1449), in his encyclopedic commentary Fatḥ al-Bārī, addresses the crucial question of what it means to "enumerate" the divine names. He reports that scholars differ significantly on this point: "Some say it means memorizing them, others say understanding their meanings, others say acting according to their implications. The strongest view combines all these: knowing them, understanding them, invoking Allah through them, and embodying their appropriate qualities while maintaining 'laysa kamithlihi shay'un.'" This comprehensive interpretation suggests that proper relationship with the divine names involves intellectual, spiritual, and practical dimensions. Memorization without understanding would be insufficient, as would theoretical knowledge without practical application. The phrase "while maintaining 'laysa kamithlihi shay'un'" is particularly significant—it indicates that even as believers seek to embody divine qualities in their own limited capacity, they must never forget the absolute difference between created and uncreated, finite and infinite.

Despite the hadith's specification of ninety-nine names, no single authoritative list appears in the earliest sources, a fact that proved both puzzling and theologically significant. The version transmitted by al-Tirmidhī in his Sunan includes a list, but al-Tirmidhī himself notes that this list represents the interpretation of one particular narrator rather than a direct prophetic specification. This absence of a fixed prophetic list led to scholarly efforts spanning centuries to derive the names from the Quran and authentic hadith. Ibn 'Arabī identifies the theological significance of this absence with characteristic insight: "The lack of a fixed prophetic list is itself instructive. It suggests that while divine names provide authentic access to divine reality, no finite enumeration can exhaust divine self-disclosure. The ninety-nine represent perfection in multiplicity, not limitation." This observation transforms what might appear as an historical accident into a profound theological truth—the divine names open onto an inexhaustible reality that cannot be completely systematized.

Major classical scholars produced various enumerations, each reflecting different methodological principles and emphases. Al-Walīd ibn Muslim's list, preserved in al-Tirmidhī's Sunan, became the most widely circulated in popular devotion, though it was criticized by some scholars for including names without clear Quranic basis. Ibn Manẓūr compiled a list based strictly on Quranic occurrence, resulting in some variations from the more popular enumeration. Al-Ghazālī's enumeration in his treatise al-Maqṣad al-Asnā represents a philosophically systematic approach, organizing the names by categories of divine perfection and providing detailed spiritual commentary on each. Ibn al-Qayyim al-Jawziyya produced a list emphasizing names with clear basis in Quran and hadith that reached the level of mutawātir (mass transmission), reflecting the more stringent textualist approach characteristic of the Ḥanbalī school. The variety of these enumerations demonstrates both the richness of the scriptural material and the challenges involved in systematizing it.

Classical scholars developed sophisticated criteria for determining what constitutes a divine name as opposed to merely a description or attribute. Al-Qurṭubī specifies three conditions: "A divine name must be: first, explicitly stated in the Quran or authentic hadith as a name of Allah; second, in the form of an adjective or noun indicating perfection; third, free from any implication of deficiency or similarity to creation." These criteria sought to maintain rigor in deriving names while preventing the proliferation of dubious attributions. Ibn Taymiyya adds an important nuance that reflects his attention to the relationship between divine attributes and actions: "Some terms describe divine actions (af'āl) rather than eternal attributes (ṣifāt). 'The Creator' (al-Khāliq) implies the act of creation. Yet even these action-names point to eternal divine perfections while the actions themselves occur in time." This distinction recognizes that some names relate primarily to God's relationship with creation and His actions within time, while still indicating eternal qualities of the divine essence.

Al-Bayhaqī (d. 458/1066), in his comprehensive treatise al-Asmā' wa-l-Ṣifāt, establishes a methodological principle that reveals the complexity involved in affirming divine names: "Every divine name implies three things: affirmation of the name itself (ithbāt al-ism), affirmation of the attribute it signifies (ithbāt al-ṣifa), and negation of its opposite (nafy al-ḍidd). Yet all must be understood through 'laysa kamithlihi shay'un.'" This formulation demonstrates that each divine name involves multiple levels of meaning. To say that God is "the Merciful" involves affirming both the name and the attribute of mercy, negating its opposite (cruelty), while simultaneously maintaining that divine mercy differs absolutely from created mercy. The theological work required to properly understand even a single divine name is thus considerable.

Perhaps no aspect of the divine names presented greater interpretive challenges than the Quranic attribution of apparently contradictory names to the One God. The Quran frequently presents divine names in complementary pairs that appear contradictory from the perspective of human logic. God is described as al-Qābiḍ and al-Bāsiṭ (the Constrictor and the Expander), al-Khāfiḍ and al-Rāfi' (the Abaser and the Exalter), al-Mu'izz and al-Mudhill (the Honorer and the Humiliator), al-Ḍārr and al-Nāfi' (the Harmer and the Benefiter). Even more philosophically challenging are the pairs al-Awwal and al-Ākhir (the First and the Last), al-Ẓāhir and al-Bāṭin (the Manifest and the Hidden). For finite human consciousness, these pairs seem to describe mutually exclusive attributes—how can something be simultaneously first and last, manifest and hidden, a constrictor and an expander?

Early commentators recognized these pairings as presenting unique theological and philosophical challenges. Al-Ḥasan al-Baṣrī, the influential early figure whose theological observations shaped later tradition, observed: "The servant's intellect struggles when told that Allah is both the Constrictor and Expander, both the Harmer and Benefiter. Yet this struggle itself teaches us that divine reality transcends the either-or logic of created existence." This formulation suggests that the apparent contradictions in divine names serve a pedagogical function—they teach believers that God transcends the categories of human logic. The struggle to understand how contradictory attributes coexist is not a defect in revelation or human reason but rather an indication that divine reality exceeds the categories through which humans ordinarily understand reality.

Al-Ghazālī provides the most systematic classical treatment of seemingly opposed names in his treatise al-Maqṣad al-Asnā, dedicated to explaining the spiritual and theological significance of the divine names. He writes, "Know that the perfection of divine essence requires that contradictory effects proceed from it without contradiction in the essence itself. When Allah constricts (qabḍ), this proceeds from His perfect wisdom and mercy. When He expands (basṭ), this too proceeds from His perfect wisdom and mercy. The opposition exists in the effects as experienced by creation, not in the divine essence or attributes themselves." This analysis locates the apparent contradiction not in God but in the diversity of created effects and creaturely experiences of divine action. What appears as contradiction from the creaturely perspective represents the single divine reality manifesting in diverse ways according to divine wisdom.

Al-Ghazālī continues with a crucial insight that connects the problem of opposed names directly to the principle of divine incomparability: "This is part of what 'laysa kamithlihi shay'un' means. Created beings cannot simultaneously be perfectly merciful and perfectly just, cannot give and withhold with equal perfection. But Allah transcends such limitations. In Him, all perfections coexist without opposition because His mode of possessing attributes differs entirely from the creaturely mode." This formulation suggests that the inability to reconcile seemingly opposed divine attributes reflects limitations in creaturely modes of existence rather than confusion in the divine nature. Created beings experience tension between justice and mercy, between expansion and contraction, because they possess these qualities in limited, creaturely modes. God's transcendence of such limitations is precisely what the apparently contradictory names are meant to convey.

Ibn 'Arabī develops perhaps the most sophisticated mystical approach to this problem in the Fuṣūṣ al-Ḥikam, his controversial masterwork of metaphysical Sufism. He writes, "The divine names that appear opposite to us are like the front and back of a single hand—distinct in appearance but one in essence. When the Real manifests as al-Qābiḍ, He is simultaneously al-Bāsiṭ from another perspective. The servant experiences constriction or expansion, but in the divine reality, these are unified aspects of a single perfection." This analogy of the two sides of a hand provides a vivid image: what appears as opposition from one angle reveals itself as complementary aspects of a unified reality when viewed more comprehensively. Ibn 'Arabī elaborates using another analogy from natural phenomena: "Consider how the same sunlight hardens clay and melts wax. The opposition lies not in the light but in the recipients. Similarly, divine manifestation through apparently opposed names reveals not divine contradiction but the diverse capacities of creation to receive the One Reality." This analysis shifts attention from the divine names themselves to the relationship between God and creation, suggesting that the diversity and apparent contradiction in divine names reflects the diverse ways creatures receive and experience the one divine reality.

The major theological schools developed distinctive approaches to this problem, each seeking to preserve both divine unity and the authenticity of the revealed names. The Ash'arite position, articulated by al-Bāqillānī, explains: "The names refer to divine actions in relation to creation, not to multiple attributes in the essence. When Allah 'harms,' this is the withholding of benefit, not a positive attribute of harmfulness. All names reduce to expressions of divine will and power, which are one in essence though multiple in effect." This solution preserves divine simplicity by reducing the multiplicity of names to expressions of a single divine will manifesting in diverse ways. The apparent multiplicity exists in the effects rather than in the divine essence itself.

The Māturīdite school, while agreeing with Ash'arites on many points, offered a slightly different emphasis. Al-Māturīdī writes: "The opposition in divine names teaches us about divine transcendence. If Allah could only show mercy but not justice, only expand but not contract, He would be limited like creation. The coexistence of seeming opposites demonstrates His absolute perfection and freedom." This formulation sees the apparently contradictory names as positive demonstrations of divine transcendence rather than merely problems requiring resolution. The coexistence of opposites becomes evidence of God's transcendence of creaturely limitations.

Philosophical theologians offered yet another perspective grounded in their metaphysical analysis of divine simplicity. Ibn Sīnā argues: "In the Necessary Existent, all perfections exist in absolute simplicity. What we perceive as multiple, even opposed attributes are human conceptualizations of a simple divine reality that transcends composition. The names are our finite ways of indicating infinite perfection." This Avicennan solution roots the problem in the relationship between divine simplicity and human conceptualization. The multiplicity exists in how human intellect necessarily apprehends divine reality, not in the reality itself.

The divine names "the Manifest" (al-Ẓāhir) and "the Hidden" (al-Bāṭin) received particular attention for appearing to present a logical impossibility more acute than other paired names. The Quran declares, "He is the First and the Last, the Manifest and the Hidden, and He has knowledge of all things" (57:3). Al-Qushayrī (d. 465/1074), in his Quranic commentary, articulates the philosophical problem: "How can the same essence be simultaneously completely manifest and completely hidden? This is impossible for created things, which must be either present or absent, known or unknown. But Allah transcends such divisions." The problem is not merely that these names appear opposed but that they seem to involve logical contradiction—to be manifest is precisely not to be hidden, and vice versa.

Al-Rāzī provides a philosophical analysis that resolves the apparent contradiction by distinguishing different senses of manifestation and hiddenness: "Al-Ẓāhir means manifest to the intellect through His effects—nothing is more evident than the Creator's existence when one contemplates creation. Al-Bāṭin means hidden from sensory perception and comprehensive knowledge—nothing is more hidden than His true essence. He is thus the most manifest in one sense, most hidden in another." This solution distinguishes between different modes of knowledge and different aspects of divine reality. God is maximally manifest in that His existence is rationally evident through its effects in creation, yet maximally hidden in that His essence transcends sensory perception and comprehensive intellectual grasp. The apparent contradiction dissolves when one recognizes that manifestation and hiddenness apply in different respects.

From the earliest period, Muslim scholars recognized that the divine names posed fundamental interpretive challenges that could not be resolved through simple rational analysis alone. The Companions of the Prophet developed principles for approaching these challenges that would guide all subsequent theological reflection. Ibn 'Abbās addressed students troubled by divine names suggesting human qualities: "When you hear that Allah has 'hands,' 'eyes,' or 'pleasure,' and when you know He is 'Merciful' and 'Angry,' remember first 'laysa kamithlihi shay'un.' Then understand that these words point to realities in Allah that transcend what these words mean regarding creation." This pedagogical approach establishes a clear priority: the principle of divine incomparability must govern interpretation of all divine names and attributes. The names are affirmed as pointing to real divine qualities, but their meaning when applied to God differs fundamentally from their meaning when applied to creation.

'Alī ibn Abī Ṭālib provided a formulation that would prove influential for later mystical theology: "The names of Allah are not Allah, yet they are not other than Allah. They are relationships (nisab) between the Creator and creation, rays from the sun of divine essence that illuminate creation while the sun itself remains transcendent." This statement navigates between two errors: identifying the names completely with the divine essence (which would make the essence multiple) and separating them completely from the divine essence (which would make them purely human constructions). Instead, the names are understood as relationships or connections between the transcendent divine essence and creation, ways in which the infinite makes itself accessible to the finite.

Several key theological debates emerged in the first centuries of Islam that would shape all subsequent discussion of divine names. The first concerned the ontological status of the names themselves: Are divine names eternal or created? If eternal, how do they relate to divine unity? If created, how can they provide true knowledge of the eternal? Wāṣil ibn 'Aṭā' (d. 131/748), the founder of the Mu'tazilite school, argued from the perspective of radical divine unity: "The names are created descriptions, not eternal attributes. Otherwise, we would have multiple eternals alongside Allah." This position sought to preserve absolute divine unity by denying eternal multiplicity in God, even the multiplicity of names and attributes. In response, Ḍirār ibn 'Amr (d. 200/815) articulated what would become the mainstream position: "The names indicate eternal divine perfections. To say Allah 'became' merciful or knowing implies He was once not so, which is impossible." This argument emphasizes that the divine names point to eternal divine qualities, not temporal acquisitions, and that denying their eternity would compromise divine perfection.

The problem of anthropomorphism presented another major challenge. How can names shared with creation not imply similarity? This question became particularly acute given that many divine names—knowing, powerful, living, hearing, seeing—use terms that also apply to creatures. Al-Junayd (d. 298/910), one of the most influential early Sufi masters, articulated what became the mainstream theological position: "The sharing is in utterance (lafẓ) only, not in meaning (ma'nā). When we say Allah is 'knowing' and humans are 'knowing,' only the word is shared. The reality differs more than the distance between heaven and earth—rather, no comparison exists at all." This formulation became foundational: the same linguistic term applies to God and creature, but it signifies radically different realities in each case. The word serves as a homonym, a single phonetic form with entirely different meanings depending on whether it applies to Creator or creation.

The question of how multiple names coexist with divine unity provoked sophisticated philosophical-theological responses. If God is absolutely one and simple, how can He possess multiple names and attributes without this multiplicity compromising His unity? Abū Hāshim al-Jubbā'ī (d. 321/933), from the Basran school of Mu'tazilite theology, proposed an influential analogy: "The names are different perspectives on one simple essence, like multiple people viewing one mountain from different angles. The perspectives are many, the mountain is one." This analogy suggests that multiplicity exists in human apprehension rather than in divine reality itself. Different names represent different human perspectives on, or conceptualizations of, a reality that remains simple and unified in itself.

Through these early discussions and debates, several methodological principles emerged that would guide later theological discourse. The principle of tafwīḍ (delegation) represented one important approach, particularly among early authorities who emphasized scriptural fidelity over philosophical speculation. Some early authorities delegated the "how" of divine attributes to divine knowledge while affirming their reality. Mālik ibn Anas, founder of the Mālikī legal school, stated regarding divine attributes: "The meaning is known, the how is unknown, asking about it is innovation." This formulation became paradigmatic for one approach to divine attributes: we know that God has the qualities indicated by His names, but we do not know the manner or modality of these divine qualities. Speculation about the "how" of divine attributes exceeds human capacity and represents blameworthy innovation.

The principle of tanzīh (transcendence) involved systematic negation of creaturely modes while affirming divine perfections. Al-Ṭaḥāwī (d. 321/933), whose creedal statement became widely accepted as representing Sunni orthodoxy, codified this principle with striking directness: "Whatever you conceive in your mind, Allah is different from that." This radical formulation suggests that any mental image or conception humans form will inevitably fall short of divine reality. The very structure of human cognition, shaped by experience of finite created things, proves inadequate when directed toward the Infinite.

The principle of ithbāt bi-lā tashbīh (affirmation without likening) sought to maintain the reality of divine names and attributes while denying any similarity to created attributes. This principle became central to mainstream Sunni theology, particularly in the Ash'arite tradition. The names affirm real divine perfections without implying similarity to creation.

One can truly say that God is merciful, knowing, and powerful while maintaining that divine mercy, knowledge, and power differ absolutely from created mercy, knowledge, and power.

Perhaps most significant was the principle of jam' bayn al-ḍiddayn (combining opposites), which represented explicit recognition that divine perfection includes what appears contradictory to human logic. This principle acknowledges that human reason, shaped by experience of created things bound by the law of non-contradiction in their creaturely mode, encounters paradox when approaching divine reality. Rather than seeing this as a defect requiring elimination, this principle treats the coexistence of apparent opposites as evidence of divine transcendence.

Early Sufi masters contributed crucial insights that enriched purely theological approaches to the divine names. Dhū al-Nūn al-Miṣrī (d. 245/859), one of the earliest systematizers of Sufi doctrine, offered a paradoxical formulation: "The divine names are veils and revelations simultaneously. They veil the essence while revealing the attributes, hide Allah from the unworthy while disclosing Him to the seekers." This statement captures a central mystical insight about the function of divine names. They serve as both revelation and concealment, making God known while preserving His transcendence. The names disclose divine attributes to those who approach with proper spiritual preparation while remaining opaque to those who lack such preparation.

Al-Bisṭāmī (d. 261/875), known for his ecstatic utterances that sometimes troubled orthodox scholars, provided a striking image: "I swam in the seas of the divine names until I realized they all pointed to one shore—the Named who transcends all naming. This is the meaning of 'Allāhu a'lam bi-asmā'ihi'—Allah knows best His own names." This formulation suggests that the multiplicity of divine names ultimately resolves in the unity of the Named, yet even this unity transcends human comprehension. The final phrase, "Allah knows best His own names," became a common way of acknowledging that complete knowledge of the divine names belongs to God alone.

Al-Junayd, whose "sober" mysticism proved more palatable to orthodox theologians than the ecstatic expressions of al-Bisṭāmī, offered an epistemological analysis of different levels of understanding: "The realized one uses the divine names while knowing they are fingers pointing at the moon. The fool argues about the fingers; the wise look where they point; the realized know that even the moon is but a metaphor for what cannot be indicated." This graduated understanding suggests three levels: those who mistake the means for the end, those who properly use the means to reach the end, and those who recognize that even the end as humanly conceived remains merely a metaphor for an ultimately transcendent reality.

From the beginning, scholars understood that a proper understanding of divine names had crucial practical implications extending beyond theoretical theology. For worship, the implications were direct and significant. Ibn 'Umar (d. 73/693), son of the second caliph, taught: "When you invoke Allah by His names, remember you are not manipulating Him through magical formulas. You are aligning yourself with divine perfections while acknowledging He transcends your understanding." This teaching guards against treating the divine names as magical incantations while affirming their efficacy when used with proper understanding and intention. The names provide legitimate means of approaching God precisely because they represent God's own self-disclosure.

For spiritual development, the divine names played a central role in classical Islamic spirituality. Al-Muḥāsibī (d. 243/857), whose psychological insight shaped later Sufi practice, developed the concept of takhalluq bi-akhlāq Allāh (adorning oneself with divine qualities). However, he maintained crucial distinctions: "When you cultivate mercy in yourself, remember that your mercy is created and finite while His is uncreated and infinite. The name is the same, the reality differs absolutely." This practice encouraged believers to embody divine attributes in their limited, creaturely capacity while never forgetting the absolute difference between created and uncreated, finite and infinite. Human mercy participates in but never equals divine mercy.

For theological discourse more broadly, clear principles emerged that would govern subsequent discussions. Every divine name must be understood through the governing principle of "laysa kamithlihi shay'un," ensuring that affirmation never slides into anthropomorphism. Multiple names do not imply multiple gods or composition in the divine essence, preserving divine unity while acknowledging multiplicity in divine self-disclosure. Apparently contradictory names demonstrate divine transcendence of ordinary logic rather than representing genuine contradictions. The "how" of divine attributes exceeds human comprehension, requiring intellectual humility in theological speculation.

The divine names in the Quran and hadith present what early Muslims recognized as both the primary means of knowing God and the greatest challenge to maintaining divine transcendence. The tradition of enumerating ninety-nine names provided a practical framework for devotion and a theoretical framework for theology while acknowledging that no enumeration could exhaust divine self-disclosure. The very incompleteness of the traditional enumerations points toward the inexhaustibility of divine reality. The presence of seemingly opposed divine attributes forced early theologians to develop sophisticated understandings that transcended simple logical categories, leading to recognition that divine reality exceeds the law of non-contradiction as it applies to finite created things.

Most significantly, the early recognition of interpretive challenges led not to despair or skepticism but to productive methodological principles that would guide Islamic theology throughout its history. Rather than seeing the tensions between divine transcendence and divine names as problems requiring elimination, early Muslims developed frameworks for living with and through these tensions in ways that proved spiritually and intellectually fruitful. The divine names became understood as authentic self-disclosures of the Incomparable that necessarily generate paradox when approached by finite human consciousness operating within categories derived from experience of finite things. The paradox itself becomes pedagogically valuable, teaching believers that they approach reality that exceeds their conceptual frameworks.

This recognition would profoundly shape all subsequent Islamic theology, philosophy, and mysticism. Later Ash'arite theologians would develop sophisticated theories of divine attributes building on these early foundations. Mu'tazilite rationalists would push the principle of divine unity in directions that sometimes troubled orthodox sensibilities, yet they too worked within frameworks established by these early discussions. Philosophers like Ibn Sīnā would provide metaphysical analyses of divine simplicity that sought to explain how multiplicity in names could coexist with absolute unity in essence. Mystical theologians like Ibn 'Arabī would develop baroque elaborations of divine self-disclosure through names, yet always grounded in principles established in this earliest period. All these later developments represented variations on and elaborations of patterns established in the first centuries of Islamic thought—patterns that preserved both the transcendence proclaimed in "laysa kamithlihi shay'un" and the intimate divine knowledge promised through "al-asmā' al-ḥusnā."

Chapter 3. The Language of Divine Description in Early Islam

The challenge of speaking appropriately about the Divine Who is "naught is like unto Him" confronted the Muslim community from its inception. How could human language, developed for mundane communication, adequately convey truths about transcendent reality? This chapter examines how the Prophet Muhammad established precedents for theological discourse, how early Muslims developed technical terminology to express subtle theological distinctions, and how the community grappled with Quranic passages that seemed to attribute human characteristics to God. These early linguistic negotiations would establish patterns that shaped all subsequent Islamic theological expression.

The Prophet Muhammad's own discourse about God, preserved in hadith literature, provided the primary model for how Muslims should speak about divine reality while maintaining divine transcendence. Analysis of authentic hadith reveals consistent patterns in prophetic theological language that demonstrate remarkable sophistication in balancing affirmation and transcendence. Al-Bukhārī and Muslim preserve numerous examples where the Prophet simultaneously affirms divine attributes while maintaining the principle of divine incomparability, establishing a template that would guide all subsequent theological discourse.

The hadith of divine descent provides a paradigmatic example of prophetic theological language. The Prophet stated, "Our Lord descends to the lowest heaven during the last third of the night and says: 'Who calls upon Me that I may respond? Who asks of Me that I may give? Who seeks forgiveness that I may forgive?'" This tradition, preserved in both Ṣaḥīḥ al-Bukhārī and Ṣaḥīḥ Muslim, appears to attribute spatial movement to God, yet the context prevents any crude physical interpretation. Ibn Ḥajar al-'Asqalānī notes in his encyclopedic commentary Fatḥ al-Bārī: "Observe how the Prophet conveys divine action (descent) and divine speech while the context—inviting prayer and forgiveness—prevents any physical understanding. This became the model: affirm the attribute, expect the benefit, avoid speculation on the mode." The hadith's purpose is clearly practical rather than metaphysical—it encourages believers to pray during the last third of the night by affirming God's special responsiveness during that time. The language of descent serves this practical purpose without requiring or supporting a literalistic spatial interpretation.

Similarly, the hadith of divine joy demonstrates the Prophet's use of comparison to convey theological truth while maintaining transcendence. The Prophet stated, "Allah is more joyful at His servant's repentance than one of you who finds his lost camel in the desert." This vivid simile appears in both major hadith collections. Al-Nawawī provides insightful commentary: "The Prophet uses comparison ('more joyful than') not to establish similarity but to help human understanding grasp the intensity of divine acceptance. The comparison points to effect, not essence—we understand God's complete acceptance of repentance without attributing human emotion to Him." The hadith employs a comparison not to suggest that divine joy resembles human joy in nature, but to convey the intensity and reality of God's acceptance of repentance in terms humans can grasp through their own experience.

The hadith literature preserves several instances where the Prophet addressed direct questions about divine nature, and his responses established methodological principles for theological discourse. In one particularly instructive incident, a bedouin asked, "O Messenger of Allah, is our Lord near so we may whisper to Him, or far so we must call out?" The Prophet remained silent until the Quranic verse was revealed: "When My servants ask about Me, indeed I am near" (2:186). This tradition, preserved in Ahmad's Musnad and authenticated by al-Albānī, became foundational for Islamic theological method. Ibn Rajab (d. 795/1393) analyzes its significance: "The Prophet's silence until revelation came teaches us methodology. Human speculation about divine modality ('is He near or far?') must yield to revealed expression that transcends the assumed categories—He is 'near' but not spatially." The Prophet's silence is as instructive as his speech, indicating that certain questions about divine nature cannot be answered through human speculation but require revelation. The revealed response transcends the either-or categories assumed in the question—God is near, but His nearness is not spatial proximity that can be measured or compared to creaturely nearness.

Another tradition that generated extensive commentary concerns the question about divine location. When asked "Where is Allah?" the Prophet responded, "Above the heavens," or in another narration, he approved a slave-girl's answer, "In the sky." This hadith, preserved in Ṣaḥīḥ Muslim, appears to locate God spatially, yet classical scholars understood it differently. Ibn 'Abd al-Barr (d. 463/1071) writes: "The scholars understand this as affirming transcendence (al-'uluww), not location (al-makān). The Prophet used language his questioners could understand while the meaning transcends their categories." The concept of 'uluww (highness or elevation) in Islamic theology came to signify transcendence and exaltedness rather than spatial position. The Prophet's response affirmed God's transcendence using language accessible to his questioners, while the true meaning exceeded the spatial categories their question assumed.

The Prophet employed several consistent methods when speaking about God that reveal sophisticated theological pedagogy. His method of negation of deficiency appears in traditions like "Allah does not sleep, nor is it befitting for Him to sleep," preserved in Ṣaḥīḥ Muslim. Al-Baghawī (d. 516/1122) notes the instructive structure: "The Prophet first negates the deficiency (sleep) then explains why it cannot apply to God (not befitting), teaching us to preserve divine perfection in our speech." The structure moves from simple negation to explanation, showing that divine transcendence is not an arbitrary exclusion but follows from divine perfection. Anything implying limitation or deficiency cannot apply to God, not merely as a stipulation but as a logical consequence of His perfection.

The Prophet's method of affirmation with qualification appears in the tradition "Allah wrote mercy upon Himself," preserved in Ṣaḥīḥ al-Bukhārī. Ibn Abī Jamra (d. 699/1300) observes the subtle theological point: "Notice 'upon Himself' (ʿalā nafsihi)—the Prophet affirms divine mercy while indicating it's self-imposed, not necessitated by anything external." This qualification preserves divine freedom and independence even while affirming divine mercy. God's mercy is not a response to external compulsion but a free divine commitment, maintaining that God is not subject to any necessity beyond His own nature and will.

The Prophet's frequent use of active participles (ism fāʿil) for divine attributes proved grammatically and theologically significant. He regularly employed forms like al-Khāliq (continuously creating), al-Rāziq (continuously providing), and al-Ghāfir (continuously forgiving). Al-Khattābī (d. 388/998) explains the theological import: "This grammatical form indicates ongoing divine action without temporal limitation—God is creating now, has always been creating, will always be creating." The active participle in Arabic denotes continuous or habitual action, making it particularly suitable for indicating eternal divine activities. Unlike the simple past tense, which might suggest completed action, or the simple present, which might suggest temporal limitation, the active participle form indicates activity that transcends temporal categories while remaining dynamically real.

The Prophet's supplications provided templates for theological language that combined comprehensiveness with humility. One particularly instructive prayer states, "O Allah, I ask You by every name that is Yours, which You have named Yourself with, or revealed in Your Book, or taught to any of Your creation, or kept hidden in the knowledge of the unseen with You." This supplication, preserved in Ahmad's Musnad, received extensive commentary. Ibn al-Qayyim (d. 751/1350) analyzes its theological structure: "This duʿā' establishes four categories of divine names: self-disclosed, revealed, taught to creation, and kept hidden. It acknowledges both divine self-revelation and the limits of human knowledge about God." The prayer recognizes that divine names exist in categories of accessibility—some God has revealed directly, some He has taught to particular creatures, and some remain in His exclusive knowledge. This acknowledges that divine self-disclosure is real but not exhaustive, preserving space for mystery while affirming genuine revelation.

Another example of prophetic supplication as a theological model appears in the morning remembrance: "O Allah, by Your knowledge of the unseen and Your power over creation, grant me life as long as You know life is better for me." This prayer, preserved in al-Nasāʾī's Sunan, demonstrates a characteristic prophetic method. Al-Sindī (d. 1138/1726) comments: "The Prophet consistently links divine attributes to their effects on creation—God's knowledge relates to the unseen, His power to creation. This teaches us to speak of divine attributes functionally rather than speculatively." Rather than abstract metaphysical speculation about divine knowledge and power in themselves, the Prophet's supplications connect divine attributes to their practical manifestations and effects in creation. This functional approach to theological language maintains focus on the relationship between God and creation rather than attempting to penetrate the mystery of divine essence itself.

As Islamic theology developed into a systematic discipline, precise technical terminology emerged to navigate the complexities of divine description while maintaining transcendence. This development of specialized vocabulary represented not innovation in doctrine but refinement in expression, providing tools to articulate more precisely what earlier' generations understood but expressed less systematically. The distinction between divine essence (dhāt) and attributes (ṣifāt) became fundamental to Islamic theological discourse. Abū Ḥanīfa (d. 150/767), the great jurist whose theological views were preserved in works like al-Fiqh al-Akbar, articulated a formulation that would prove foundational: "Allah has attributes (ṣifāt) subsisting in His essence (dhāt). They are neither Him nor other than Him." This paradoxical formulation seeks to avoid two errors—identifying attributes with essence (which would make divine simplicity problematic) and completely separating them (which would suggest composition in God or make attributes independent entities).

Al-Tahāwī explains the significance of this subtle formulation: "This language preserves divine unity while allowing meaningful discourse about divine perfections. The terminology transcends the binary of identity and difference." The phrase "neither Him nor other than Him" deliberately refuses the either-or categories that would apply to created things. Created attributes are either identical with the thing possessing them (an accidental property that has no existence apart from its substrate) or separate from it (a distinct entity). Divine attributes fit neither category, requiring a unique theological grammar that acknowledges their reality while preserving divine simplicity and unity.

The paired terms tanzīh (transcendence) and tashbīh (comparison or affirmation of similarity) became crucial for maintaining theological balance. Al-Qāḍī 'Iyāḍ (d. 544/1149), the distinguished Mālikī scholar, defines their proper relationship: "Tanzīh is declaring Allah free from all creaturely attributes. Tashbīh is affirming what Allah has affirmed for

Himself. Sound theology requires both without falling into either extreme (taʿṭīl or tajsīm)." The terms represent complementary rather than contradictory principles. Tanzīh without tashbīh leads to ta'ṭīl (negation or emptying)—denying that one can say anything positive about God. Tashbīh without tanzīh leads to tajsīm (anthropomorphism)—understanding divine attributes in creaturely terms. Orthodox theology requires both movements simultaneously: affirming what God has revealed about Himself while denying creaturely modality.

The phrase bilā kayf—"without asking how"—became perhaps the most important piece of technical terminology in Islamic theology. Though associated particularly with Mālik ibn Anas's famous statement about divine "establishment on the throne" (istiwā'), the phrase came to represent a comprehensive methodological principle. Al-Bayhaqī traces its development: "From Mālik's statement about istiwā', scholars derived a comprehensive methodology: affirm the attribute (ithbāt), negate the modality (nafy al-kayfiyya), and avoid speculation (tark al-taʾwīl al-muḥdath)." The bilā kayf approach refuses to explain away scriptural language while simultaneously refusing to understand it in anthropomorphic terms. It maintains that we know that God has the attributes He claims for Himself, but we do not know and should not speculate about how He possesses these attributes.

As Muslims encountered other theological traditions, they adapted terminology while maintaining Islamic distinctiveness. Terms from Greek philosophy entered Islamic usage but were transformed in the process. Al-Ash'arī articulates this selective appropriation: "We use the philosophers' terms but not their meanings. When we say Allah is not jawhar, we mean He is not composed of matter and form, not that He lacks existence." The term jawhar (substance) in Greek philosophy refers to the underlying substrate of a thing, composed of matter and form. Islamic theologians employed the term to deny that God is a substance in this technical sense—not to deny His reality but to affirm His transcendence of categories applicable to created things.

Pre-Islamic Christian Arabic provided some vocabulary that Muslims encountered and selectively adopted. Terms like lāhūt (divinity) and nāsūt (humanity) existed in Christian Arabic theological discourse, but Muslims developed distinct usage. Al-Juwaynī (d. 478/1085) notes the selective process: "We adopt useful terms while filling them with Islamic meaning, guided always by 'laysa kamithlihi shay'un.'" The borrowed terminology was recontextualized within Islamic theological frameworks, ensuring that linguistic borrowing did not entail doctrinal compromise.

Some terms were uniquely Islamic innovations without precedent in Arabic or in other religious traditions. The term tawḥīd, derived from the verb "to make one," became the comprehensive term for Islamic monotheism, conveying not just divine unity but the active process of affirming and maintaining that unity against all forms of associationism. The term iḥdāth (temporal origination) became crucial for Islamic creation theology, denoting the bringing into existence of something that previously did not exist. The term qidam (pre-eternity or eternity without beginning) distinguished divine existence, which has no beginning, from temporal existence, which begins at some point. These terms provided precise theological vocabulary that could articulate distinctively Islamic doctrines.

Early grammarians contributed significantly to theological precision, recognizing that grammatical structures carry theological implications. Al-Zamakhsharī notes a significant verbal pattern: "The Quran uses the imperfect tense for divine action—'yakhluqu' (He creates), not just 'khalaqa' (He created)—indicating continuous divine activity transcending temporal limitations." The imperfect aspect in Arabic can denote ongoing or habitual action, making it particularly suitable for describing divine activities that are not confined to particular moments in time. The grammatical choice reflects and reinforces the theological understanding that divine creative activity is continuous rather than confined to some primordial moment of creation.

Sībawayh (d. 180/796), the foundational figure of Arabic grammar, observes theological significance in the shifting divine pronouns in the Quran: "The shift between third person ('He') and first person ('I') in divine speech serves theological purposes—third person maintains transcendence, first person enables direct address without compromising divine incomparability." When the Quran speaks about God in the third person, it maintains a certain distance appropriate to divine transcendence. When God speaks in the first person, the directness conveys divine accessibility and intimacy. The shifting pronouns thus balance transcendence and immanence within a single discourse.

Al-Farrā' analyzes the theological work performed by conditional statements in the Quran: "When Allah says 'If there were gods besides Allah, they would have sought a way to the Lord of the Throne' (17:42), the impossible condition teaches through negation what direct statement cannot convey." The counterfactual conditional—stating the consequences of an impossible condition—serves as a form of argumentation that demonstrates the impossibility of the condition itself. The verse doesn't directly assert "There are no other gods" but demonstrates it through showing the absurd consequences if there were, making the theological point through logical implication rather than mere assertion.

Perhaps no issue challenged early theological language more than Quranic passages attributing apparently human characteristics to God. The Quran contains numerous verses that seem to attribute physical form or human qualities to God. References to divine "hand" appear in verses like "The hand of Allah is above their hands" (48:10). The Throne receives multiple mentions, as in "The Throne of your Lord will be carried above them" (69:17). Divine rest or settling appears in "To your Lord on that day will be the place of rest" (75:12). The controversial term istiwā' (often translated as "rose over" or "established Himself upon") appears in "Then He rose over (istawā) the Throne" (7:54) and similar verses.

Additionally, hadith literature contains language that appears even more anthropomorphic. The famous tradition states, "Allah created Adam in His image" (found in both Ṣaḥīḥ al-Bukhārī and Ṣaḥīḥ Muslim). Another hadith reports, "The hearts of the children of Adam are between two fingers of the Most Merciful" (Ṣaḥīḥ Muslim). Yet another states, "Our Lord laughs at His servant's despair while relief is near" (Sunan Ibn Mājah). These traditions use vivid anthropomorphic language that posed significant interpretive challenges for early Muslims committed to divine transcendence.

Different groups developed distinct approaches to this challenging material. Many early authorities, whom later scholars called ahl al-ithbāt (the affirmers), affirmed these descriptions while denying any similarity to creation. Ibn Khuzayma (d. 311/924) states this position clearly: "We affirm what Allah and His Messenger have affirmed—hands, eyes, pleasure, anger—while believing 'laysa kamithlihi shay'un.' We affirm the names and attributes without likening, modality, or comparison." This approach takes the principle of divine incomparability as governing hermeneutical principle while refusing to explain away scriptural language. The attributes mentioned in scripture are real divine attributes, but they differ absolutely from any creaturely attribute sharing the same name.

Others, whom later scholars called ahl al-ta'wīl (the interpreters), interpreted anthropomorphic language metaphorically from the earliest period. Even Muqātil ibn Sulaymān (d. 150/767), generally known for literalistic exegesis, interpreted "hand" as power and "eye" as knowledge in specific contexts where the text seemed to require such interpretation. This approach saw metaphorical interpretation as sometimes necessary to preserve divine transcendence and as consistent with ordinary Arabic usage, where "hand" commonly means power or control and "eye" means watchful care.

A significant group, known as ahl al-tafwīḍ (the delegators), delegated the precise meaning to God while affirming the general sense. Sufyān ibn 'Uyayna (d. 198/814), a respected early authority, said about anthropomorphic verses: "Their recitation is their interpretation"—meaning we recite them as revealed without claiming to understand their precise meaning. This approach combines affirmation of scriptural language with agnosticism about its precise referent, maintaining that God knows what He means by these expressions while we affirm them without full comprehension.

Through debate and reflection across these different approaches, several principles emerged that would guide mainstream Islamic theology. The principle of appropriateness (mā yalīqu bi-Allāh) holds that whatever interpretation preserves divine perfection and transcendence is preferred over what compromises it. Al-Muḥāsibī articulated this principle: "Whatever interpretation preserves divine perfection and transcendence is preferred over what compromises it. This is not changing God's word but understanding it appropriately." The principle provides a criterion for evaluating competing interpretations—the interpretation that best preserves divine transcendence and perfection deserves preference.

The context principle emphasized that apparently anthropomorphic language must be read in its scriptural context. Ibn Qutayba (d. 276/889) in Ta'wīl Mukhtalif al-Ḥadīth argued: "Look at the context. When the Prophet says 'Allah laughs,' he immediately mentions divine mercy. The context prevents physical understanding and points to the meaning—divine approval and grace." The broader context of scriptural passages often provides interpretive guidance, suggesting how particular expressions should be understood. When divine "laughter" appears in contexts discussing mercy and acceptance, the context suggests that "laughter" signifies divine pleasure and approval rather than physical expression.

The principle of Arabic language usage emphasized that the Quran was revealed in Arabic and should be interpreted according to established Arabic usage. Al-Ash'arī emphasized: "The Quran was revealed in Arabic. Arabs say 'the hand of the king', meaning his power, 'under my eye', meaning my protection. Why abandon known Arabic usage when interpreting divine speech?" This principle recognizes that figurative and metaphorical language is intrinsic to Arabic (as to all languages), and that interpreting divine speech according to established Arabic usage does not constitute distortion but rather proper understanding.

Several specific controversies shaped the development of theological language in decisive ways. The trial of Ahmad ibn Ḥanbal (d. 241/855) during the Mu'tazilite inquisition (miḥna) over the createdness of the Quran involved fundamental questions about divine speech and attributes. Ibn Ḥanbal's position—"The Quran is the uncreated speech of Allah"—eventually prevailed, but with important nuances that prevented crude literalism. Al-Ṭabarī explains the resulting consensus: "The words we recite are created, the meanings they convey are eternal. This preserves both divine transcendence and the reality of revelation." The Quran as meaning, as divine speech in itself, is uncreated and eternal. The Quran as physical book, as recited sounds, as written letters, participates in creation. This distinction allowed affirming both the eternity of God's speech and the obvious created nature of physical Quranic manuscripts.

The controversy over the Ḥashwiyya, groups accused of crude anthropomorphism, demonstrated the boundaries of acceptable belief. Al-Ka'bī (d. 319/931) reports debates with those who claimed "Allah sits on the Throne physically, leaving space for the Prophet." The mainstream response, articulated by al-Ash'arī and others, rejected such views decisively: "Such beliefs violate 'laysa kamithlihi shay'un' and have no basis in authentic understanding." While the majority affirmed that God's relationship to the Throne is real (not merely metaphorical), they rejected any physical or spatial interpretation that would liken God to creatures who occupy space.

At the opposite extreme, the Jahmite tendency toward complete negation of attributes also faced rejection. The followers of Jahm ibn Ṣafwān negated all positive attributes in the name of preserving divine transcendence. Al-Dārimī (d. 280/894) responded: "In fleeing from tashbīh, they fell into ta'ṭīl (negation). The correct path affirms what Allah affirmed while maintaining transcendence." This represented the other extreme, so emphasizing divine transcendence that nothing positive could be said about God at all. Mainstream theology rejected this path as effectively denying the revealed divine names and attributes.

By the third and ninth centuries, balanced formulations emerged that would characterize mainstream Islamic theology across different schools. Al-Ṭaḥāwī's creed (d. 321/933) articulates what became widely accepted as orthodox: "Allah is exalted beyond having limits, boundaries, sides, organs, or limbs. The six directions do not contain Him as they contain created things. The 'establishment on the Throne' is real, but its modality is unknown. To deny it is kufr, to discuss its modality is bid'a." This formulation affirms the reality of what scripture affirms (the istiwā' or establishment on the Throne) while denying any spatial or physical understanding, and it declares that speculation about the precise mode constitutes blameworthy innovation.

Al-Māturīdī developed a sophisticated synthesis that recognized anthropomorphic expressions as constituting a unique category of language. He proposed that "the anthropomorphic expressions in Quran and Sunnah are neither purely literal (ḥaqīqa) nor purely metaphorical (majāz) but a special category—divine description (waṣf ilāhī) that transcends ordinary language categories." This formulation refuses to accept the binary of literal versus metaphorical, suggesting instead that language applied to God functions in a unique way that cannot be reduced to ordinary categories of human speech. Divine descriptions are neither straightforwardly literal (which would imply anthropomorphism) nor merely metaphorical (which would imply they don't really apply to God) but constitute a third category requiring its own interpretive principles.

Ibn Abī Zayd al-Qayrawānī (d. 386/996), the distinguished Mālikī scholar, provides practical guidance in his famous Risāla: "It is obligatory to believe in the names and attributes mentioned in the Quran and Sunnah, to pass them on as they came without explanation (tafsīr), to believe in them without comparison (tamthīl), and to avoid saying what they mean while knowing they don't resemble human attributes." This formulation became characteristic of Mālikī theology—affirm scriptural language, transmit it unchanged, avoid claiming to explain precisely what it means, but maintain firmly that it doesn't mean what similar language means when applied to creatures.

Early scholars developed several linguistic strategies for handling anthropomorphic language that balanced affirmation with transcendence. The distinction between attribute (ṣifa) and the one described (mawṣūf) proved important. Al-Bāqillānī explains: "When we say 'Allah has a hand,' we affirm the attribute (hand) while the reality of how this attribute subsists in the divine essence transcends our understanding." This distinction separates the question of whether God has the attribute from the question of how He possesses it. The first question receives an affirmative answer based on scripture; the second exceeds human comprehension.

The practice of reading anthropomorphic verses alongside transcendent verses became a standard interpretive method. Ibn 'Abbās established the principle: "Interpret the ambiguous (mutashābih) by the clear (muḥkam). 'Nothing is like Him' is clear; it governs all else." This hermeneutical principle gives interpretive priority to verses clearly establishing divine transcendence, using them as the lens through which all other verses must be read. Since "laysa kamithlihi shay'un" is unambiguous in meaning, it governs the interpretation of verses whose meaning might be ambiguous, ensuring that no interpretation compromises divine incomparability.

The development of technical qualifiers that became standard in theological discourse represented another linguistic solution. Terms like bilā kayf (without asking how), bilā tashbīh (without likening), and bi-ḥadd yaḍu'uhu li-nafsihi (in a manner He has determined for Himself) became standard qualifiers preserving meaning while negating crude understanding. These qualifiers could be attached to any affirmation of divine attributes, simultaneously affirming the reality of the attribute and denying any creaturely mode of understanding it.

The early Islamic period witnessed remarkable linguistic creativity as Muslims developed ways to speak about the Incomparable God. The Prophet's own discourse provided models of balanced expression that affirmed divine attributes while maintaining transcendence, establishing patterns that would guide all subsequent theological language. His methods combined affirmation with qualification, employed grammatical forms that suggested continuity and transcendence, used analogies while preventing literalistic misunderstanding, and connected divine attributes to their practical effects in creation. As theology became more systematic, technical terminology emerged that could capture the subtle distinctions necessary for preserving orthodox understanding. Terms like dhāt and ṣifāt, tanzīh and tashbīh, bilā kayf, and others provided precise vocabulary for articulating theological truths that earlier generations understood but expressed less systematically.

The challenge of anthropomorphic language, rather than creating insurmountable obstacles, led to sophisticated interpretive principles that would guide Islamic theology for centuries. Different approaches emerged—affirmation without inquiry into modality, metaphorical interpretation, and delegation of precise meaning to God—yet all shared commitment to preserving divine transcendence while maintaining scriptural fidelity. The controversies that erupted over these issues ultimately led to balanced formulations that avoided both extremes of crude anthropomorphism and complete negation of attributes. These formulations recognized that scriptural language about God is neither straightforwardly literal nor merely metaphorical but functions according to unique principles appropriate to divine speech.

These early linguistic negotiations established several enduring principles that would characterize Islamic theological discourse across its diverse schools and periods. Human language can meaningfully refer to God while acknowledging its fundamental limitations when applied to infinite reality. Apparent contradictions in divine description often point to transcendent realities beyond human categories rather than representing genuine logical problems. Maintaining divine incomparability requires not the abandonment of scriptural language but its proper understanding according to principles that balance affirmation with transcendence. The patterns established in this formative period—balancing affirmation with negation, meaning with mystery, accessibility with transcendence—would continue to characterize Islamic theological discourse throughout its history, demonstrating that the challenge of speaking about the One who is "naught is like unto Him" generates not linguistic poverty but creative abundance. The very difficulty of the task stimulated sophisticated reflection on the nature and limits of theological language, producing a rich tradition of linguistic and hermeneutical analysis that remains instructive for contemporary theology.

Chapter 4. Revelation, Interpretation, and the Preservation of Mystery

The Quranic principle "naught is like unto Him" extends beyond theological description to encompass the very nature of divine communication itself. How does the Incomparable God reveal Himself to finite human consciousness? How should believers approach a revelation that simultaneously discloses and conceals, clarifies and mystifies? This chapter examines how Islamic tradition developed sophisticated hermeneutical principles that preserve divine mystery within the interpretive process, recognizing that authentic engagement with divine revelation requires acknowledging both what can be understood and what necessarily transcends human comprehension.

The science of Quranic interpretation (tafsīr) developed elaborate methodologies for approaching divine revelation while maintaining consciousness of human interpretive limitations. These methodologies represent not merely technical procedures but embody profound theological convictions about the relationship between finite human understanding and infinite divine communication. Ibn Taymiyya (d. 728/1328), in his influential Muqaddima fī Uṣūl al-Tafsīr, articulates what became the standard hierarchy of interpretive sources: "The Quran is explained by the Quran itself, then by the Sunnah, then by the statements of the Companions, then by the statements of the Successors. Each level involves greater human involvement and thus greater possibility of interpretive limitation." This hierarchy itself embodies a principle of interpretive humility, acknowledging that human understanding becomes increasingly fallible as it moves away from the immediacy of divine revelation. The progression from Quranic self-interpretation to prophetic explanation to Companion understanding to Successor commentary represents degrees of mediation between divine intent and human comprehension.

The principle of tafsīr al-Qur'ān bi-l-Qur'ān (interpreting the Quran through the Quran itself) holds privileged position in this hierarchy. Al-Suyūṭī (d. 911/1505) in his encyclopedic al-Itqān provides numerous examples of this methodology: "What is stated generally in one place is specified elsewhere, what is summarized in one verse is elaborated in another. This internal interpretation preserves divine intent without human interference." The Quran's self-interpretation represents the most authoritative form of exegesis precisely because it involves no human mediation. Al-Ṭabarī demonstrates this principle specifically regarding divine transcendence: "'Nothing is like unto Him' (42:11) interprets every anthropomorphic expression. 'Allah is the Light of the heavens and the earth' (24:35) is immediately followed by 'The parable of His light'—the Quran itself indicates this is similitude, not literal description." This internal Quranic hermeneutic provides interpretive keys that prevent misunderstanding, particularly regarding divine attributes. The juxtaposition of apparently anthropomorphic language with explicit affirmations of divine transcendence guides interpretation without requiring external human speculation.

The Prophet's interpretations, preserved in authentic hadith, carry special authority as the second level of the interpretive hierarchy. Al-Baghawī (d. 516/1122) notes a crucial feature of prophetic exegesis: "When the Prophet explained 'al-ṣirāṭ al-mustaqīm' as 'the Book of Allah,' he provided authoritative interpretation while preserving the verse's multiple valid meanings—it remains guidance, Islam, and truth simultaneously." Prophetic interpretation characteristically opens meaning rather than closing it, providing authoritative guidance while acknowledging that Quranic language often encompasses multiple valid significations. This multiplication rather than reduction of meaning became a characteristic feature of classical Islamic exegesis.

Classical exegetes recognized that Quranic verses often carry multiple valid interpretations without contradiction, a recognition that serves the preservation of divine mystery by preventing any single human interpretation from claiming exclusive truth about divine meaning. Ibn al-Jawzī (d. 597/1201) articulates this principle in Zād al-Masīr: "When interpretations do not contradict each other or established principles, they may all be intended. The Quran's miraculous nature (i'jāz) includes its capacity to communicate multiple truths simultaneously." This understanding of Quranic polysemy differs from mere ambiguity or vagueness. Rather, it suggests that divine speech possesses a richness and depth that can support multiple meanings simultaneously, each valid within its proper context and framework.

Al-Rāzī exemplifies this approach in interpreting the verse "He is with you wherever you are" (57:4). He presents multiple interpretations without suggesting they are mutually exclusive: the verse means with you by His knowledge, indicating that He knows all you do; it means with you by His power, indicating that He controls all that happens to you; it means with you by His care, indicating that He protects and guides you. Al-Rāzī then observes that all these interpretations are true simultaneously without contradicting the fundamental principle that "naught is like unto Him." The "withness" indicated by the verse does not suggest spatial proximity, which would compromise divine transcendence, but rather knowledge, power, and care that operate without spatial limitation. This multiplicity of valid meanings preserves divine transcendence by preventing any single interpretation from exhausting divine intent or reducing it to creaturely categories.

The principle of linguistic precedence holds that the apparent meaning takes precedence unless there is evidence requiring departure from it. Al-Zarkashī (d. 794/1392) in al-Burhān fī 'Ulūm al-Qur'ān articulates this principle: "The apparent meaning (ẓāhir) takes precedence unless there is evidence (dalīl) requiring departure from it. This evidence may be rational, textual, or based on necessary preservation of divine transcendence." He provides a crucial example that demonstrates how the principle of divine incomparability functions as decisive evidence affecting interpretation: "Allah's 'hand' (yad) apparently means the bodily limb. But 'laysa kamithlihi shay'un' provides decisive evidence against this apparent meaning, requiring either metaphorical interpretation or delegation of the true meaning to Allah." This formulation shows how different types of evidence interact in interpretation. Linguistic evidence suggests one meaning, but theological evidence rooted in the principle of divine transcendence provides compelling reason to understand the term differently.

Al-Shāṭibī (d. 790/1388) develops sophisticated contextual analysis in his influential al-Muwāfaqāt, recognizing that proper interpretation requires attention to multiple levels of context. He writes that "the Quran was revealed over twenty-three years addressing specific situations while providing eternal guidance." The interpreter must therefore understand the specific context of revelation (sabab al-nuzūl) without limiting meaning to it, recognizing that while revelation addresses particular historical circumstances, its meaning transcends those circumstances. The interpreter must also consider whether the passage is Meccan or Medinan, as this affects emphasis and style. The immediate textual context (siyāq) surrounding any verse influences its interpretation, as does the overall Quranic context (naẓm al-Qur'ān) in which themes and concepts recur throughout the text. This contextual awareness preserves mystery by acknowledging that divine communication transcends its historical occasions while working through them. The eternal meaning operates through but is not exhausted by the temporal occasion of revelation.

Al-Ghazālī, in his treatise Qānūn al-Ta'wīl, provides crucial guidelines for understanding the limits of rational interpretation. He writes that "reason ('aql) serves interpretation but within limits." Reason can determine what is impossible for Allah, such as ignorance or inability, as these contradict divine perfection. Reason can recognize when literal meaning contradicts established principles, necessitating an alternative interpretation. However, reason cannot determine the true nature (ḥaqīqa) of divine attributes, as this exceeds its capacity. Nor can reason exhaust the meanings Allah intended, as divine intent transcends finite human comprehension. This framework preserves divine mystery by explicitly acknowledging where human reason must yield to divine transcendence. Reason plays a legitimate but limited role in interpretation—it can identify impossibilities and contradictions, but it cannot penetrate to the ultimate reality of divine attributes or exhaust divine meaning.

The Quranic distinction between clear (muḥkam) and ambiguous (mutashābih) verses provides the foundational framework for understanding how divine revelation preserves mystery within clarity. This distinction, explicitly articulated in the Quran itself, became central to Islamic hermeneutical theory. The locus classicus appears in Sūrat Āl 'Imrān: "It is He who has sent down to you the Book; in it are verses that are precise (muḥkamāt)—they are the foundation of the Book—and others ambiguous (mutashābihāt). As for those in whose hearts is deviation, they follow that which is ambiguous thereof, seeking discord and seeking its interpretation. And none knows its interpretation except Allah. And those firm in knowledge say, 'We believe in it. All is from our Lord.' And none will remember except those of understanding" (3:7).

This verse itself became subject to extensive commentary, particularly regarding the crucial question of whether to pause after "except Allah" or continue to include "those firm in knowledge" among those who know the interpretation. This grammatical ambiguity in a verse about ambiguity itself demonstrates the self-referential complexity of the issue. The placement of the pause determines whether ultimate knowledge of mutashābihāt verses belongs exclusively to God or whether those firmly grounded in knowledge share in this understanding to some degree.

Al-Ṭabarī presents multiple scholarly opinions before concluding: "Muḥkam verses are those whose meaning is clear and univocal, requiring no interpretation. Mutashābih verses are those admitting multiple meanings or whose true significance is known only to Allah." This definition identifies two types of ambiguity: verses that admit multiple valid meanings and verses whose ultimate significance transcends human understanding entirely. Al-Māturīdī provides a more developed categorization, dividing mutashābih verses into three types. First, linguistic ambiguity involves words with multiple established meanings in Arabic usage. Second, conceptual ambiguity concerns meanings that transcend human experience, where the words themselves may be clear, but what they signify exceeds ordinary human understanding. Third, purposeful ambiguity reflects divine wisdom in not revealing certain matters fully, suggesting that some ambiguity serves theological and spiritual purposes rather than representing a deficiency in divine communication.

Al-Rāghib al-Iṣfahānī (d. 502/1108) provides philosophical depth to the discussion of mutashābihāt: "Mutashābih verses are those where the divine intent transcends what human language can definitively convey. They point to realities (ḥaqā'iq) beyond the forms (ṣuwar) of expression." This formulation recognizes that language itself faces inherent limitations when attempting to convey realities that transcend ordinary human experience. The linguistic forms available in human speech cannot fully capture certain divine realities, necessitating a mode of expression that points toward meaning without completely containing it.

Classical scholars recognized that mutashābih verses serve essential functions rather than representing defects in revelation. The existence of ambiguous verses performs important theological and spiritual work. Al-Qurṭubī notes the function of spiritual testing and development: "The existence of mutashābihāt tests the servants—will they submit to Allah's knowledge or follow their own speculations? This develops spiritual humility essential for approaching divine reality." The presence of verses whose meaning is not immediately transparent requires believers to make a choice between humble submission and arrogant speculation. This choice reveals and shapes spiritual character, developing the humility necessary for proper relationship with divine reality.

Ibn 'Aṭiyya (d. 541/1147) observes how ambiguous verses prevent claims to comprehensive understanding: "If all verses were muḥkam, humans might claim complete comprehension of divine revelation. Mutashābihāt remind us that divine communication exceeds our full understanding." The very existence of verses that resist definitive interpretation functions as a safeguard against human pretensions to exhaustive knowledge of divine revelation. No matter how advanced human understanding becomes, the mutashābihāt remain as permanent reminders of the limits of human comprehension before divine reality.

Al-Rāzī argues that ambiguous verses encourage continued reflection across generations: "Mutashābih verses require ongoing contemplation, preventing the Quran from becoming a closed book. Each generation discovers new meanings within divine parameters." Rather than representing deficiency, ambiguity ensures that the Quran remains an inexhaustible source of meaning that cannot be reduced to any single interpretation or confined to any particular historical understanding. Each generation brings new questions and new insights to the text, discovering meanings that previous generations may not have perceived.

Al-Bayhaqī states simply but profoundly: "Many mutashābihāt relate to divine attributes and actions, preserving the principle 'laysa kamithlihi shay'un' by preventing definitive human statements about divine nature." The connection between ambiguous verses and divine incomparability is direct and essential. If humans could speak definitively about divine nature using clear, univocal language, this would compromise divine transcendence. The preservation of ambiguity in verses concerning divine attributes ensures that human speech about God never becomes so confident that it forgets the absolute difference between Creator and creation.

Classical exegetes examined specific examples of mutashābih verses and the various approaches scholars developed for handling them. The verse stating "The Most Merciful rose over the Throne (istawā 'alā al-'arsh)" (20:5) became perhaps the most discussed example of interpretive approaches to ambiguous language. Some early authorities adopted what might be called a literalist approach, though this term requires careful qualification. Ibn Ḥāmid (d. 403/1012) articulated this position: "We affirm rising without asking how or comparing to creation." This approach affirms the reality of what the verse states while systematically refusing to specify its mode or compare it to creaturely actions. The affirmation is literal in the sense that it accepts the verse's language, but it refuses to specify what this language ultimately means.

Others adopted a metaphorical approach, interpreting the term according to its established meanings in Arabic usage. Al-Ṭabarī records interpretations of istawā as "conquered," "subdued," or "established authority," noting that all these represent known Arabic meanings of the term. This approach sees metaphorical interpretation not as explaining away revelation but as understanding it according to the flexibility inherent in Arabic linguistic usage. The third major approach involved delegation of precise meaning to God while affirming general sense. Mālik ibn Anas's famous statement became paradigmatic for this position: "Istiwa' is known, the modality is unknown, belief in it is obligatory, questioning it is innovation." This formulation affirms that something real is being communicated by the term while denying that humans can know the precise nature of this divine reality. The statement also includes prescriptive elements—belief is obligatory, speculation is forbidden—indicating that this represents not merely an interpretive choice but a theological principle.

The verse "And your Lord comes with the angels, rank upon rank" (89:22) posed similar challenges. Al-Bayḍāwī (d. 685/1286) presents three interpretive approaches without decisively choosing among them. The first understands "His command comes" as metonymy for divine decree, with the divine "coming" representing the manifestation of divine command rather than spatial movement. The second interprets "signs of His power come" as the manifestation of divine authority through created effects. The third maintains "He comes in a manner befitting His transcendence, which we cannot comprehend," affirming the reality of what the verse states while denying human capacity to understand its mode. The presentation of multiple approaches without definitive selection itself embodies interpretive humility, acknowledging that human understanding cannot definitively capture divine intent.

The disjointed letters (al-muqaṭṭa'āt) opening certain sūras represent perhaps the most mysterious element of the Quranic text. Ibn Kathīr summarizes scholarly positions without resolving the matter: these are names of the sūras; they indicate the miraculous nature of the Quran, demonstrating that it is composed of ordinary letters yet remains inimitable; they are mysteries known only to Allah. He notes that each position acknowledges human interpretive limitation, suggesting that the letters serve precisely to indicate the limits of human understanding. Their very inscrutability reminds readers that revelation contains depths that exceed human comprehension.

The classical period witnessed sophisticated debate about the proper approach to mutashābihāt, crystallizing around the grammatical question of where to pause in verse 3:7. The stop position (waqf) involved pausing after "except Allah," excluding "those firm in knowledge" from those who know the interpretation. This position was advocated by Ibn 'Abbās in one narration, Ubayy ibn Ka'b, and other early authorities. Al-Suyūṭī explains the theological rationale: "This preserves Allah's exclusive knowledge of ultimate meanings while allowing scholarly engagement with possible interpretations." This approach maintains a sharp distinction between human interpretive efforts, which remain always tentative and limited, and divine knowledge of ultimate meaning, which remains absolute and exclusive.

The continuation position (waṣl) involved including "those firm in knowledge" among those who know interpretation. This position was supported by Mujāhid and Ibn 'Abbās in another narration, demonstrating that even individual Companions held varying views on this question. Al-Ṭabarī, who favored this interpretation, argues: "They know the interpretation (ta'wīl) but not the ultimate reality (ḥaqīqa) it points to." This formulation allows "those firm in knowledge" to possess genuine interpretive understanding while denying them exhaustive knowledge of divine reality. The distinction between interpretation and ultimate reality becomes crucial—scholars can understand what verses mean in a practical sense without penetrating to the ultimate metaphysical reality they indicate.

Al-Ghazālī provides what became an influential synthesis of these positions: "Those firm in knowledge know interpretations within human capacity while acknowledging that ultimate meanings transcend their comprehension. They know and don't know simultaneously—this is true wisdom." This paradoxical formulation captures the complexity of human relationship to revelation. Scholars genuinely know something—they are not complete agnostics before the text. Yet they simultaneously do not know in an absolute sense—their knowledge remains limited and partial. The coexistence of knowledge and ignorance, rather than representing confusion, constitutes true wisdom about the nature of revelation and human understanding.

The recognition that divine revelation necessarily exceeds human comprehension led to the development of sophisticated approaches embodying interpretive humility. These approaches were not merely intellectual positions but represented comprehensive methodologies for engaging revelation while preserving its mystery. The methodology of tafwīḍ (delegation) represents perhaps the most explicit acknowledgment of interpretive limitation. Al-Safārīnī (d. 1188/1774) provides a classical definition: "Tafwīḍ is affirming what Allah and His Messenger affirmed while delegating knowledge of the true nature and modality to Allah." This approach maintains the reality of what revelation affirms while denying human capacity to comprehend fully its ultimate nature.

Early authorities practiced tafwīḍ naturally before it became systematized as a formal methodology. Sufyān al-Thawrī's statement about anthropomorphic verses became paradigmatic: "We narrate these hadiths and believe in them without saying 'how' or 'why.'" This formulation emphasizes transmission and belief while systematically refusing speculation about mode or reason. The practitioner of tafwīḍ accepts and affirms what revelation states without claiming to understand how it can be or why it must be so. Al-Juwaynī provides a systematic theological rationale for this approach: "Tafwīḍ is not intellectual defeat but recognition that finite minds cannot encompass infinite reality. It preserves both revealed content and divine transcendence." This formulation is crucial because it reframes what might appear as intellectual resignation or failure. Rather than representing the inability to answer questions that should be answerable, tafwīḍ recognizes questions that by their nature exceed human capacity. The limitation lies not in human intellectual weakness but in the necessary difference between finite human understanding and infinite divine reality.

Ibn Qudāma (d. 620/1223) describes the practical application of tafwīḍ methodology: "When encountering Allah's 'hand' or 'face,' the practitioner of tafwīḍ affirms these are Allah's attributes as stated, negates any resemblance to creation, refrains from claiming knowledge of their reality, and focuses on practical guidance rather than speculation." This four-step process embodies balanced engagement with revelation. Affirmation ensures that scriptural language is not denied or explained away. Negation of resemblance preserves divine transcendence. Refusal to claim knowledge maintains epistemic humility. Focus on practical guidance ensures that theology serves spiritual and ethical purposes rather than degenerating into empty speculation.

Beyond specific methodologies, a general principle of apophatic restraint characterized traditional interpretation. Al-Qushayrī warns against interpretive overconfidence: "Beware of saying 'This verse definitely means...' about matters touching divine nature. Say instead 'It may mean...' or 'The apparent meaning suggests...' preserving space for meanings beyond your comprehension." This linguistic restraint embodies theological humility. By using probabilistic rather than definitive language, interpreters acknowledge that their understanding remains tentative and that divine meaning may exceed what they have grasped.

Ibn 'Arabī systematizes what many scholars practiced intuitively, recognizing multiple levels of meaning in revelation: "Every verse has an outward aspect (ẓāhir) accessible to all, an inward aspect (bāṭin) for those with insight, a limit (ḥadd) where human understanding stops, and a point of ascent (maṭla') where divine meaning begins." This framework acknowledges that verses operate on multiple levels simultaneously. The outward meaning provides basic guidance accessible to all believers. The inward meaning yields deeper insights to those with spiritual and intellectual preparation. Yet even the most advanced understanding encounters limits beyond which it cannot pass, and at this boundary divine meaning properly begins—a meaning that remains with God and transcends all human comprehension.

Al-Sha'rānī (d. 973/1565) articulates the principle of generational humility: "Each generation discovers meanings previous generations missed, not because earlier scholars were deficient but because divine revelation continually unfolds its treasures. This should humble every interpreter." This recognition that new meanings emerge across generations prevents interpretive closure. No generation can claim to have exhausted the Quran's meaning, and the discoveries of one generation do not invalidate the insights of previous generations. Rather, divine revelation proves inexhaustible, continually yielding new meanings as it encounters new questions and new contexts. This historical consciousness about interpretation itself embodies humility—each generation recognizes itself as standing within a continuous tradition while acknowledging that the tradition itself never achieves final, complete understanding.

Traditional scholarship developed ethical guidelines for approaching divine revelation, recognizing that proper interpretation requires not only intellectual capacity but spiritual preparation. Al-Ghazālī, in his masterwork Iḥyā' 'Ulūm al-Dīn lists prerequisites for interpreters that extend beyond technical competence. The interpreter requires purification of the heart from envy, pride, and worldliness, as these spiritual defects distort perception and judgment. The interpreter must seek knowledge for Allah's sake rather than reputation, as improper motivation corrupts the interpretive process. Recognition of one's limitations before divine mystery remains essential, preventing the presumption that leads to false certainty. The interpreter should consult earlier authorities while remaining open to new understanding, balancing respect for tradition with intellectual honesty about contemporary questions.

Ibn al-Ṣalāḥ (d. 643/1245) warns against the dangers of purely rational speculation divorced from tradition: "Interpreting by mere opinion (ra'y) about divine matters is prohibited. The Prophet ﷺ said: 'Whoever speaks about the Quran by his opinion has erred even if correct.'" This hadith establishes that proper interpretation requires grounding in tradition rather than individual speculation. Even an accidentally correct interpretation arrived at through an improper method represents error because the method itself violates the reverence and humility required when approaching divine speech. Al-Ṭaḥāwī emphasizes communal considerations: "In matters of ambiguity touching divine nature, maintaining community unity supersedes individual interpretive claims. Better to remain silent than cause division over incomprehensible matters." This principle recognizes that theology serves communal purposes and that interpretive speculation that fractures community represents failure, even if intellectually sophisticated.

The tradition developed institutional practices preserving interpretive humility beyond individual ethical guidelines. The isnād system, requiring chains of transmission for interpretations, prevented individual speculation from claiming unwarranted authority. Al-Dhahabī (d. 748/1348) notes: "Even in tafsīr, the isnād protects against those who would explain divine mystery through mere reason." By requiring that interpretations be traceable to earlier authorities, the system ensures that interpretation remains rooted in tradition rather than individual innovation. This does not eliminate interpretive creativity but channels it within communal constraints that prevent radical individualism.

Major interpretive works often emerged from scholarly circles rather than individual authors working in isolation. Al-Qurṭubī describes his method: "I gathered interpretations from previous authorities, compared them, and indicated where scholars differed—no single human can exhaust divine meaning." This collective approach to interpretation acknowledges that divine revelation exceeds any individual's capacity to comprehend. By presenting multiple interpretive positions rather than claiming definitive understanding, such works embody interpretive humility at the structural level.

Emphasis on studying with teachers rather than books alone preserved interpretive wisdom that could not be fully captured in written form. Al-Nawawī states: "Books contain words; teachers convey understanding, including consciousness of what transcends understanding." This principle recognizes that interpretive tradition includes not only explicit content but tacit knowledge—understanding of what questions should not be pressed, awareness of the limits of interpretation, consciousness of mystery. Teachers transmit not only information but an attitude toward knowledge itself, including recognition of its limits. This tacit dimension of interpretive tradition cannot be fully codified in texts and requires personal transmission from teacher to student.

Several case studies demonstrate how major authorities applied principles of interpretive humility to specific questions. The tradition that Allah has a "greatest name" (ism Allah al-a'ẓam) by which prayers are answered generated extensive speculation about which name this might be. Yet major authorities demonstrated remarkable restraint despite the practical importance of the question. Al-Ṭabarī observed that various hadiths suggest different names, concluding: "This itself indicates divine wisdom in concealing it, teaching us to use all divine names with reverence." Rather than seeing the uncertainty as a deficiency, al-Ṭabarī interprets it as pedagogical—the concealment serves to encourage comprehensive devotion to all divine names rather than mechanical focus on a single formula.

Ibn Ḥajar suggested that "perhaps it changes according to the caller's state and need. Divine response transcends mechanical formulas." This interpretation recognizes that the relationship with God cannot be reduced to technique. If the greatest name were definitively known, it might be treated as a magical formula for guaranteed response. The uncertainty preserves the personal, relational dimension of prayer, where God responds to the heart's sincerity rather than the correct pronunciation of particular words. Al-Nawawī adds: "The search for the greatest name may be more valuable than finding it, developing the servant's relationship with all divine names." This suggests that the process of seeking, which involves comprehensive engagement with divine names and attributes, may serve spiritual development better than definitive knowledge, which might short-circuit the process of deepening the relationship with God.

When questioned about the spirit, the Quran provides minimal information: "The spirit is from the command of my Lord, and you have not been given knowledge except a little" (17:85). This verse itself establishes that certain matters remain beyond human comprehension, and commentators demonstrated remarkable restraint in approaching it. Al-Rāzī, after presenting seventeen different philosophical opinions about the nature of the rūḥ, concludes: "After presenting these opinions, we must conclude that its reality remains with Allah. Human speculation cannot pierce this divine secret." The extensive presentation of philosophical positions serves not to resolve the question but to demonstrate that even sophisticated philosophical analysis cannot penetrate certain divinely-maintained mysteries. Al-Ālūsī comments: "The verse itself teaches methodology—some matters Allah has chosen not to reveal fully. Accepting this limitation is wisdom." The verse functions as a model for approaching other questions where divine wisdom maintains mystery rather than providing complete explanation.

Scholars debated which night in Ramadan is the Night of Power (laylat al-qadr), with textual evidence supporting multiple possibilities. Rather than seeing this uncertainty as problematic, authorities interpreted it as embodying divine mercy and wisdom. Ibn 'Abd al-Barr observed: "The disagreement itself may be divine mercy, encouraging worship throughout the possible nights rather than limiting devotion to one." The uncertainty prevents believers from concentrating all effort on a single night, instead encouraging sustained devotion throughout the month. Al-Suyūṭī developed this observation into a broader pattern: "Allah concealed this night within Ramadan as He concealed His greatest name among all names and His pleasure within acts of obedience—teaching us comprehensive devotion." This pattern of divine concealment within revelation serves pedagogical purposes, encouraging comprehensive rather than selective practice while acknowledging that ultimate certainty about some matters remains with God alone.

The Islamic tradition's approach to revelation, interpretation, and the preservation of mystery demonstrates remarkable sophistication in balancing human understanding with divine transcendence. The development of classical hermeneutical principles provided frameworks for meaningful engagement with revelation while acknowledging its ultimate transcendence of human comprehension. These principles were not abstract theoretical positions but practical guidelines that shaped how generations of Muslims approached scripture. The Quranic category of mutashābihāt verses institutionalized recognition that divine communication necessarily includes elements that exceed finite understanding, ensuring that the preservation of mystery became not an unfortunate side effect but an essential feature of revelation itself.

Traditional approaches to interpretive humility—whether through tafwīḍ, apophatic restraint, or ethical guidelines—ensured that the principle "laysa kamithlihi shay'un" governed not only theological content but the very process of interpretation itself. The principle of divine incomparability shaped not only what Muslims said about God but how they approached the task of understanding revelation. Interpretive humility became not a concession to ignorance but a positive theological virtue, recognizing that proper relationship with divine reality requires acknowledgment of its transcendence of human comprehension.

This examination reveals that preserving mystery within revelation serves not as an obstacle to religious understanding but as its essential condition. By acknowledging what cannot be fully comprehended, the tradition creates space for continual discovery across generations. It prevents claims to divine comprehension that would compromise transcendence, guarding against the presumption that finite human understanding could exhaust infinite divine meaning. It maintains the reverential distance necessary for an authentic divine-human relationship, ensuring that familiarity with revelation never degenerates into presumption about exhaustive understanding. The patterns established in classical Islamic hermeneutics—affirming while acknowledging limitation, interpreting while preserving mystery, understanding while maintaining humility—continue to guide Islamic engagement with revelation, demonstrating that the challenge of interpreting communication from the Incomparable generates not frustration but profound wisdom about the nature of human understanding and its limits before the divine.

Chapter 5. Ash'arite Contributions to Understanding Divine Transcendence

The Ash'arite school, founded by Abū al-Ḥasan al-Ash'arī (d. 324/936), represents one of the most influential theological movements in Islamic history. Emerging from a context of intense theological debate, the Ash'arites developed sophisticated methodologies for preserving the principle "laysa kamithlihi shay'un" while maintaining fidelity to scriptural sources that seemed to attribute human-like qualities to God. This chapter examines how Ash'arite theologians navigated between the rationalist reductionism of the Mu'tazilites and the literalist tendencies of some traditionalists, establishing principles that would profoundly shape mainstream Sunni theology.

Al-Ash'arī emerged in a period of unprecedented theological controversy during the third and ninth centuries in Baghdad. The Mu'tazilite school, with its emphasis on rational theology and rigorous application of philosophical principles to theological questions, had gained significant political support during the miḥna (inquisition) that extended from 218 to 234 in the Hijri calendar, corresponding to 833 to 849 in the Common Era. This period saw the Abbasid caliphate attempt to enforce Mu'tazilite doctrine, particularly regarding the createdness of the Quran, as official state orthodoxy. Meanwhile, traditionalist scholars, represented most prominently by Aḥmad ibn Ḥanbal (d. 241/855), insisted on accepting scriptural descriptions of God without rational speculation or philosophical elaboration, maintaining that human reason should not presume to explain or qualify what God has revealed about Himself.

Al-Khaṭīb al-Baghdādī (d. 463/1071) preserves vivid accounts of the theological climate in the capital: "In Baghdad, theological sessions (majālis al-kalām) were battlegrounds. The Mu'tazilites denied divine attributes as incompatible with unity. The Ḥashwiyya affirmed them with crude literalism. The Muslims sought a middle path." This characterization captures the polarization that characterized theological discourse. The Mu'tazilites, in their zeal to preserve divine unity and transcendence, denied that God possesses real attributes distinct from His essence, arguing that affirmation of multiple eternal attributes would compromise absolute divine unity. At the opposite extreme, groups pejoratively labeled Ḥashwiyya (literally "stuffers" or those who stuff their minds with traditions without understanding) affirmed divine attributes in ways that seemed to compromise divine transcendence by understanding them too literally according to their creaturely meanings.

Al-Ash'arī spent forty years as a prominent Mu'tazilite theologian before his famous conversion to traditionalist positions, though his adoption of traditionalist conclusions did not mean abandonment of rational methodology. Ibn 'Asākir (d. 571/1176) in his defense of al-Ash'arī, Tabyīn Kadhib al-Muftarī, records multiple accounts of this transformation. The most famous account involves prophetic dreams in which the Prophet Muhammad appeared commanding al-Ash'arī to "support what is related from me," meaning to defend the theological positions grounded in authentic prophetic traditions rather than those derived primarily from rational speculation.

Al-Ash'arī himself explains his methodological shift in al-Ibāna, one of his major works written after his conversion: "I used to uphold the doctrine of the negation of divine attributes, the createdness of the Quran, and that human acts are not created by Allah. Then Allah guided me and showed me the truth. I found that the Book of Allah and the Sunnah of His Prophet affirm divine attributes, the eternity of divine speech, and that Allah creates human actions." This statement indicates a fundamental reorientation in his theological approach. However, this transformation was not a simple switch from rationalism to traditionalism, from philosophical theology to naive literalism. Rather, it represented the development of a new methodology that would employ rational argumentation in service of traditional doctrine, using the tools of philosophical theology to defend positions grounded in scripture and prophetic tradition.

Al-Ash'arī established several core methodological principles that would characterize his school and distinguish it from both Mu'tazilite rationalism and traditionalist literalism. The principle of rational defense of traditional belief became foundational. Al-Bayhaqī reports al-Ash'arī's programmatic statement: "My method is to establish by rational proof what the traditionalists believe by transmitted proof. The content is theirs; the demonstration is mine." This formulation captures the distinctive Ash'arite approach. The theological conclusions derive from scripture and tradition, but the defense and systematic articulation of these conclusions employs rational argumentation. The Ash'arites accepted traditionalist conclusions about what to believe but rejected the traditionalist reluctance to engage in rational theology.

The concept of the middle position (al-mawqif al-wasaṭ) became central to Ash'arite self-understanding. Ibn Fūrak (d. 406/1015), one of al-Ash'arī's prominent students, articulates this positioning: "Our teacher took from the Mu'tazilites their rational method while rejecting their conclusions. He took from the traditionalists their conclusions while providing them rational support." This characterization suggests a synthetic methodology that combines elements from both approaches while avoiding what Ash'arites saw as the errors of each extreme. From the Mu'tazilites, Ash'arism adopted rational argumentation, philosophical terminology, and systematic presentation. From the traditionalists, it adopted substantive theological positions about divine attributes, the eternity of the Quran, and divine determination of human acts.

However, as al-Juwaynī emphasizes, this should not be understood as mere compromise or eclecticism: "Al-Ash'arī did not merely find a middle ground between extremes. He developed a comprehensive methodology that transcended the limitations of both pure rationalism and naive literalism." The Ash'arite position represents not splitting the difference between two existing approaches but creating a new synthesis with its own internal logic and coherence. The school claimed to preserve what was valid in both rationalism and traditionalism while avoiding the defects of each.

The Ash'arite methodology evolved and was refined through successive generations of scholars who expanded and systematized their master's insights. Al-Bāqillānī (d. 403/1013) systematized Ash'arite theology in major works like al-Tamhīd and al-Inṣāf, providing comprehensive presentations of Ash'arite positions with detailed argumentation. He articulates the methodological principle: "Our method requires affirming what revelation affirms while using reason to understand how these affirmations preserve divine transcendence rather than compromise it." This formulation indicates that reason serves not to judge or modify revelation but to demonstrate how revealed truths about God preserve rather than violate divine incomparability.

Al-Juwaynī (d. 478/1085), known by the honorific Imām al-Ḥaramayn (Imam of the Two Sanctuaries), further refined the methodology in works like al-Irshād. He articulates a three-fold approach: "We employ three tools: scriptural text (naql), rational proof (dalīl 'aqlī), and the principle of divine transcendence (tanzīh). When these seem to conflict, we seek interpretations that harmonize all three." This formulation recognizes that apparent conflicts may arise between what scripture seems to say, what reason seems to require, and what divine transcendence demands. The Ash'arite method seeks interpretations that satisfy all three criteria simultaneously rather than privileging one at the expense of others.

Al-Ghazālī (d. 505/1111) brought Ash'arism to its classical maturity, integrating theological doctrine with Islamic spirituality and demonstrating how Ash'arite theology could ground profound mystical practice. In al-Iqtiṣād fī al-I'tiqād, he states: "The highest achievement is to affirm divine attributes as revelation presents them while understanding them in ways that preserve absolute divine transcendence." For al-Ghazālī, proper theology balances affirmation and transcendence, neither denying what God has revealed about Himself nor understanding it in ways that compromise His incomparability.

The doctrine of bilā kayf (without asking how) became central to Ash'arite methodology, providing a technical principle for handling scriptural descriptions of God that seem anthropomorphic. Though the phrase and concept predate the Ash'arite school, al-Ash'arī and his followers transformed it from an individual response into systematic methodology. The phrase originates with early authorities, most famously Mālik ibn Anas (d. 179/795), founder of the Mālikī legal school. When asked about the verse "The Most Merciful rose over the Throne (istawā)," Mālik responded with a formulation that became paradigmatic: "Al-istiwā' is not unknown (ghayr majhūl), the modality (kayf) is not comprehensible (ghayr ma'qūl), belief in it is obligatory (wājib), and asking about it is innovation (bid'a)."

This response embodies several crucial principles. First, the term istiwā' itself is not unknown—it has established meanings in Arabic and appears in revelation. Second, the precise modality of divine istiwā' is not comprehensible to human understanding. Third, belief in what the verse affirms is religiously obligatory. Fourth, speculation about the how or mode of divine istiwā' constitutes blameworthy innovation. Al-Ash'arī transformed this response to a specific question into a general methodological principle applicable across all divine attributes. In Maqālāt al-Islāmiyyīn, he writes: "We affirm that Allah has two hands, as He said, 'Nay, His two hands are spread wide' (5:64), without asking how (bilā kayf) and without comparison (bilā tashbīh)."

Al-Bāqillānī provides the theoretical foundation for the bilā kayf methodology in al-Inṣāf, articulating what the principle entails. When Ash'arites say bilā kayf, they mean three related things. First, they do not ask about the modality (kayfiyya) because such questioning implies that divine attributes operate according to created modalities, which would compromise transcendence. Second, they do not imagine (tawahhum) any specific form, as imagination is necessarily limited to created experiences and cannot grasp the uncreated. Third, they do not compare (qiyās) divine attributes to created attributes, as comparison violates the fundamental principle that "naught is like unto Him." These three negations—of asking about mode, of imagining form, of comparing to creation—preserve divine transcendence while allowing affirmation of what revelation states.

The Ash'arites applied the bilā kayf methodology to specific scriptural descriptions that seemed to attribute physical characteristics to God. Regarding references to divine hand, al-Ash'arī states in al-Ibāna: "We affirm that Allah has a hand, as the Quran states. This hand is an attribute neither identical to nor separate from His essence. Its reality (ḥaqīqa) differs entirely from created hands. We affirm the attribute, negate the modality, and avoid speculation about its nature." This formulation demonstrates the characteristic Ash'arite move: affirm what scripture affirms, deny that it means what it would mean if applied to creatures, and refuse to speculate about what it does mean in divine reality.

Regarding references to divine face, al-Bayhaqī records the Ash'arite position in al-Asmā' wa-l-Ṣifāt: "His face is an eternal attribute subsisting in His essence. It is not a limb, part, or dimension. When creatures perish,

'Everything will perish except His face' (28:88)—His face remains, indicating an attribute of the eternal essence, not a physical feature." The verse's statement that everything perishes except God's face is taken as evidence that "face" indicates something eternal about God rather than a physical feature, as physical features belong to the created realm that perishes.

The case of divine establishment on the throne (istiwā') received particularly extensive treatment. Al-Juwaynī explains the Ash'arite understanding: "When we affirm that Allah 'rose over the Throne,' we understand that this is true information from Allah about Himself, that it does not imply physical sitting, contact, or location, that the Throne does not bear Him, for He bears the Throne and its bearers, and that we affirm establishment (istiwā') while negating all creaturely modes of establishment." This interpretation maintains the reality of what the verse affirms while systematically negating all the implications that would follow from creaturely establishment.

Al-Ghazālī extended the bilā kayf principle beyond obviously anthropomorphic attributes to all divine attributes, demonstrating its comprehensive applicability. In Qawā'id al-'Aqā'id, he writes: "The principle applies to all divine attributes—His knowledge is bilā kayf (not like human knowledge involving acquisition or change), His power is bilā kayf (not involving potential or exertion), His existence is bilā kayf (not involving location or duration). This comprehensive application preserves divine transcendence across all theological discourse." Even attributes that do not seem anthropomorphic on their face—like knowledge, power, and existence—must be understood bilā kayf, because even these attributes as understood in creaturely terms involve limitations that cannot apply to God.

The bilā kayf methodology faced criticisms from multiple directions, requiring Ash'arite scholars to defend and clarify their approach. The Mu'tazilites charged that bilā kayf represents intellectual abdication, affirming contradictions without resolution. If one affirms that God has attributes like hand, face, and establishment on a throne while denying that these mean what they ordinarily mean, one seems to affirm words without meaning. Al-Bāqillānī responds to this criticism: "Rather, it is intellectual precision. We distinguish between what revelation affirms (thabata) and what reason can comprehend (aḥāṭa). Affirming the former while acknowledging limits on the latter is wisdom, not abdication." The distinction between knowing that something is true and comprehending how it is true becomes crucial. Ash'arism claims to affirm genuine attributes without claiming to comprehend their divine mode of existence.

From the opposite direction, some traditionalists, particularly those in the Ḥanbalī tradition, worried that bilā kayf might open the door to ta'wīl (metaphorical interpretation that departs from apparent meaning). Al-Bayhaqī clarifies the distinction: "Bilā kayf is not ta'wīl. Ta'wīl claims to know the true meaning by departing from the apparent. Bilā kayf affirms the apparent meaning while denying knowledge of the modality. We neither change the meaning nor claim comprehensive understanding." This clarification maintains that bilā kayf represents a distinct approach, neither literalistic affirmation that compromises transcendence nor metaphorical interpretation that explains away scriptural language.

The Ash'arite school developed nuanced approaches to scriptural passages that seemed to attribute human characteristics to God, recognizing that different types of anthropomorphic expressions required different analytical strategies. Al-Juwaynī in al-Irshād classifies anthropomorphic expressions into distinct categories. References to limbs and organs include mentions of God's hand, eye, face, shin, and side. Spatial relations concern God's coming, going, descending, ascending, and sitting. Emotional states involve God's pleasure, anger, love, hatred, and laughter. Temporal actions refer to God's creating "then," responding "when," and apparently changing decisions. Each category required specific interpretive strategies while maintaining the overarching principle of transcendence.

The Ash'arites developed a comprehensive interpretive framework for handling these expressions. The principle of possibility (tajwīz) recognizes that Arabic expressions often bear multiple meanings. Al-Bāqillānī establishes: "An expression may bear multiple meanings in Arabic. We select the meaning that preserves divine transcendence while remaining within linguistic possibility." This principle grounds Ash'arite interpretation in Arabic linguistic usage rather than foreign philosophical categories, claiming that metaphorical and figurative interpretation follows established patterns in the Arabic language itself.

The principle of scriptural coherence holds that no verse can contradict fundamental Quranic teachings. Al-Juwaynī states: "No verse can contradict 'laysa kamithlihi shay'un.' Apparent contradictions indicate our misunderstanding, not scriptural inconsistency." Since the Quran explicitly affirms divine incomparability, any interpretation of other verses that compromises this principle must be mistaken. The clear verses about transcendence govern interpretation of ambiguous verses about divine attributes.

The principle of functional understanding recognizes that anthropomorphic expressions often convey functional rather than descriptive meaning. Al-Ghazālī articulates this principle: "Often, anthropomorphic expressions convey functional rather than descriptive meaning. 'God's hand' conveys His power and generosity, not physical form." This approach distinguishes between what anthropomorphic language does—communicating truths about God's relationship to creation—and what it seems to describe—physical features. The expressions function to convey theological truths without requiring literalistic interpretation.

The Ash'arites applied these principles to specific challenging verses. The verse "The hand of Allah is over their hands" (48:10) appears in the context of believers pledging allegiance to the Prophet. Al-Māturīdī records the Ash'arite approach: "The context involves pledge-taking (bay'a). God's 'hand over their hands' means His acceptance and support of their pledge. The hand signifies power, favor, and confirmation—meanings established in Arabic usage." The contextual interpretation recognizes that when humans pledge allegiance by placing hands together, God's "hand over their hands" signifies His witnessing, accepting, and supporting their covenant.

Al-Rāzī adds philosophical depth through reductio ad absurdum: "If taken literally, would God's hand be above only the Companions' hands at that moment? The absurdity reveals that spatial, physical understanding fails. The verse conveys divine witness, support, and acceptance of their covenant." The literalistic interpretation leads to absurd conclusions—that God's hand was spatially positioned above certain human hands at a particular historical moment—demonstrating that such interpretation cannot represent the verse's actual meaning.

The verse "To what I created with My two hands" (38:75) posed particular challenges due to the dual form, which might seem to indicate two physical hands. Al-Ash'arī himself addressed this: "The dual indicates emphasis and honor, not physical duality. Allah distinguished Adam's creation through direct divine action without intermediaries." The dual form serves rhetorical purposes, emphasizing that God created Adam directly rather than through secondary causes or intermediaries.

Al-Juwaynī elaborates using comparative Arabic usage: "The Arabs say 'I built this house with my two hands' to emphasize personal involvement. God's 'two hands' emphasizes that Adam's creation received special divine attention, not that God has physical limbs." This appeal to established Arabic usage demonstrates that the dual form functions idiomatically to indicate special care and direct involvement rather than literally describing physical appendages.

The verse "And your Lord comes with the angels, rank upon rank" (89:22) describes Judgment Day using language of divine coming. Al-Bāqillānī analyzes the semantic range of the term: "Coming (al-majī') has multiple meanings: the arrival of a person, the arrival of a command, the arrival of signs. Since physical locomotion is impossible for Allah, we understand this as the coming of His command or the manifestation of His signs on Judgment Day." The term "coming" in Arabic can indicate the arrival of various things, not only physical movement of bodies through space.

Al-Ghazālī provides a synthesis that recognizes the experiential dimension: "The verse describes Judgment Day when veils are lifted and divine majesty becomes manifest. 'Coming' expresses the experiential reality for creation—they experience divine presence in unprecedented ways. The anthropomorphism conveys experiential truth without implying physical movement." This interpretation acknowledges that the language captures something real about creaturely experience of Judgment Day—the overwhelming sense of divine presence—without requiring that God literally moves from one location to another.

Within Ash'arism itself, debate arose about the extent of permissible metaphorical interpretation (ta'wīl). Conservative Ash'arites like al-Bayhaqī preferred minimal interpretation: "We affirm 'hand' as an attribute while negating physicality. Going further risks replacing God's description with human speculation." This conservative approach maintains that one should affirm the attribute "hand" without specifying whether this means power, favor, or something else. The affirmation plus negation of physicality suffices without requiring positive interpretation of what "hand" does mean.

Progressive Ash'arites like al-Rāzī engaged in more extensive interpretation: "Reason, which God gave us, demands that we understand 'hand' as power when literalism contradicts divine transcendence. This serves revelation rather than opposing it." This progressive approach sees interpretation not as departing from revelation but as properly understanding it. Since God gave humans reason, using reason to interpret revelation in ways that preserve divine transcendence represents piety rather than presumption.

Al-Ghazālī mediates between these positions in Fayṣal al-Tafriqa: "Ta'wīl is obligatory when literal meaning is rationally impossible, permissible when it better preserves transcendence, and forbidden when it serves only intellectual comfort. The goal is preserving divine transcendence, not displaying cleverness." This formulation provides criteria for when interpretation is required, allowed, or forbidden. The deciding factor is preservation of divine transcendence rather than satisfaction of human curiosity or intellectual preferences.

The Ash'arite treatment of divine attributes (ṣifāt) represents their most distinctive and influential theological contribution. Al-Ash'arī established the basic position in al-Luma': "We affirm that Allah has attributes (ṣifāt) subsisting in His essence (qā'ima bi-dhātihi). These attributes are neither He Himself (fa-laysat hiya huwa) nor are they other than He (wa-lā hiya ghayruhu). They are eternal with His eternity, necessary with His necessity." This formulation, though appearing paradoxical, addresses crucial concerns from multiple directions. Against the Mu'tazilites who denied real attributes to preserve unity, it affirms that attributes are real. Against philosophers who reduced attributes to mere concepts, it maintains that they subsist in the divine essence. Against anthropomorphists who conceived attributes as separable parts, it denies that they are other than God.

Al-Bāqillānī systematized seven essential attributes in al-Tamhīd, providing detailed analysis of each. Life (ḥayāt) is described as follows: "Allah's life is an eternal attribute by which He is living (ḥayy). It involves neither blood, breath, nor biological processes. It is the condition for other attributes—knowledge and power subsist only in the living." Divine life provides the ontological ground for other attributes while differing absolutely from biological life.

Knowledge ('ilm) receives this characterization: "Allah's knowledge is eternal, encompassing all things—past, present, future, actual, possible. It neither increases (no learning) nor decreases (no forgetting). He knows universals and particulars without the knowledge being universal or particular itself." Divine knowledge is comprehensive without acquisition, exhaustive without composition, detailed without particularity—modes of knowledge that transcend creaturely epistemology.

Power (qudra) is explained: "Allah's power relates to all possibles. It does not relate to impossibles (like making Himself non-existent) or necessities (which need no power to exist). His power involves no effort, instruments, or stages." Divine power extends to everything possible but does not extend to logical impossibilities or to necessities that exist by their own nature. The limitation reflects not deficiency but the nature of power itself.

Will (irāda) is described: "Allah's will eternally specifies possibles for existence or non-existence. It involves no deliberation, desire, or compulsion. What He wills occurs; what occurs He has willed." Divine will determines without deliberation, specifies without external constraint, and operates with complete efficacy—whatever God wills to exist comes into existence.

Hearing (sam') receives this explanation: "Allah hears all sounds simultaneously without organs, waves, or medium. His hearing is not conditioned by distance, volume, or time." Divine hearing involves no physical mechanism and suffers no limitation from spatial or temporal factors that constrain creaturely hearing.

Sight (baṣar) is characterized: "Allah sees all visible things without light, organ, or perspective. He sees the hidden as clearly as the manifest, darkness as clearly as light." Divine vision requires no illumination, depends on no physical structure, and makes all things equally visible without gradations based on concealment or distance.

Speech (kalām) receives particularly detailed treatment: "Allah's speech is an eternal attribute, neither letters nor sounds. The Quran is His speech—eternal in attribute, created in recitation and inscription." This formulation distinguishes between the eternal divine attribute of speech and its temporal manifestations in recited or written form, allowing Ash'arites to affirm both the eternity of God's speech and the obvious created nature of physical Qurans.

The relationship between divine essence and attributes generated extensive philosophical and theological discussion. Al-Juwaynī analyzes the paradoxical formulation "neither Him nor other than Him": "When we say attributes are 'neither Him nor other than Him,' we mean the attribute of knowledge is not identical to the attribute of power—so they are not simply identical to Him—yet they do not constitute additional entities alongside God—so they are not other than Him. This preserves both the reality of attributes and divine unity." The formulation seeks to avoid both absolute identity, which would make all attributes the same, and absolute otherness, which would introduce multiplicity into the Godhead.

Al-Ghazālī attempts clarification through analogy while acknowledging its limitations: "Consider the sun, its heat, and its light. The heat is not the light, yet both are inseparable from the sun. This analogy limps—as all analogies must regarding Allah—but suggests how multiplicity of attributes need not compromise essential unity." The sun analogy provides a mental model for how distinct attributes can belong to a single reality, though al-Ghazālī immediately qualifies that all analogies fail when applied to divine reality.

Beyond the seven essential attributes, Ash'arites recognized attributes of action (ṣifāt al-fi'l) that relate to divine effects in creation. Al-Baghdādī (d. 429/1037) explains in Uṣūl al-Dīn: "Creating, providing, giving life, causing death—these relate to divine effects in time while grounded in eternal attributes of power and will. The effects are temporal; the power and will eternal." This distinction proved crucial for maintaining divine immutability while affirming real divine action in time. The eternal divine power and will remain unchanging, but their effects in creation occur temporally.

Debate arose within Ash'arism about the ontological status of divine attributes. The reality position, held by al-Ash'arī and al-Bāqillānī, maintained that attributes have real existence (wujūd) while subsisting in the divine essence. Al-Bāqillānī argues: "To deny real existence to divine attributes is to empty religious language of meaning. When the Quran calls Allah 'All-Knowing,' this must refer to real knowledge, not merely the absence of ignorance." This position sees robust realism about attributes as necessary for maintaining the meaningfulness of theological language.

Later Ash'arites like al-Juwaynī adopted a more cautious modality position: "We affirm attributes as true of Allah without speculating on their ontological status. Whether they 'exist' or 'subsist' or bear some other relation to the essence exceeds our comprehension." This position maintains that humans can affirm attributes without claiming to understand precisely how they relate to the divine essence ontologically.

Al-Ghazālī navigates between these positions with characteristic subtlety: "Divine attributes are neither existent entities added to God nor mere mental concepts we project. They are aspects (wujūh) of the divine reality—truly there but not there as creatures and their attributes are there. This mystery is part of 'laysa kamithlihi shay'un.'" This formulation refuses both absolute realism, which might compromise divine simplicity, and nominalism, which would make attributes mere human constructions. The attributes are real aspects of divine reality without being additional entities.

The Ash'arites faced various philosophical objections requiring sophisticated responses. The simplicity objection charges that multiple attributes compromise divine simplicity by introducing composition. Al-Shahrastānī (d. 548/1153) responds: "Divine simplicity differs from mathematical simplicity. God is simple in having no parts, no composition, no division. Multiple attributes no more divide Him than multiple names divide the named." This response distinguishes between simplicity as lack of composition and simplicity as absolute undifferentiated unity. The former is necessary for God; the latter would make all attributes identical.

The redundancy objection argues that if God is necessarily perfect, attributes add nothing and thus seem redundant. Al-Rāzī answers: "Attributes explicate perfection rather than adding to it. Saying 'God is necessarily perfect' conveys less than explaining He is knowing, powerful, merciful. The attributes reveal perfection's content without implying its absence without them." Attributes do not add to a previously incomplete divine essence but rather articulate what divine perfection means concretely.

The Ash'arite doctrine of attributes profoundly influenced subsequent Islamic theology across multiple dimensions. Their careful formulations became standard in creedal statements ('aqā'id) and theological manuals throughout the Sunni world, shaping how ordinary Muslims understood and articulated belief in God. Their framework enabled sophisticated dialogue with philosophers while maintaining orthodox commitments, demonstrating that philosophical sophistication need not lead to heterodoxy. Sufi masters like al-Ghazālī showed how Ash'arite theology could ground profound spiritual practice, integrating systematic theology with experiential religion. Ash'arite works became central to madrasa curricula, shaping centuries of Islamic theological education and ensuring transmission of Ash'arite approaches across generations and regions.

The Ash'arite contribution to understanding divine transcendence represents a masterful balance between rational argumentation and scriptural fidelity. Through the bilā kayf methodology, they affirmed divine attributes while preserving mystery, demonstrating that one need not choose between affirmation and transcendence. Their responses to anthropomorphism demonstrated how reason could serve rather than subvert traditional belief, using philosophical tools to defend rather than undermine scriptural teaching. Their sophisticated analysis of divine attributes provided frameworks for theological discourse that maintained both intellectual rigor and appropriate recognition of divine transcendence, showing that systematic theology need not sacrifice either precision or piety.

Most significantly, the Ash'arites showed that preserving "laysa kamithlihi shay'un" did not require either crude literalism that compromises transcendence or radical abstraction that empties revelation of content. Through careful methodology, precise language, and intellectual humility, they developed approaches that honored both the human need to understand and the divine right to transcend understanding. Their legacy continues to influence Islamic theology, providing resources for contemporary Muslims seeking to articulate divine transcendence within modern contexts while maintaining fidelity to classical principles. The Ash'arite achievement demonstrates that the most profound theology emerges not from resolving all tensions but from learning to maintain productive tensions that preserve both divine mystery and human meaning. By holding together affirmation and negation, reason and revelation, systematic articulation and acknowledgment of limits, Ash'arism established patterns of theological discourse that continue to guide Muslims seeking to speak faithfully about the One who is "naught is like unto Him."

Chapter 6. Mu'tazilite Rationalism: Achievements and Limitations

The Mu'tazilite school of Islamic theology, which flourished from the early 2nd/8th to the 4th/10th centuries, represents one of the most significant attempts in Islamic intellectual history to articulate divine transcendence through systematic rational demonstration. Their approach to the principle "laysa kamithlihi shay'un" sought to preserve divine incomparability through rigorous philosophical argumentation, generating both remarkable theological insights and instructive limitations that would shape subsequent Islamic thought. This chapter examines how the Mu'tazilite engagement with divine transcendence reveals essential patterns in Islamic theological discourse, demonstrating how their rational methodology both illuminated and encountered the inherent challenges of approaching the incomparable divine reality through finite human reason.

The emergence of Mu'tazilite thought in the cosmopolitan centers of Basra and Baghdad during the early Abbasid period reflects the dynamic intellectual environment in which Muslim scholars engaged with both internal theological questions and external philosophical challenges. The traditional account of the school's founding, preserved in heresiographical literature, traces its origins to Wāṣil ibn 'Aṭā' (d. 131/748) and his "withdrawal" (i'tizāl) from the teaching circle of al-Ḥasan al-Baṣrī over the question of the grave sinner's status.

Al-Ṭabarī reports: "Wāṣil ibn 'Aṭā' was asked about the one who commits a grave sin: Is he a believer or an unbeliever? He withdrew (i'tazala) and said: 'He is in a position between the two positions (manzila bayn al-manzilatayn).'" This foundational moment established a pattern of independent theological reasoning that would characterize the school.

The early generations of Mu'tazilite thinkers developed increasingly sophisticated approaches to divine transcendence through successive figures whose contributions built upon one another. Wāṣil ibn 'Aṭā' (d. 131/748) established the principle of the intermediate position and began developing rational approaches to divine unity. His student 'Amr ibn 'Ubayd (d. 144/761) emphasized divine justice and human responsibility within a framework of divine transcendence, laying groundwork for what would become central Mu'tazilite concerns. The systematic development of these principles accelerated with Abū al-Hudhayl al-'Allāf (d. 235/849-50), who developed rigorous arguments for divine unity and the created nature of the Quran. His contemporary al-Naẓẓām (d. 231/845) advanced increasingly sophisticated philosophical arguments about divine nature and human knowledge, while al-Jāḥiẓ (d. 255/869) applied Mu'tazilite principles to broader cultural and literary contexts, demonstrating the school's expanding intellectual reach.

The Mu'tazilite theological system crystallized around five fundamental principles, each reflecting their approach to preserving divine transcendence through rational demonstration. Al-Qāḍī 'Abd al-Jabbār (d. 415/1025) provides the classical formulation in his Al-Mughnī. The first and most foundational principle, tawḥīd (divine unity), affirmed that God is one, eternal, without body, form, or accidents, and that nothing resembles Him in any way. The second principle, 'adl (divine justice), maintained that God acts only in accordance with wisdom and justice, neither committing evil nor commanding it. The third principle, al-wa'd wa-l-wa'īd (promise and threat), held that God necessarily fulfills His promises of reward and threats of punishment. The fourth principle, al-manzila bayn al-manzilatayn (the intermediate position), addressed the specific question that had sparked the school's founding by maintaining that the grave sinner is neither believer nor unbeliever but occupies an intermediate state. Finally, the fifth principle, al-amr bi-l-ma'rūf wa-l-nahy 'an al-munkar (commanding good and forbidding evil), established the obligation to command good and forbid evil through appropriate means.

The Mu'tazilite development occurred within a rich intellectual environment that shaped their distinctive approach to divine transcendence. Their engagement with Greek philosophy proved particularly significant, as al-Kindī notes: "The Mu'tazila were among the first to systematically employ

Aristotelian logic in theological argumentation, seeking to demonstrate religious truths through universal rational principles." Equally important was their dialogue with other religions, as their emphasis on rational theology partly emerged from debates with Christians, Jews, and Zoroastrians in urban centers. Al-Jāḥiẓ's Kitāb al-Ḥayawān preserves records of such inter-religious theological discussions. Much of their theology also developed in response to what they perceived as anthropomorphic tendencies in popular religion and some hadith literature, driving them toward increasingly abstract and philosophical formulations of divine nature.

The Mu'tazilite approach to divine unity (tawḥīd) represents their most systematic attempt to preserve divine transcendence through rational demonstration. Their arguments reveal both the power and limitations of rational theology in approaching the incomparable divine reality. Abū al-Hudhayl al-'Allāf articulated one of the most influential Mu'tazilite arguments for absolute divine unity: "If God possessed distinct attributes separate from His essence, He would be composite. But composition implies dependence on parts, and the Necessary Existent cannot be dependent. Therefore, God's attributes are not distinct from His essence."

This argument, preserved in detail by al-Ash'arī in his Maqālāt al-Islāmiyyīn, demonstrates the characteristic Mu'tazilite method. They began by identifying a potential threat to divine transcendence, in this case the multiplicity of attributes. They then conducted rational analysis of the implications, demonstrating that composition implies dependence. Finally, they reached a conclusion that preserved transcendence by affirming that attributes are identical with essence. This methodological pattern would recur throughout their theological system.

The Mu'tazilite position on divine attributes generated extensive internal debate despite their shared commitment to absolute unity. Al-Shahrastānī records in Al-Milal wa-l-Niḥal: "The Mu'tazila agreed that God is knowing, powerful, and living through His essence, not through knowledge, power, and life that are additional to His essence. They said: 'If the attributes were additional eternal entities, there would be multiple eternals, which contradicts tawḥīd.'" Yet within this shared framework, different Mu'tazilite scholars developed various formulations to articulate precisely how divine attributes relate to the divine essence. Abū al-Hudhayl maintained that God is knowing through Himself (bi-nafsihi), not through knowledge ('ilm). Al-

Naẓẓām took a more negative approach, arguing that the meaning of saying "God is knowing" is simply the negation of ignorance from Him. Abū 'Alī al-Jubbā'ī developed yet another position, proposing that God is knowing means He is in a state (ḥāl) that necessitates His being knowing.

The Mu'tazilites also developed sophisticated arguments for God's existence that sought to preserve divine transcendence while establishing rational grounds for belief. Al-Qāḍī 'Abd al-Jabbār presents a typical formulation: "The world contains originated events (ḥawādith). Everything originated requires an originator. This originator must be either originated or eternal. If originated, it requires another originator, leading to infinite regress, which is impossible. Therefore, there must be an eternal originator who is God." This argument carefully preserves divine transcendence by establishing God as categorically different from all originated existence, belonging to an entirely distinct ontological category.

Perhaps the most controversial Mu'tazilite position was their insistence that the Quran is created. Their argument, as preserved by al-Ash'arī, demonstrates how their concern for absolute divine unity drove even their most contentious conclusions: "The Mu'tazila said: The Quran is the speech of God, created and originated. They argued: Everything other than God is created, for if it were eternal, it would be a second eternal alongside God, violating tawḥīd." Bishr ibn al-Mu'tamir elaborated this reasoning by focusing on the nature of speech itself: "The Quran consists of arranged letters and sequential words. What has arrangement and sequence must be temporal, not eternal." This position would ultimately lead to the infamous miḥna (inquisition) under the Abbasid caliph al-Ma'mūn and contribute to the eventual decline of Mu'tazilite influence.

The Mu'tazilite school was far from monolithic, containing significant internal diversity that reveals the complexity of their engagement with divine transcendence. Two major centers of Mu'tazilite thought developed distinct approaches. The Basra School, following Abū al-Hudhayl and the Jubbā'ī family, tended toward more systematic philosophical positions. Al-Ash'arī, who studied under Abū 'Alī al-Jubbā'ī before his conversion to what would become the Ash'arī school, preserves their positions in detail. The Baghdad School, influenced by Bishr ibn al-Mu'tamir, showed more flexibility on certain issues. Ibn al-Murtaḍā records in Ṭabaqāt al-Mu'tazila: "The Baghdad school allowed that God could perform the optimal (aṣlaḥ) without being obligated, while the Basrans insisted on obligation." This debate over whether God is obligated to do what is best for His creation reveals deeper tensions within Mu'tazilite thought about how to balance divine transcendence with divine justice.

A major internal debate concerned how God knows particulars without compromising divine unity. Al-Ash'arī records the diversity of positions within the school. Al-Naẓẓām argued that God knows things through the things themselves, not through knowledge within Himself. Abū al-Hudhayl maintained that God knows things through a knowledge that is Himself. Al-Ka'bī offered yet another formulation, proposing that God's knowledge of things is the things' being known by Him. These subtle distinctions reveal Mu'tazilite struggles to preserve both divine omniscience and absolute unity, demonstrating how even within a shared commitment to rational demonstration, the complexity of divine reality generated multiple sophisticated responses.

While united in affirming human free will against predestinarian views, Mu'tazilites debated its precise nature and implications. Bishr ibn al-Mu'tamir developed the theory of "generation" (tawallud), arguing that human actions generate effects that extend beyond the immediate act. Al-Naẓẓām rejected this theory, maintaining that each effect has its own direct cause and that humans are only responsible for their immediate actions. 'Abbād ibn Sulaymān offered a middle position, arguing that humans create their actions, but the capacity (istiṭā'a) comes from God. These debates demonstrate how the Mu'tazilite commitment to human agency, itself rooted in their understanding of divine justice, generated its own complex set of theological questions.

The Mu'tazilite approach to divine transcendence generated significant critique from other theological schools, revealing essential patterns in Islamic theological discourse about the limits of rational approaches to the divine. Al-Ash'arī, after leaving the Mu'tazilite school, developed comprehensive critiques that would shape Sunni theology for centuries. In his Al-Ibāna, he argues: "The Mu'tazila, in attempting to preserve God's transcendence through negating attributes, actually limit God. To say God knows without knowledge is to affirm ignorance, for knowledge is the opposite of ignorance, not its mere negation." He particularly criticized their position on divine speech: "If the Quran is created, then at some point God was without speech. But speech is a perfection, so this implies God was once imperfect." Al-Ash'arī's critique thus turned the Mu'tazilite method against itself, arguing that their rational approach to transcendence actually diminished divine perfection.

Al-Māturīdī offered more nuanced critiques in his Kitāb al-Tawḥīd, acknowledging the legitimacy of Mu'tazilite concerns while questioning their method: "The Mu'tazila err not in their concern for divine transcendence but in their method. Reason alone cannot determine what is possible or impossible for God. We need revelation to guide reason." He specifically addressed their theodicy: "To obligate God to do the optimal (aṣlaḥ) is to subject Him to external standards. True transcendence means God acts according to His wisdom, which may transcend human understanding of optimality." This critique identifies what Māturīdī saw as a fundamental flaw in the Mu'tazilite project—the attempt to make human rational categories authoritative over divine reality itself.

In Tahāfut al-Falāsifa, al-Ghazālī extends his critique of philosophical rationalism to encompass Mu'tazilite theology: "The Mu'tazila share with the philosophers the error of subjecting God to rational categories. But 'laysa kamithlihi shay'un' means God transcends even the categories of logic. Their rational unity becomes a limitation when it denies God's ability to have attributes while remaining one." Al-Ghazālī's critique thus challenges the very foundation of the Mu'tazilite project, questioning whether rational demonstration can adequately preserve what it seeks to protect.

Ibn Taymiyya provides historical perspective in Dar' Ta'āruḍ al-'Aql wa-l-Naql: "The Mu'tazila arose from sincere desire to defend divine transcendence against anthropomorphism. But they went to the opposite extreme, denying what God affirmed about Himself. The truth lies in affirming what God affirmed while maintaining 'laysa kamithlihi shay'un.'" This assessment, while critical, acknowledges the sincerity and theological legitimacy of the Mu'tazilite project while identifying what Ibn Taymiyya saw as its methodological error.

Modern scholarly reassessments have provided more sympathetic readings of Mu'tazilite contributions, recognizing their significance within the broader development of Islamic thought. George Hourani notes: "The Mu'tazilites were not simply rationalists imposing Greek philosophy on Islam. They were profoundly concerned with Quranic values of justice and divine transcendence, using reason to articulate these values systematically." Richard Frank observes: "The subtlety of Mu'tazilite positions is often lost in polemical sources. Their theory of 'states' (aḥwāl) represents a sophisticated attempt to preserve both divine unity and the reality of divine attributes." Josef van Ess, in his magisterial Theologie und Gesellschaft, demonstrates: "Mu'tazilite theology must be understood in its historical context—responding to real challenges from dualists, Christians, and anthropomorphists while developing Islamic theology's technical vocabulary." These modern assessments recognize that the Mu'tazilite project cannot be adequately understood through the lens of later polemical accounts alone, but must be appreciated within its own intellectual and historical context.

The Mu'tazilite experience reveals several crucial patterns in Islamic approaches to divine transcendence that extend beyond their specific doctrinal positions. First, their very rigor in applying reason revealed reason's limitations when approaching divine reality. As al-Juwaynī observed: "The Mu'tazilite failure was not in using reason but in expecting reason alone to comprehend 'mā laysa kamithlihi shay'un.'" Second, their emphasis on absolute transcendence sometimes made God seem remote, creating tensions with the Quranic presentation of divine accessibility and relationship with creation. Al-Qushayrī notes: "In fleeing from tashbīh (anthropomorphism), they fell into ta'ṭīl (denial of attributes), making God unknowable." Third, the productive nature of theological tension becomes evident in how their debates with other schools sharpened Islamic theological vocabulary and method. Even critics like al-Ash'arī adopted their philosophical tools while rejecting certain conclusions, demonstrating how theological development occurs through creative engagement with opposed positions. Fourth, their experience demonstrated that authentic Islamic theology requires both rational reflection and revelatory guidance, neither alone proving sufficient for approaching divine transcendence adequately.

Despite theological defeat and the eventual marginalization of their school, Mu'tazilite contributions remain significant within the broader Islamic intellectual tradition. The theological vocabulary they developed, including terms like ḥāl (state), ma'nā (meaning), and ṣifa (attribute), entered Islamic theology through their analysis and became standard terminology across all schools. Their rigorous, systematic method established standards for theological discourse that were adopted by all subsequent schools, even those most opposed to their specific conclusions. Their concern for divine justice influenced Islamic ethical thought broadly, even among their critics who developed alternative frameworks for understanding divine justice. Perhaps most significantly, Ash'arī and Māturīdī theology developed partly in response to Mu'tazilite challenges, creating more nuanced positions that attempted to preserve Mu'tazilite insights while avoiding what their critics saw as their methodological errors.

The Mu'tazilite engagement with divine transcendence demonstrates how the principle "laysa kamithlihi shay'un" challenges even the most sophisticated rational approaches. Their sincere attempt to preserve divine incomparability through systematic reason revealed essential patterns: that divine transcendence exceeds rational categories while remaining accessible through appropriate integration of reason and revelation. Their experience does not discredit rational theology but rather demonstrates its proper scope and limitations. As al-Ghazālī concluded: "The Mu'tazila were like those who, to protect a precious gem from thieves, locked it away so securely that even its owner could not access it. Divine transcendence must be preserved, but in a way that maintains the divine-human relationship established through revelation."

The Mu'tazilite legacy thus lies not in their specific doctrinal positions but in their demonstration that approaching the One who is "naught is like unto Him" requires methodological humility that acknowledges the limits of human reason while employing it faithfully within those limits. Their very failures illuminate the nature of divine transcendence more clearly than unchallenged success might have done, contributing essentially to the Islamic tradition's sophisticated understanding of how finite human consciousness can authentically approach the incomparable divine reality.

Chapter 7. Maturidite Synthesis: Mediating Positions in Classical Theology

The Maturidite school, founded by Abū Manṣūr al-Māturīdī (d. 333/944) in Samarqand, represents a crucial yet often underappreciated strand of Islamic theological thought. Emerging contemporaneously with Ash'arism but developing independently in the eastern Islamic lands, the Maturidite approach to divine transcendence demonstrates how the principle "laysa kamithlihi shay'un" could be preserved through a distinctive synthesis of rational argumentation and traditional fidelity. This chapter examines how Maturidite theology developed mediating positions that would profoundly influence Hanafi thought and provide alternative frameworks for understanding divine incomparability.

The Maturidite school emerged in Transoxiana (Mā warā' al-nahr) during a period of intense theological ferment, developing approaches that would distinguish it from both Ash'arism and Mu'tazilism while sharing concerns with both. Al-Māturīdī lived and taught in Samarqand, a major center of Hanafi jurisprudence far from the Baghdad-Basra axis where Ash'arism and Mu'tazilism primarily developed. This geographical separation allowed for independent theological development. Al-Nasafi (d. 537/1142) notes in Tabṣirat al-Adilla: "The scholars of Transoxiana, following the methodology of Abū Ḥanīfa, developed their theological positions through engagement with local challenges—Manicheans, Buddhists, and various dualist sects—while maintaining connection to the broader Islamic tradition."

Limited biographical information survives about al-Māturīdī himself.

Al-Sam'ānī (d. 562/1166) provides a brief notice: "Abū Manṣūr Muḥammad ibn Muḥammad al-Māturīdī, the Imam of the theologians, author of Kitāb al-Tawḥīd and Ta'wīlāt Ahl al-Sunna. He studied under Abū Naṣr al-'Iyāḍī and other students of Abū Ḥanīfa's companions." This intellectual genealogy proves significant. Through his teachers, al-Māturīdī inherited Abū Ḥanīfa's approach to theology, which emphasized reason's legitimate role in understanding revelation, restraint in making takfīr (excommunication), focus on divine justice and human responsibility, and careful balance between divine transcendence and accessibility. These inherited emphases would shape the distinctive character of Maturidite theology as it developed into a comprehensive theological system.

Al-Māturīdī's theology emerged with several distinctive features that positioned it as a middle way between competing schools. The first of these was an epistemological optimism that set Maturidite thought apart from Ash'arite caution about reason's capacities. Unlike the Ash'arites who limited reason's role, al-Māturīdī argued for reason's capacity to know certain truths independently. In Kitāb al-Tawḥīd, he states: "Sound reason ('aql ṣaḥīḥ) can know the existence of the Creator, the obligation of gratitude to Him, and the wrongness of oppression without revelation. This does not diminish revelation's role but shows God's wisdom in creating humans with faculties aligned to truth." This confidence in reason's proper functioning within its sphere would become a hallmark of Maturidite methodology.

The second distinctive feature was al-Māturīdī's insistence that his approach represented genuine synthesis rather than mere compromise. He explicitly rejected the notion of finding truth simply by splitting the difference between extremes. He writes: "The truth is not found by simply taking a middle position between two errors. Rather, we must examine each position, accept what is sound, reject what is false, and synthesize truth wherever it is found." This methodological commitment ensured that Maturidite positions emerged from principled analysis rather than diplomatic accommodation.

The third characteristic feature was an emphasis on divine wisdom that distinguished Maturidite thought from Ash'arite voluntarism. While Ash'arites emphasized divine will, Maturidites stressed divine wisdom. Al-Māturīdī argues: "Every divine act proceeds from perfect wisdom (ḥikma), even if that wisdom transcends human comprehension. God does not act arbitrarily but always in accordance with wisdom that encompasses all existence." This emphasis on wisdom rather than bare will would have significant implications for Maturidite approaches to theodicy, ethics, and the purposes of Islamic law.

Al-Māturīdī developed a sophisticated theological methodology that would characterize the school and provide its distinctive epistemological framework. In the introduction to Kitāb al-Tawḥīd, he outlines three sources of knowledge that must work in harmony. Sensory perception (ḥiss) provides knowledge of the material world, offering humanity direct access to empirical reality. Reason ('aql) grasps universal truths and logical relationships, enabling human beings to move from particular observations to general principles. Authentic transmission (khabar ṣādiq) conveys knowledge beyond reason's reach, providing access to realities that transcend human experience and rational demonstration. He explains: "These three sources must work in harmony. Reason without revelation leads to speculation; revelation without reason leads to blind imitation; sensation without both leads to materialism." This triadic epistemology provided the foundation for all subsequent Maturidite theological reflection.

The Maturidite school developed through several generations of scholars who refined and systematized al-Māturīdī's insights, each contributing to the elaboration and defense of the school's distinctive positions. Abū al-Yusr al-Bazdawī (d. 493/1099) wrote Uṣūl al-Dīn, providing systematic presentation of Maturidite theology. He clarifies the school's position: "We follow the methodology of al-Māturīdī, who followed Abū Ḥanīfa. This is not blind following but reasoned acceptance of sound principles." His work established the canonical formulation of Maturidite doctrine for subsequent generations.

Abū al-Mu'īn al-Nasafī (d. 508/1114) authored Tabṣirat al-Adilla, one of the most comprehensive Maturidite theological works. He emphasizes: "Our school seeks to preserve the transcendence emphasized by the Mu'tazila while maintaining the divine attributes affirmed by the Ahl al-Ḥadīth, showing these are not contradictory but complementary truths." His massive work demonstrates the sophistication that Maturidite theology had achieved by the early sixth/twelfth century, engaging with philosophical, Mu'tazilite, and Ash'arite positions while developing distinctively Maturidite responses.

'Alā' al-Dīn al-Samarqandī (d. 539/1144) in Mīzān al-Uṣūl developed Maturidite legal theory, showing how theological principles influenced jurisprudential methodology. His work demonstrates the deep integration between Maturidite theology and Hanafi jurisprudence, illustrating how theological commitments shaped approaches to legal reasoning and how legal methodology reflected underlying theological convictions.

The Maturidite approach to divine attributes represents perhaps their most distinctive contribution to Islamic theology, developing nuanced positions that sought to preserve both divine transcendence and the reality of divine qualities. Al-Māturīdī affirmed the reality of divine attributes while developing a unique understanding of their relationship to the divine essence. In Kitāb al-Tawḥīd, he argues: "The attributes of God are neither He Himself nor other than Him. They are eternal qualities subsisting in His essence (ṣifāt azaliyya qā'ima bi-dhātihi). To say they are Him would be to deny their distinctiveness; to say they are other than Him would be to affirm multiple eternals." This formulation resembles the Ash'arite position but with crucial differences in emphasis and explanation, particularly in how it maintains the reality of attributes while avoiding the multiplication of eternal entities.

Al-Nasafī elaborates the Maturidite classification of attributes in Tabṣirat al-Adilla through a distinction that proved crucial for maintaining divine immutability while affirming real divine action in the world. Essential attributes (ṣifāt dhātiyya) are those inseparable from the divine essence. He explains: "These are inseparable from the divine essence—life, knowledge, power, will, hearing, sight, speech. God is never without these attributes; they are eternal with His eternity." By contrast, active attributes (ṣifāt fi'liyya) relate to God's actions in time. He clarifies: "These relate to God's actions in time—creating, sustaining, giving life, causing death. The capacity for these actions is eternal; their actual occurrence is temporal." This distinction enabled Maturidite thinkers to affirm that God truly acts in history without compromising divine immutability or introducing change into the divine essence.

The Maturidite position on divine speech and the nature of the Quran demonstrates their mediating approach between Mu'tazilite and extreme traditionalist positions. Al-Māturīdī writes: "The speech of God (kalām Allah) is an eternal attribute. The Quran, as God's speech, is uncreated in its attribute-aspect (ṣifa) but created in its letter-and-sound aspect (ḥarf wa-ṣawt). When we recite the Quran, our recitation is created, but what we recite—God's eternal speech—is uncreated." Al-Bazdawī clarifies this complex position: "This preserves the Quran's divine status while acknowledging the created nature of its physical manifestation. We neither say the Quran is entirely created (like the Mu'tazila) nor that the physical book is eternal (like some extreme traditionalists)." This nuanced formulation sought to preserve both the divine origin of the Quran and the obvious temporal nature of its physical manifestation.

Maturidite scholars developed sophisticated approaches to apparently anthropomorphic divine descriptions, navigating between crude literalism and excessive allegorization. Al-Māturīdī states: "When the Quran mentions God's 'hand,' 'face,' or 'eyes,' these are real attributes whose modality (kayfiyya) we cannot comprehend. We neither interpret them as mere metaphors nor understand them as physical organs. They are attributes appropriate to divine perfection, understood through 'laysa kamithlihi shay'un.'" Al-Nasafī expands: "The error of the anthropomorphists (mujassima) is not in affirming these attributes but in understanding them through human analogy. The error of the extreme allegorists is in denying their reality. We affirm their reality while denying comparability." This balanced position sought to honor the Quranic text while maintaining absolute divine transcendence.

A distinctive Maturidite contribution was their emphasis on the unity underlying divine attributes, a position that influenced later discussions about divine simplicity in Islamic theology. Al-Māturīdī argues: "All divine attributes are unified in the divine essence without confusion or separation. God's knowledge, power, and will are distinct in concept (mafhūm) but united in reality (ḥaqīqa). This is part of the mystery indicated by 'laysa kamithlihi shay'un'—in creation, attributes are truly distinct; in God, they are mysteriously one." This formulation acknowledges that human language and conceptual categories inevitably introduce distinctions that do not correspond to any real multiplicity in the divine being itself.

The Maturidite school's most significant contribution may be its sophisticated balance between rational argumentation and traditional authority, developing principles that would influence Islamic theology far beyond Hanafi circles. Al-Māturīdī articulated a nuanced view of reason's capabilities and limitations, distinguishing carefully between what reason can and cannot achieve. In Kitāb al-Tawḥīd, he identifies several truths accessible to unaided reason: the existence of the Creator through contemplating creation, basic moral truths concerning good and evil in general terms, the necessity of prophetic guidance, and the coherence of revealed truths. These represent truths that sound reason, functioning properly, can grasp independently of revelation, though revelation confirms and clarifies them.

By contrast, al-Māturīdī identifies other domains that exceed reason's independent capacity. Reason cannot know the specific details of divine nature, the particular forms of worship pleasing to God, the details of eschatology, or the wisdom behind specific divine commands. These realities require revelation for human access, lying beyond what reason can discover through its own operations. He explains the relationship between reason and revelation through a luminous analogy: "Reason is like the eye—it can see when there is light but requires light to function. Revelation is that light, enabling reason to perceive truths it could not discover independently." This image captures the Maturidite understanding that reason is a genuine faculty of knowledge that nonetheless requires revelation's guidance to function optimally.

Al-Nasafī develops this theme of harmony between reason and revelation in Baḥr al-Kalām, articulating a principle that would become foundational for Maturidite theological method: "True reason and authentic revelation can never contradict, for both originate from God. When they appear to conflict, either our reasoning is flawed, our understanding of revelation is incorrect, or we have not properly understood the relationship between universal principles and particular applications." This principle of necessary harmony provided the foundation for Maturidite confidence in employing rational arguments while maintaining reverence for revealed texts.

This principle of harmony led to distinctive Maturidite positions on several contested issues. On human free will, Maturidites argued: "Reason indicates human responsibility; revelation confirms it. We affirm real human choice (ikhtiyār) while maintaining divine creation of human acts. This is not contradiction but mystery appropriate to the divine-human relationship." On divine justice, they maintained: "Reason grasps that God is just; revelation details what divine justice entails. We neither subject God to human concepts of justice nor make His justice arbitrary." These positions sought to honor both rational insight and revealed teaching without subordinating either to the other.

The Maturidites developed sophisticated hermeneutical principles balancing literal and interpretive approaches to scripture. Al-Samarqandī in Sharḥ al-Fiqh al-Akbar outlines several key principles that guided

Maturidite interpretation. The presumption of apparent meaning held that scripture should be understood according to its apparent meaning unless compelling evidence requires otherwise, establishing a default respect for the plain sense of the text. The principle of divine perfection required that any interpretation compromising divine perfection must be rejected, ensuring that textual interpretation never undermined core theological commitments. The harmony principle demanded that interpretation must harmonize all relevant texts rather than privileging some while ignoring others, preventing selective reading of scripture. Finally, the practical principle insisted that theological interpretation must support rather than undermine religious practice, maintaining the connection between theology and lived religion.

The Maturidite approach to the divine throne illustrates their balanced methodology in practice. Al-Māturīdī writes: "God's establishment (istiwā') on the Throne is real, as the Quran states. However, it does not involve physical sitting or location. The Throne does not contain or support God. God was perfect before creating the Throne and remains unchanged after. We affirm what revelation states while reason prevents us from understanding it corporeally. This is neither crude literalism nor empty allegorism but appropriate affirmation with transcendent understanding." This approach exemplifies how Maturidite theology sought to honor the Quranic text without compromising divine transcendence, affirming the reality of what scripture describes while denying any similarity between divine and creaturely modes of being.

The Maturidite synthesis profoundly shaped Hanafi theology, creating a distinctive theological tradition that would dominate vast regions of the Islamic world. The natural affinity between Maturidite theology and Hanafi jurisprudence stemmed from shared methodological principles rooted in their common genealogy. Al-Kāsānī (d. 587/1191) in Badā'i' al-Ṣanā'i' notes: "The principles Abū Ḥanīfa applied in fiqh—the use of reason within revelation's framework, emphasis on divine wisdom, and practical consideration—align perfectly with Maturidite theological method."

This integration appeared in several areas that demonstrate the deep connection between theological and jurisprudential commitments. In legal theory, Maturidite emphasis on divine wisdom influenced Hanafi understanding of the purposes of Islamic law (maqāṣid al-sharī'a), encouraging jurists to seek the rationale behind legal rulings. In ethical theory, the Maturidite position on natural knowledge of good and evil supported Hanafi views on legal reasoning and equity (istiḥsān), providing theological grounding for juristic preference based on rational assessment of benefit. In the theological implications of legal rulings, Hanafi jurists increasingly incorporated Maturidite theological principles in their legal works, creating an integrated tradition where theology and law mutually informed each other.

Several major figures exemplify the Hanafi-Maturidite synthesis and its development over centuries. Najm al-Dīn al-Nasafī (d. 537/1142) authored the famous 'Aqā'id al-Nasafī, which became the most widely studied Maturidite creed. Its concise formulations spread Maturidite theology throughout the Hanafi world, providing generations of students with their foundational theological education.

Al-Taftāzānī (d. 792/1390) wrote extensive commentaries on Nasafī's creed, demonstrating the vitality of Maturidite theology centuries after al-Māturīdī. His Sharḥ al-'Aqā'id states: "The Maturidite school preserves the balance our religion requires—affirming divine attributes without anthropomorphism, human responsibility without denying divine creation, reason's role without diminishing revelation's authority." His commentaries engaged with philosophical developments and responded to new challenges while maintaining core Maturidite commitments.

Ibn Kamāl Pāshā (d. 940/1534), the Ottoman Shaykh al-Islam, reinforced Maturidite theology as Ottoman official doctrine. His treatises defended Maturidite positions while addressing contemporary challenges, ensuring that Maturidite theology remained the dominant framework in Ottoman lands. His influence helped solidify the identification between Hanafi jurisprudence and Maturidite theology in Ottoman consciousness.

The Maturidite synthesis spread throughout regions where Hanafism dominated, becoming the theological complement to Hanafi legal thought across vast geographical and cultural domains. Central Asia, the original heartland, remained strongly Maturidite, with madrasas in Bukhara and Samarqand teaching al-Māturīdī's works alongside Hanafi fiqh. The Ottoman Empire's adoption of Hanafi-Maturidite theology as official doctrine ensured its spread throughout Ottoman territories from the Balkans to North Africa. In the Indian subcontinent, Hanafi predominance made Maturidite theology standard in madrasas from Delhi to Bengal, shaping the theological education of countless scholars. In the modern period, the majority of Hanafis worldwide follow Maturidite theology, though many may not explicitly identify as such, demonstrating the school's successful integration into normative Sunni consciousness.

The Maturidite synthesis contributed several enduring elements to Islamic theology that extend beyond specifically Hanafi contexts. Their epistemological balance, articulating a middle way between extreme rationalism and anti-rational traditionalism, influenced discussions about natural theology and ethics throughout Islamic intellectual history. Their emphasis on divine wisdom rather than mere will provided resources for engaging philosophical traditions while maintaining theological integrity. Their integration of theology with jurisprudence ensured that theological reflection remained connected to religious practice rather than becoming abstract speculation divorced from lived religion. Finally, their generally irenic approach, less polemical than other schools, facilitated broader acceptance and made their positions attractive to those seeking theological stability without excessive controversy.

Modern Muslim thinkers have found resources in Maturidite thought for addressing contemporary challenges facing Islamic theology. The Maturidite balance between reason and revelation provides frameworks for engaging modern science and philosophy while maintaining traditional commitments, offering a model for how Muslims might appropriate modern knowledge without abandoning classical theology. Maturidite optimism about reason's universal capacity offers resources for interfaith dialogue, suggesting that rational discussion across religious boundaries remains possible because all humans share basic rational capacities. Their position on natural knowledge of good and evil informs contemporary discussions of Islamic ethics, providing theological grounding for ethical discourse that can engage with secular ethics while maintaining Islamic distinctiveness.

The Maturidite synthesis represents a crucial development in Islamic theological thought, demonstrating how the principle "laysa kamithlihi shay'un" could be preserved through careful balance between rational reflection and traditional fidelity. Neither purely rationalist like the Mu'tazilites nor strictly traditionalist like some Ahl al-Hadith, the Maturidites developed sophisticated frameworks that maintained divine transcendence while affirming divine attributes, preserved human responsibility while acknowledging divine sovereignty, and employed reason while respecting revelation's authority.

Their influence on Hanafi thought created a theological tradition that would shape Muslim belief and practice across vast regions for centuries. The Maturidite achievement lies not in resolving all theological tensions but in developing frameworks for maintaining productive tensions that preserve both divine transcendence and accessibility. Their synthesis demonstrates that the most enduring theology emerges not from choosing between reason and tradition but from understanding their complementary roles in approaching the One who is "naught is like unto Him."

The patterns established by Maturidite thought—the emphasis on divine wisdom, confidence in reason's proper role, integration of theology with practice, and irenic spirit—continue to offer resources for contemporary Islamic theology. In an age requiring both authentic tradition and thoughtful engagement with modern challenges, the Maturidite synthesis provides a model of how classical Islamic theology can remain vibrantly relevant while maintaining its core commitment to divine transcendence.

Chapter 8. The Development of Apophatic Theology (Tanzīh) in Classical Islam

The principle of tanzīh—declaring God free from all creaturely attributes and limitations—represents one of the most fundamental aspects of Islamic theology. Rooted in the Quranic declaration "laysa kamithlihi shay'un" (naught is like unto Him), tanzīh developed from scattered precedents in early Islam into sophisticated systematic formulations that would profoundly shape Muslim understanding of divine transcendence. This chapter examines how apophatic theology emerged in Islamic thought, exploring its early precedents, systematic development, complex relationship with affirmative theology (tashbīh), and the classical debates that refined its application.

The foundations of Islamic apophatic theology appear in the earliest sources, where the Prophet Muhammad and his Companions established patterns of speaking about God through negation that would guide all subsequent theological reflection. The hadith literature preserves numerous examples of the Prophet employing apophatic language when discussing divine nature. These precedents established tanzīh not as philosophical speculation but as prophetic practice.

Al-Tirmidhī reports that the Prophet said: "Allah was, and there was nothing besides Him" (kāna Allāhu wa lam yakun shay'un ghayrahu). Ibn Ḥajar comments in Fatḥ al-Bārī: "This hadith establishes the ultimate tanzīh—God's existence precedes all else, sharing no common ground with creation that would enable comparison." This foundational statement places divine existence in a category utterly distinct from all created being, establishing the radical otherness that would characterize Islamic understanding of transcendence.

Muslim reports the Prophet's statement concerning divine attributes: "Allah does not sleep, nor is it befitting for Him to sleep. He lowers and raises the scale. The deeds of the night are raised to Him before the deeds of the day, and the deeds of the day before the night." Al-Nawawī explains the significance of this hadith's formulation: "Notice the Prophet's method—he negates sleep absolutely, then adds that it is 'not befitting,' teaching us that divine tanzīh involves not merely factual negation but the recognition that certain attributes are incompatible with divine perfection." This dual structure of negation establishes that apophatic theology concerns not just what God happens not to be, but what is fundamentally inappropriate to divine nature.

In a profound hadith qudsī reported by Muslim, Allah says: "I am as My servant thinks of Me" (anā 'inda ẓanni 'abdī bī). Al-Qurṭubī observes: "This indicates that all human conceptualization of God falls short of His reality. The hadith implies tanzīh by suggesting that divine reality transcends even the highest human conception." This statement reveals the inherent limitation of all human attempts to comprehend the divine, establishing a humility that would characterize the best Islamic theological reflection.

The Companions developed sophisticated apophatic expressions that would influence all later theology. 'Alī ibn Abī Ṭālib's sermons in Nahj al-Balāgha contain extensive apophatic passages demonstrating remarkable theological sophistication. He states: "He who points to Him limits Him; he who limits Him numbers Him; he who numbers Him negates His eternity; he who asks 'how?' seeks to describe Him; he who asks 'where?' seeks to contain Him." Al-Sharīf al-Raḍī comments: "This cascading negation demonstrates how each attempted affirmation about God leads to limitation, requiring perpetual tanzīh." 'Alī's formulation reveals how even innocent-seeming questions about divine nature involve problematic assumptions that compromise transcendence.

When asked about the meaning of "laysa kamithlihi shay'un," Ibn 'Abbās responded: "This means Allah shares with His creation neither essence (dhāt), nor attributes (ṣifāt), nor actions (af'āl). Whatever you understand about creation, understand that Allah is utterly different (bi-khilāf dhālik)." This comprehensive statement established that divine incomparability extends to every aspect of divine reality, not merely to particular attributes. Abū Bakr's famous statement, "The inability to comprehend is itself comprehension" (al-'ajz 'an dark al-idrāk idrāk), became paradigmatic for apophatic theology. Al-Ghazālī later explains: "This is the highest human achievement regarding divine knowledge—to know certainly that we cannot know Him as He knows Himself." This recognition of necessary limitation became foundational for all subsequent Islamic theology.

The first generations developed technical vocabulary for apophatic theology that would provide the linguistic tools for systematic theological reflection. The term tanzīh, from the root n-z-h meaning to declare free or pure from something, became the standard designation for apophatic discourse. Sa'īd ibn Jubayr (d. 95/714) defined it: "Tanzīh is declaring Allah free from whatever does not befit His majesty—whether limitations, needs, or resemblances to creation." The related term taqdīs, from q-d-s meaning to sanctify or declare holy, carried additional connotations. Mujāhid ibn Jabr (d. 104/722) explained: "Taqdīs goes beyond tanzīh—it is not merely negating imperfection but affirming absolute holiness that transcends human understanding."

The concept of salb al-ṣifāt, the negation of attributes, required careful differentiation to avoid theological error. Early theologians distinguished between negating deficient attributes such as ignorance, weakness, or injustice from God; negating creaturely modes of perfect attributes, recognizing that God's knowledge is not acquired and His power not potential; and negating the applicability of categorical descriptions by asserting that God is neither substance nor accident. These distinctions enabled sophisticated theological discourse that could employ negation precisely rather than indiscriminately.

Several methodological principles emerged from these early precedents that would guide later theological development. Wahb ibn Munabbih (d. 114/732) articulated the priority of negation: "Begin knowing Allah by knowing what He is not. Only then can you appreciate what the names and attributes convey while maintaining transcendence." Al-Ḥasan al-Baṣrī observed the dialectical relationship between negation and affirmation: "Every negation about Allah implies an affirmation. 'He does not sleep' affirms His perfect vigilance; 'He does not forget' affirms His perfect knowledge." However, Ja'far al-Ṣādiq (d. 148/765) warned against excess: "Excessive negation (ifrāṭ fī al-tanzīh) can lead to denying what Allah affirmed about Himself. True tanzīh maintains the balance." These principles established that apophatic theology, properly understood, serves affirmation rather than negation of divine reality.

As Islamic theology matured, scattered apophatic insights coalesced into systematic approaches that would characterize different theological schools. The Mu'tazilites developed perhaps the most rigorous systematic negative theology. Al-Qāḍī 'Abd al-Jabbār in Al-Mughnī presents their comprehensive approach: "The foundation of theology is tanzīh. We begin by negating from Allah: all attributes of bodies—location, direction, movement, rest, color, taste, smell; all attributes of accidents—temporal origination, change, development; all attributes implying need—composition, causation, potentiality; all attributes implying limitation—ignorance, weakness, injustice." He continues with positive principles derived from negation: "From negating ignorance, we derive infinite knowledge; from negating weakness, infinite power; from negating injustice, perfect justice." This systematic approach sought to preserve divine transcendence through a comprehensive rational analysis of what God cannot be.

The Ash'arites developed a more nuanced negative theology that operated at multiple levels simultaneously. Al-Juwaynī in Al-Irshād articulates their position: "Tanzīh operates at multiple levels. Essential tanzīh declares that God's essence is utterly unlike created essences. Attributive tanzīh maintains that divine attributes, while real, operate in modes entirely unlike creaturely attributes. Active tanzīh affirms that divine actions proceed without the conditions that govern created actions. Relational tanzīh asserts that God's relationship to creation involves no dependence or change in Him." This multilayered approach enabled Ash'arites to maintain divine transcendence while affirming the reality of divine attributes.

Al-Ghazālī synthesizes the Ash'arite position in Al-Maqṣad al-Asnā: "Perfect tanzīh means understanding that even our negations are inadequate. When we say God is 'not limited,' we must not imagine we comprehend unlimited existence. The negation points beyond itself to incomprehensible perfection." This meta-apophatic insight recognizes that negation itself remains a human conceptual operation that cannot fully capture divine reality.

Al-Māturīdī developed a balanced approach in Kitāb al-Tawḥīd that distinguished between different degrees of apophatic necessity. Tanzīh has necessary, revealed, and precautionary dimensions. Necessary tanzīh encompasses what reason demands, including the negation of corporeality, location, and change. Revealed tanzīh includes what scripture teaches through specific negations like "He begets not." Precautionary tanzīh involves avoiding expressions that might mislead, even if technically permissible. Al-Nasafī elaborates: "The Māturīdite method maintains that tanzīh should never negate divine perfections or render God unknowable. Balanced tanzīh declares God free from imperfection while affirming His self-revealed attributes." This graduated approach enabled careful navigation between excessive negation and insufficient transcendence.

Muslim philosophers developed highly abstract negative theology that pushed apophatic discourse to its conceptual limits. Ibn Sīnā in Al-Ishārāt wa-l-Tanbīhāt writes: "The Necessary Existent admits no positive predication in the ordinary sense. We can only say what It is not—not composite, not multiple, not potential; how It relates—as cause to effect, known to knower; and that It transcends—beyond all categories of existence applicable to possibles." This philosophical approach sought to articulate divine transcendence through metaphysical categories that transcend ordinary predication.

Al-Suhrawardī refines this in Ḥikmat al-Ishrāq: "Even negation fails to capture divine transcendence. God is not merely 'not-darkness' but Light beyond the opposition of light and darkness, Being beyond the distinction of existence and non-existence." This radical formulation suggests that divine reality transcends even the most fundamental metaphysical distinctions, including the very opposition between being and non-being.

Sufi thinkers developed experiential negative theology grounded in spiritual realization rather than purely conceptual analysis. Al-Qushayrī in his Risāla states: "The people of realization (ahl al-taḥqīq) practice tanzīh in three ways. Verbal tanzīh involves careful speech about God, ensuring that language respects divine transcendence. Conceptual tanzīh requires purifying the heart from anthropomorphic imaginings that compromise true understanding. Experiential tanzīh means witnessing divine transcendence in spiritual unveiling, where theoretical knowledge becomes lived reality." This threefold approach integrates intellectual, psychological, and spiritual dimensions of apophatic theology.

Ibn 'Arabī deepens this in Fuṣūṣ al-Ḥikam: "True tanzīh transcends both negation and affirmation. God is munazzah (transcendent) even from tanzīh itself. This is the meaning of 'Glorified be your Lord, the Lord of Might, above what they describe' (37:180)." This ultimate apophatic move suggests that even the act of declaring divine transcendence remains inadequate to divine reality, which exceeds all human operations, including negation itself.

The relationship between tanzīh (transcendence/ dissimilarity) and tashbīh (immanence/similarity) represents one of the most nuanced aspects of Islamic theology, requiring careful balance to avoid extremes. Al-Ghazālī explains in Mishkāt al-Anwār why both are necessary: "Pure tanzīh without tashbīh leads to ta'ṭīl—negating divine attributes until God becomes an abstract concept. Pure tashbīh without tanzīh leads to tajsīm—anthropomorphism that compromises divine transcendence. The Quran employs both, teaching us their proper relationship." This recognition that neither pure negation nor pure affirmation suffices established the dialectical character of Islamic theological discourse.

Different schools articulated this balance distinctively while sharing the conviction that both moments remain essential. The Ash'arite position, articulated by al-Bāqillānī, maintains: "We affirm what Allah affirmed (tashbīh in the linguistic sense) while negating the modality (tanzīh in the conceptual sense). God has a 'hand' but not as creatures have hands—the word is similar, the reality utterly different." This formula of "affirmation without modality" became standard in Ash'arite theology.

The Māturīdite nuance, expressed by al-Nasafī, emphasizes the functional complementarity of the two moments: "Tashbīh in language serves human understanding; tanzīh in meaning preserves divine transcendence. We need anthropomorphic language to relate to God, but must understand it through the lens of 'laysa kamithlihi shay'un.'" This formulation recognizes that human language necessarily employs familiar categories while theological understanding must transcend literal interpretation.

The Sufi integration, articulated by al-Junayd, grounds the dialectic in spiritual experience: "The realized one affirms tashbīh in his spiritual need and tanzīh in his theological understanding, knowing that both point to a reality transcending either." This approach recognizes that the relationship to God requires both intimacy enabled by tashbīh and reverence preserved by tanzīh.

Ibn 'Arabī developed the most comprehensive treatment of the tanzīh-tashbīh relationship through a synthetic vision that transcends simple alternation. He states: "He who affirms tanzīh alone worships the Absolute (al-muṭlaq); He who affirms tashbīh alone worships the determinate (almuqayyad); He who affirms both worships the Real (al-Ḥaqq). For God says 'Nothing is like Him'—this is tanzīh; And He says 'He is the Hearing, the Seeing'—this is tashbīh. The complete servant affirms both, following the Quran." He explains further: "Tanzīh without tashbīh is deficiency in knowing God; tashbīh without tanzīh is deficiency in unifying God. The perfect knowledge combines both while transcending both." This dialectical synthesis recognizes that authentic theology must hold both moments together in productive tension.

The tanzīh-tashbīh relationship had practical consequences for religious life, demonstrating that this theological dialectic was not merely abstract speculation. In worship, al-Ghazālī notes: "In prayer, we face the qibla (tashbīh—as if God were in a direction) while believing 'wherever you turn, there is the Face of Allah' (tanzīh—God is not limited to direction)." In supplication, Ibn 'Aṭā' Allah states: "We raise our hands in du'ā' (tashbīh) while knowing 'He is closer than the jugular vein' (tanzīh). The physical gesture expresses spiritual orientation, not divine location." In understanding scripture, al-Rāzī explains: "When reading anthropomorphic verses, the heart experiences divine nearness through tashbīh while the intellect maintains divine transcendence through tanzīh. Both operate simultaneously." These practical applications demonstrate how the theological dialectic shapes lived religious experience.

The development of apophatic theology generated significant debates that refined Islamic understanding of divine transcendence. The first major debate concerned the extent of permissible negation, with different schools drawing the boundaries of legitimate apophatic discourse differently. The Mu'tazilites argued for extensive negation, with Abū Hāshim al-Jubbā'ī stating: "We must negate from God not only deficiencies but any attribute that could imply limitation, including distinct attributes themselves." This position sought to preserve absolute divine unity through comprehensive negation of multiplicity.

Critics like al-Ash'arī responded that such extensive negation exceeded proper bounds: "Excessive negation denies what God affirmed about Himself. If God says He is 'Knowing,' we cannot negate knowledge from Him in the name of tanzīh." This critique established limits on apophatic theology, insisting that negation must never contradict divine self-revelation.

The second debate concerned the status of divine names and whether they necessarily involve problematic similarity. The Ḥashwiyya argued: "If God calls Himself 'the Merciful' and humans can be merciful, this is explicit tashbīh that must be accepted." This position emphasized the apparent meaning of shared terminology. The mainstream response, articulated by al-Māturīdī, distinguished between linguistic and semantic similarity: "Divine names involve linguistic similarity (ishtirāk lafẓī) but absolute difference in meaning (tabāyun ma'nawī). God's mercy differs from human mercy more than existence differs from non-existence." This solution preserved both the meaningfulness of divine names and absolute divine transcendence.

The third major debate concerned the interpretation of anthropomorphic texts, generating three major positions with different strategies for preserving transcendence. The Ẓāhirī position, articulated by Ibn Ḥazm, argued: "We affirm the apparent meaning without interpretation, adding only 'laysa kamithlihi shay'un.'" The Ash'arī-Māturīdī position maintained: "We affirm the texts while negating anthropomorphic understanding, sometimes through ta'wīl when necessary to preserve tanzīh." The philosophical position held that "all anthropomorphic language is purely metaphorical, requiring consistent allegorical interpretation." Each approach sought to balance respect for revelation with preservation of transcendence.

Despite these disagreements, certain consensual positions emerged that defined the parameters of acceptable Islamic theology. The primacy of transcendence gained universal acceptance, with all schools agreeing that "laysa kamithlihi shay'un" governs all theological discourse. As al-Tahāwī's creed states: "Whoever describes Allah with any human attribute has committed kufr." This fundamental commitment unified all mainstream Islamic theology.

The necessity of balance between extremes achieved consensus status, with mainstream theology rejecting both extreme tanzīh resulting in ta'ṭīl (negation of attributes) and extreme tashbīh resulting in tajsīm (anthropomorphism). Ibn Taymiyya summarizes this consensus: "The saved sect affirms what Allah affirmed while maintaining transcendence." The mystery of divine nature received universal acknowledgment, with consensus emerging that ultimate divine reality transcends human comprehension. Al-Ghazālī expresses this agreement: "The endpoint of gnosis is recognizing the inability to achieve gnosis."

Several methodological principles gained wide acceptance as guides for theological reflection. Scripture must interpret scripture (al-Qur'ān yufassiru ba'ḍuhu ba'ḍan), ensuring that interpretation remains grounded in revelation itself. Clear verses judge ambiguous ones, providing hermeneutical priority to unambiguous texts. Transcendence governs all interpretation, ensuring that "laysa kamithlihi shay'un" functions as the supreme interpretive principle. Practical piety takes precedence over speculation, maintaining the connection between theology and lived religion.

These consensual positions were codified in creeds and teaching texts that became standard across Islamic education. Al-Ṭaḥāwī's Creed became widely accepted across schools: "Allah is exalted beyond having limits, boundaries, corners, limbs, or organs. The six directions do not contain Him as they contain all created things." Al-Nasafī's Creed provided the standard Māturīdī formulation: "Allah is not a body, not a substance, not an accident. He has no limit, no opposite, no equal, no peer." Educational institutions developed curricula balancing tanzīh and appropriate tashbīh, teaching students to navigate this theological complexity with sophistication.

Post-classical scholars continued refining apophatic theology through increasingly systematic presentations. Al-Sanūsī (d. 895/1490) developed the categorization of attributes into necessary (wājib), impossible (mustaḥīl), and possible (jā'iz) regarding God, providing systematic framework for tanzīh that became standard in theological education. Al-Bājūrī (d. 1277/1860) in his popular commentary emphasized: "The science of tawḥīd begins with knowing what is impossible for Allah—this is the foundation of sound belief." This pedagogical emphasis on negative theology demonstrated its enduring centrality.

The development of apophatic theology in Islam demonstrates sophisticated engagement with the fundamental challenge of speaking about the One who is "naught is like unto Him." From early precedents in prophetic practice and Companion statements through systematic elaboration in classical texts, tanzīh emerged as an essential aspect of Islamic theology. The relationship between tanzīh and tashbīh reveals Islam's nuanced approach to divine transcendence—neither pure negation that empties religious language of meaning nor naive affirmation that compromises divine incomparability. The classical debates, while generating diverse positions, produced consensual frameworks that continue to guide Islamic theology.

The patterns observed—the priority of transcendence, the necessity of balance, the recognition of mystery, and the integration of theory with practice—demonstrate that apophatic theology in Islam serves not merely as philosophical exercise but as essential guidance for authentic divine-human relationship. Tanzīh preserves the awe, reverence, and mystery appropriate to the divine while enabling meaningful worship and spiritual development.

This examination reveals that Islamic negative theology, far from being purely negational, opens space for the most profound affirmation—that the divine reality infinitely exceeds all human conception while remaining accessible through divine self-disclosure. The achievement of classical Islamic theology lies in maintaining this productive tension, ensuring that the principle "laysa kamithlihi shay'un" continues to guide believers toward ever-deeper appreciation of divine transcendence.

Chapter 9. Al-Ghazali's Integration of Philosophy and Traditional Theology

Abū Ḥāmid al-Ghazālī (d. 505/1111) stands as one of the most influential figures in Islamic intellectual history, earning the honorific "Proof of Islam" (Ḥujjat al-Islām). His sophisticated integration of philosophical methodology with traditional Ash'arite theology while maintaining deep spiritual commitment represents a watershed moment in Islamic thought. This chapter examines how al-Ghazālī navigated between philosophical rationalism and traditional theology, using the very tools of philosophy to establish its limits while preserving the transcendent mystery proclaimed in "laysa kamithlihi shay'un."

Al-Ghazālī's Tahāfut al-Falāsifa (The Incoherence of the Philosophers) emerged from a specific historical context where philosophical thought had gained significant influence in Islamic intellectual circles, raising concerns about its compatibility with revealed theology. By al-Ghazālī's time, falsafa (Islamic philosophy) had developed into a sophisticated tradition. Al-Fārābī (d. 339/950) and Ibn Sīnā (d. 428/1037) had created comprehensive philosophical systems that claimed to demonstrate religious truths through pure reason. Ibn Sīnā's influence was particularly pervasive. Al-Ghazālī himself acknowledges in Al-Munqidh min al-Ḍalāl: "The philosophy of Ibn Sīnā had become so widespread among the intellectual elite that many considered his views as established truth. Students of religious sciences felt intellectually inferior if they could not engage with philosophical arguments."

Understanding the Tahāfut requires appreciating al-Ghazālī's unique preparation for this monumental critique. In Al-Munqidh, he describes his systematic study: "I dedicated myself to studying philosophy until I mastered it completely. For nearly two years, alongside my teaching duties, I read the philosophers' books. I would spend my nights writing Maqāṣid al-Falāsifa, summarizing their doctrines accurately. Only one who truly understands a position can effectively critique it." This preparation was unprecedented. Earlier critics of philosophy often attacked strawmen. Al-Ghazālī's Maqāṣid al-Falāsifa presented philosophical positions so accurately that later Latin translators mistook it for advocacy rather than preparation for refutation.

Al-Ghazālī identified twenty philosophical positions he considered problematic, focusing on three as warranting takfīr (declaration of unbelief). These were the eternity of the world, God's knowledge only of universals rather than particulars, and the denial of bodily resurrection. He explains his selective approach: "I do not oppose the philosophers in matters of logic, mathematics, or even much of their physics. These are demonstrative sciences where opposition would be foolish. I challenge them where they transgress into metaphysics and theology without demonstrative proof." This discrimination demonstrated that his critique was principled rather than a wholesale rejection of philosophical inquiry.

Al-Ghazālī's approach was revolutionary in its philosophical sophistication, employing multiple strategies that would make his critique uniquely effective. Rather than opposing philosophy with scripture, he demonstrated internal contradictions within philosophical systems through what might be called internal critique. He explains: "I show that philosophers contradict each other and themselves, that their metaphysical 'demonstrations' rest on unproven premises." He employed logical rigor by using the philosophers' own logical tools against them. "I use their syllogistic method to show where their syllogisms fail, their demonstrative science to reveal where demonstration ends and conjecture begins." Most significantly, the critique centered on knowledge claims through its epistemological focus. "My goal is not to establish counter-positions but to show that philosophical metaphysics lacks the certainty it claims. In matters touching divine transcendence, pretended certainty becomes dangerous falsehood."

While critiquing philosophical overreach, al-Ghazālī masterfully employed philosophical tools to articulate and defend traditional Ash'arite positions. In Mi'yār al-'Ilm (The Standard of Knowledge), al-Ghazālī argues for logic's religious neutrality: "Logic is to the intellectual sciences what grammar is to language and prosody to poetry. Just as grammar serves equally the poet praising wine and the preacher condemning it, logic serves both truth and falsehood. The tool itself is neutral; its application determines its value."

He systematically showed how logical argumentation could support traditional theology through specific applications to contested doctrines. On divine attributes, he argued: "The philosophers claim that affirming multiple attributes compromises divine unity. But logical analysis shows that conceptual distinction need not imply real multiplicity. The Ash'arite position—attributes neither identical to nor separate from the essence—is logically coherent." On creation, he demonstrated: "Philosophers argue that 'from one only one proceeds.' But this principle, even if granted, applies to natural causation, not divine creative action which transcends natural patterns." These demonstrations proved that traditional theology need not fear rigorous logical analysis.

Al-Ghazālī distinguished between legitimate demonstrative science and philosophical speculation, establishing crucial epistemological boundaries: "Mathematics provides certain knowledge through demonstration. When philosophers apply mathematical reasoning to metaphysics, they mistake methodological similarity for equal certainty. But metaphysical premises lack mathematical self-evidence." He illustrated this through specific examples drawn from central philosophical arguments. Regarding the eternity argument, he observed: "Philosophers argue: 'Change implies temporal origination; God is changeless; therefore the world, as His effect, must be eternal.' This appears demonstrative but assumes that divine creative action parallels natural causation—an undemonstrated premise." Regarding divine knowledge, he noted: "Their argument that knowing particulars implies change in the knower applies only to human knowledge, which is receptive and temporal. Divine knowledge, being creative and eternal, need not follow this pattern."

One of al-Ghazālī's most influential philosophical contributions was his critique of necessary causation, which would have profound implications for Islamic theology: "The connection between what is habitually believed to be cause and effect is not necessary. Fire does not burn by its nature but by divine action through it. God could create burning without fire or prevent burning despite fire's presence." This position, developed in detail in the Tahāfut, served traditional doctrine by preserving divine omnipotence against philosophical determinism, grounding miracles in coherent metaphysics, and maintaining divine transcendence by denying that God acts under compulsion of natures. This occasionalist metaphysics would become characteristic of later Ash'arite thought.

Al-Ghazālī's magnum opus demonstrates positive integration of philosophical insights with traditional theology, moving beyond mere critique to constructive synthesis. In the book on divine names, he writes: "Understanding God's names requires three levels of apprehension: linguistic (the grammarian's level), conceptual (the theologian's level), and experiential (the mystic's level). Philosophy serves the conceptual level, preparing the heart for experiential knowledge."

He employs philosophical analysis to deepen traditional understanding across multiple theological domains. On divine mercy, he argues: "The philosophers correctly note that divine mercy differs categorically from human emotion. But they err in making it merely metaphorical. Divine mercy is real—more real than human mercy—but its mode transcends human categories." On divine unity, he maintains: "Philosophical analysis helps us understand that divine unity is not numerical (like one among many) but absolute (precluding real multiplicity). This serves the traditional affirmation of tawḥīd." These applications demonstrate how philosophical precision could enhance rather than undermine traditional doctrine.

Al-Ghazālī's position on reason was nuanced—neither rationalist nor anti-rational, but carefully delineating reason's proper scope and inherent limitations. In Mishkāt al-Anwār, al-Ghazālī presents a sophisticated epistemology through a hierarchical understanding of human knowledge: "Human faculties form a hierarchy: sensation, imagination, estimation, reason, and finally the prophetic faculty. Each transcends the previous while building upon it. As imagination grasps what escapes sensation, and reason what escapes imagination, the prophetic faculty grasps what escapes reason."

This hierarchy establishes reason's dignity while acknowledging its limits: "Reason is humanity's glory, elevating us above animals. But those who deny what transcends reason resemble those born blind who deny color's existence because it escapes their experience." This analogy became influential in later Islamic thought, providing a framework for understanding the relationship between natural and revealed knowledge.

Al-Ghazālī carefully delineated where reason operates legitimately across different domains of human concern. In worldly matters, he affirmed reason's excellence: "Reason excellently judges practical affairs, mathematical truths, and logical relationships. Here it serves as God's gift for human flourishing." In basic religious truths, he recognized reason's capacity: "Reason can know God exists, that He is one, powerful, and knowing. It can recognize the possibility of prophecy and the coherence of moral principles." In theological defense, he valued reason's protective function: "Reason protects faith from sophistry, distinguishes sound from unsound arguments, and articulates belief coherently." These affirmations demonstrate that al-Ghazālī's delimitation of reason was not born of hostility but of precision.

Al-Ghazālī identified specific areas where reason must yield to revelation, establishing boundaries that would shape subsequent theological discourse. Regarding divine nature, he argued: "Reason can know that God exists and is perfect, but cannot determine the specific nature of divine perfection. That God is 'samī'' (All-Hearing) without organs or sound waves transcends rational categories." Regarding eschatological details, he maintained: "Reason can demonstrate the soul's immortality and the coherence of afterlife, but specific details of paradise and hell come only through revelation." Regarding ritual specifications, he observed: "Reason grasps the value of worship but cannot determine that prayer involves specific movements at specific times. These specifications require prophetic instruction." These distinctions enabled Muslims to employ reason confidently within its proper sphere while respecting revelation's authority beyond it.

Al-Ghazālī's deepest critique targeted not reason itself but philosophical presumption about reason's capacities: "The philosophers' error is not using reason but exceeding its competence. Like someone who uses a perfectly good scale to weigh mountains—the fault lies not in the scale but in misapplication."

He identified specific overreaches that characterized philosophical error. Philosophers erred in claiming demonstrative certainty where none existed: "In metaphysics, philosophers present probable arguments as demonstrations, conjectures as certainties. This misleads students who assume philosophical conclusions carry mathematical certainty." They erred in reducing mystery to logic: "They subject divine transcendence to logical categories, forgetting that 'laysa kamithlihi shay'un' means God transcends even the laws of logic that govern created thought." Most dangerously, they erred in dismissing revelation: "Most dangerously, they consider revealed knowledge inferior to philosophical, not recognizing that revelation provides what reason cannot—specific knowledge of transcendent reality."

Al-Ghazālī advocated intellectual humility as reason's perfection rather than its abdication: "The intelligent person uses reason to recognize reason's limits. As eyes need light to see, reason needs revelation's light to perceive transcendent truths. Acknowledging this need demonstrates reason's health, not sickness." In Iḥyā', he provides practical guidance for how reason should function in the religious life of the believer. Reason should be used to understand what can be understood, to recognize what cannot be understood, to accept revealed knowledge about what transcends understanding, and to experience through spiritual practice what transcends both reason and ordinary revelation. This fourfold program integrated intellectual, religious, and spiritual dimensions into a comprehensive approach to knowledge.

Al-Ghazālī's synthesis profoundly influenced subsequent Islamic thought, generating both adoption and adaptation across theological, philosophical, and mystical traditions. The initial reception was mixed but intense, demonstrating the work's immediate impact. The philosophical response came most notably from Ibn Rushd (d. 595/1198), who wrote Tahāfut al-Tahāfut defending philosophy against al-Ghazālī's critique. Yet even this defense acknowledged: "Al-Ghazālī raised legitimate concerns about philosophical method in theology. His critique forced greater precision in distinguishing demonstration from dialectic."

Theological embrace came quickly from Ash'arite theologians who adopted al-Ghazālī's synthesis. Al-Rāzī (d. 606/1210) extensively used philosophical argumentation while maintaining al-Ghazālī's boundaries: "Al-Ghazālī showed us how to use philosophical tools without becoming philosophers, to employ reason without succumbing to rationalism." Sufi integration found in al-Ghazālī a model for combining intellectual and spiritual life. 'Abd al-Qādir al-Jīlānī (d. 561/1166) praised: "Al-Ghazālī united what others separated—sharp intellect with burning heart, philosophical precision with spiritual submission."

Al-Ghazālī's influence reshaped Islamic theology in lasting ways through methodological transformation. Post-Ghazālī Ash'arism incorporated philosophical sophistication while maintaining traditional commitments. Works like al-Ījī's al-Mawāqif show this influence: "We follow al-Ghazālī in using philosophical analysis to clarify, not replace, traditional doctrine."

Educational reform followed as his approach influenced madrasa curricula. Logic became standard preparatory study, but within frameworks emphasizing its instrumental nature. Al-Suyūṭī notes: "After al-Ghazālī, denying logic's utility became as untenable as granting it absolute authority." Creedal formulations reflected his nuanced positions, with later creeds like al-Sanūsī's widely-studied text showing clear influence in its philosophical precision serving traditional ends.

Despite his critique, al-Ghazālī inadvertently enriched Islamic philosophy by forcing it to become more rigorous and self-aware. In the eastern lands, philosophers like Naṣīr al-Dīn al-Ṭūsī (d. 672/1274) engaged seriously with his criticisms: "Al-Ghazālī's challenges forced us to strengthen philosophical foundations and clarify metaphysical demonstrations." The illuminationist response came from al-Suhrawardī (d. 587/1191), who developed illuminationist philosophy partly responding to al-Ghazālī's critique of Peripatetic rationalism: "Where al-Ghazālī showed discursive reason's limits, we seek direct illuminative knowledge." Later synthesis emerged with Mullā Ṣadrā (d. 1050/1640), who achieved a comprehensive integration incorporating al-Ghazālī's insights: "Al-Ghazālī correctly identified pure reason's limitations. But reason illuminated by revelation and spiritual experience transcends those limits."

Al-Ghazālī's greatest influence may be in Islamic mysticism, where he legitimized Sufism by integrating it with orthodox theology and law, making mystical practice respectable in mainstream circles. Ibn 'Arabī acknowledged: "Al-Ghazālī opened doors for us by showing that experiencing divine mysteries accords with, rather than contradicts, sound theology." His methodological influence shaped all subsequent Sufi manuals, as works like al-Qushayrī's Risāla were reread through Ghazālian lenses. He established a tradition of intellectual mysticism, with later figures like 'Abd al-Karīm al-Jīlī combining philosophical analysis with mystical experience while following al-Ghazālī's model.

Al-Ghazālī's influence extends into contemporary Islamic thought through multiple channels. Reformist appropriation came from modern reformers like Muhammad 'Abduh and Rashīd Riḍā, who invoked al-Ghazālī's balanced use of reason against both pure traditionalism and excessive rationalism. Neo-Ghazālian movements emerged as thinkers like Muhammad Iqbal explicitly built on al-Ghazālī while adapting to modern contexts: "Al-Ghazālī's critique of philosophical presumption remains valid against modern materialism." Academic study has increasingly recognized al-Ghazālī's philosophical sophistication. As Frank Griffel notes: "Al-Ghazālī was not philosophy's enemy but its most sophisticated internal critic."

Not all reception was positive, however. Rationalist critique came from Mu'tazilite-influenced thinkers who argued al-Ghazālī weakened Islam's rational foundations. Modern critics like Fazlur Rahman worried: "Al-Ghazālī's delimiting of reason, however nuanced, contributed to later intellectual stagnation." Traditionalist concerns emerged from some traditional scholars who felt he conceded too much to philosophy. Ibn Taymiyya, despite general appreciation, criticized: "Al-Ghazālī sometimes let philosophical categories shape his theology even while critiquing philosophers." The problem of mystical excess arose as later antinomian Sufis claimed al-Ghazālī's authority for positions he would have rejected, leading to debates about his true legacy.

Al-Ghazālī's integration of philosophy and traditional theology represents a crucial moment in Islamic intellectual history. His sophisticated engagement with philosophy—mastering it to critique it, using it to serve tradition—established patterns that continue to influence Islamic thought. His approach to reason's limits was neither obscurantist nor rationalist but profoundly nuanced. By showing where demonstration ends and faith begins, where reason serves and where it must yield, he preserved space for the transcendent mystery expressed in "laysa kamithlihi shay'un" while maintaining intellectual rigor.

The Tahāfut did not end Islamic philosophy but transformed it, forcing greater precision and humility. His positive integration in works like the Iḥyā' showed how philosophical tools could deepen rather than threaten traditional understanding. Most significantly, he demonstrated that engaging seriously with challenging intellectual traditions need not compromise authentic faith but can strengthen and clarify it.

Al-Ghazālī's legacy lies not in specific positions but in his method—rigorous engagement, careful distinction, synthetic integration, and ultimate submission to transcendent truth. In an age where Muslims again face challenging intellectual systems, his model remains relevant: neither retreating into isolation nor uncritically embracing foreign frameworks, but engaging thoughtfully while maintaining authentic Islamic commitments. His life and work embody the recognition that approaching the One who is "naught is like unto Him" requires all human faculties—reason and revelation, philosophy and tradition, intellect and spirit—working in proper harmony. This integration, rather than any single insight, may be al-Ghazālī's greatest contribution to Islamic thought.

Chapter 10. Ibn Sina's Necessary Existent: A Philosophical Approach

Abū 'Alī al-Ḥusayn ibn 'Abd Allāh ibn Sīnā (d. 428/1037), known in the Latin West as Avicenna, developed perhaps the most influential philosophical articulation of divine transcendence in Islamic thought. His concept of the Necessary Existent (wājib al-wujūd) provided a rigorously philosophical approach to understanding the One who is "naught is like unto Him," employing demonstration rather than tradition to establish divine incomparability. This chapter examines how Ibn Sīnā's metaphysics engaged with Islamic theology, his doctrine of divine simplicity, the reception and critiques his thought generated, and his profound influence on subsequent Islamic philosophy.

Ibn Sīnā's philosophical system emerged from a unique synthesis of Aristotelian philosophy, Neoplatonic thought, and Islamic theological concerns, creating a metaphysics that claimed to demonstrate rationally what revelation taught about divine nature. The cornerstone of Avicennan metaphysics lies in the fundamental distinction between existence (wujūd) and essence (māhiyya). In al-Najāt, Ibn Sīnā explains: "In everything whose essence is other than its existence, existence is something that happens to the essence. The essence in itself neither exists nor does not exist—it is neutral regarding existence. When we conceive 'human' or 'horse,' we conceive what they are, not whether they exist."

This distinction proves crucial for understanding divine transcendence: "There must be something whose essence is existence itself, where 'what it is' and 'that it is' are identical. This is the Necessary Existent, whose reality is pure existence without any essence to which existence is added." Al-Ṭūsī, commenting on Ibn Sīnā's al-Ishārāt, clarifies: "This means God's reality cannot be conceptualized as essence plus existence. He is existence itself, subsisting without qualification or determination." This metaphysical insight would become foundational for subsequent Islamic philosophy.

Ibn Sīnā developed multiple proofs for God's existence, but his most original was the "Proof of the Truthful" (burhān al-ṣiddīqīn), which begins from the concept of existence itself rather than from creation. In al-Shifā', he argues: "Existence is either necessary or possible. If necessary, our conclusion is reached. If possible, it requires a cause. This cause is either necessary (and we have our conclusion) or possible (requiring another cause). An infinite regress of possible causes is impossible. Therefore, a Necessary Existent exists." He emphasizes this proof's superiority: "Other proofs proceed from effects to cause—from motion to Prime Mover, from design to Designer. This proof proceeds from the very concept of existence to necessary existence. It is more certain because it relies on fewer premises."

From the concept of necessary existence, Ibn Sīnā derives all divine attributes through pure rational analysis. Regarding unity, he argues: "If there were two necessary existents, each would need a differentiating factor. But whatever has compositional factors is caused, not necessary. Therefore, the Necessary Existent is absolutely one." Regarding simplicity, he maintains: "The Necessary Existent cannot have parts—physical, conceptual, or essential. Any composition implies dependence on parts, but the Necessary is absolutely independent." Regarding immateriality, he demonstrates: "Matter is pure potentiality awaiting actualization. The Necessary Existent is pure actuality with no potentiality. Therefore, It is absolutely immaterial." Regarding intelligence, he concludes: "The Necessary Existent must be intelligent, for It is free from matter, and immateriality is the root of intellectuality. Moreover, It knows Itself through Itself, for knower and known are one in It."

Ibn Sīnā explicitly connected his philosophical conclusions with Quranic teaching. In his Risāla fī Ithbāt al-Nubuwwāt, he writes: "What demonstration establishes about the Necessary Existent—Its unity, knowledge, power, and will—corresponds precisely to what the Prophet [ﷺ] taught about Allah. Philosophy confirms revelation through independent rational proof." He addressed apparent tensions through careful interpretation. On divine names, he explained: "The many names of Allah refer to various relationships between the Necessary Existent and Its effects, not to multiple attributes in the essence. 'The Merciful' refers to the relationship of existence-giving; 'The Wise' to the relationship of order-giving." On creation, he argued: "The Quranic teaching that Allah creates by command—'Be! and it is'—philosophically means that His knowledge of the good order is itself the cause of that order's existence. No temporal deliberation is implied."

However, certain positions created controversy that would generate extensive debate. On eternal creation, he maintained: "From an eternal, unchanging Necessary Existent, the effect must also be eternal. The world is eternally created, not created in time." On knowledge of particulars, he argued: "The Necessary Existent knows all things, but in a universal way that encompasses particulars without being subject to temporal change." These positions would become focal points for theological critique.

Ibn Sīnā's doctrine of absolute divine simplicity represents his most radical preservation of divine transcendence, pushing the principle "laysa kamithlihi shay'un" to its logical limits. In al-Shifā', Metaphysics IX.4, Ibn Sīnā argues: "The Necessary Existent is simple in every conceivable way: no physical parts (not a body), no metaphysical parts (no matter and form), no logical parts (no genus and differentia), no distinction between essence and attributes, and no distinction between essence and existence."

He explains the radical nature of this simplicity: "In the Necessary Existent, power is not something It has but something It is. The same for knowledge, will, and life. These are not attributes added to an essence but identical with the simple reality that is pure necessary existence." This formulation represented the most extreme philosophical articulation of divine transcendence in Islamic thought.

This raised the classical problem of how God can have multiple attributes if He is absolutely simple. Ibn Sīnā's solution was revolutionary: "The attributes are conceptually distinct but really identical. Our minds, proceeding from effects, conceive different aspects of the one simple reality. We see existence-giving and call it 'power,' order-giving and call it 'wisdom.' But in the Necessary Existent, these are one simple act of being." He uses the analogy of light: "Light illuminates, warms, and reveals colors. These seem like different activities but are all just light being light. Similarly, the Necessary Existent's various attributes are just necessary existence being necessary existence."

Divine simplicity profoundly affects the understanding of divine action in ways that would generate significant theological controversy. Regarding temporal activity, Ibn Sīnā argues: "The Necessary Existent cannot act in time, for temporal action implies change from potency to act. Its action is eternal—one timeless act that temporal beings experience sequentially." Regarding the plurality of acts, he maintains: "Creating Zayd and creating 'Amr are not two acts in God but one eternal act perceived as multiple from the side of effects." Regarding the nature of creation itself, he concludes: "Given absolute simplicity, creation occurs through necessary emanation (fayḍ) rather than voluntary choice between alternatives. The Necessary Existent emanates existence as the sun emanates light—naturally and eternally."

Ibn Sīnā's account of divine knowledge preserves simplicity while affirming omniscience through a sophisticated analysis: "The Necessary Existent knows all things through knowing Itself. In knowing Itself as the cause of all things, It knows all effects. This knowledge is not discursive (moving from premise to conclusion), not conceptual (through universal concepts), not temporal (changing with objects), but one simple intuition of all reality." He clarifies in al-Ta'līqāt: "God's knowledge of things is the cause of their existence, not—as with us—their existence the cause of our knowledge. His simple self-knowledge, as source of all, contains all multiplicity in absolute unity."

Ibn Sīnā's philosophical theology generated intense debate across the Islamic intellectual spectrum, from enthusiastic adoption to fierce critique. Among philosophers, Ibn Sīnā's system gained rapid acceptance. Bahmanyār ibn al-Marzubān (d. 458/1066), Ibn Sīnā's student, defended and systematized his master's thought in al-Taḥṣīl: "The Master's great achievement was demonstrating rationally what prophets taught through symbol—the absolute transcendence and simplicity of the Necessary Existent." 'Umar Khayyām (d. 526/1131), better known as a poet, wrote philosophical treatises defending Avicennan positions: "Those who attack Ibn Sīnā for making God too abstract fail to understand that 'laysa kamithlihi shay'un' demands such transcendence."

Theologians raised serious objections to specific Avicennan positions that they saw as incompatible with Islamic revelation. Al-Ghazālī's systematic critique in Tahāfut al-Falāsifa devoted three of his twenty discussions to what he considered Ibn Sīnā's gravest errors. On eternal creation, al-Ghazālī argued: "Ibn Sīnā's eternal world contradicts the Quranic teaching of creation's temporal beginning. His argument that change in God would result from temporal creation fails—God can eternally will a temporal effect." On divine knowledge, he maintained: "To say God knows particulars only 'in a universal way' effectively denies His knowledge of individuals. The Quran teaches that not a leaf falls without His knowledge—particular, detailed knowledge." On bodily resurrection, he objected: "By making the soul alone immortal, Ibn Sīnā denies bodily resurrection, contradicting explicit Quranic teaching."

Al-Ghazālī's deeper critique targeted the entire method: "Ibn Sīnā subjects God to philosophical categories—necessary existence, simplicity, emanation. But 'laysa kamithlihi shay'un' means God transcends even these philosophical concepts." Al-Shahrastānī (d. 548/1153) offered nuanced critique in Kitāb al-Muṣāra'a: "Ibn Sīnā correctly emphasizes divine transcendence but errs in two ways. He makes God too abstract—a philosophical principle rather than the living God of revelation. He binds God to logical necessity, denying real divine freedom."

Sufi thinkers showed ambivalent responses to Avicennan thought. Al-Qushayrī (d. 465/1074) warned against philosophical abstraction: "The philosophers' Necessary Existent may satisfy the intellect but leaves the heart cold. The God experienced in dhikr and murāqaba transcends philosophical categories." However, later Sufis like 'Ayn al-Quḍāt al-Hamadhānī (d. 525/1131) integrated Avicennan concepts: "Ibn Sīnā's Necessary Existent, properly understood, points to the same reality we experience in fanā'—absolute unity beyond all multiplicity."

Philosophical defenses emerged from various quarters. Ibn Rushd (Averroes) (d. 595/1198), while developing his own positions, defended Ibn Sīnā against some of al-Ghazālī's critiques: "Al-Ghazālī misunderstands Ibn Sīnā on divine knowledge. The claim is not that God is ignorant of particulars but that His knowledge transcends the temporal, changeable knowledge that 'particular' implies for us." Naṣīr al-Dīn al-Ṭūsī (d. 672/1274) wrote extensive defenses, particularly in his commentary on al-Ishārāt: "Those who claim Ibn Sīnā's Necessary Existent is not the God of Islam fail to see that rational demonstration and revealed description approach the same reality from different angles. The God who is 'laysa kamithlihi shay'un' must transcend anthropomorphic conception—precisely what Ibn Sīnā establishes."

Ibn Sīnā's concept of the Necessary Existent profoundly shaped subsequent Islamic philosophy, influencing even thinkers who rejected specific Avicennan positions. In the Eastern lands, Avicennan philosophy became the foundation for continued philosophical development. The School of Isfahan produced philosophers like Mīr Dāmād (d. 1040/1631) and his student Mullā Ṣadrā, who built on Avicennan foundations while addressing critiques. Mullā Ṣadrā writes in al-Asfār: "Ibn Sīnā established the primacy of existence but didn't fully develop its implications. The Necessary Existent is not just necessary existence but the source of existence's dynamic self-unfolding (tashkīk al-wujūd)."

The illuminationist revision undertaken by al-Suhrawardī (d. 587/1191) transformed Avicennan metaphysics: "Ibn Sīnā correctly identified the Necessary Existent but erred in making It mere existence. The Necessary Existent is Light of Lights (nūr al-anwār), and existence is Its first emanation. This preserves transcendence while making God more than abstract being."

Later theologians increasingly incorporated Avicennan insights into their systematic presentations. Fakhr al-Dīn al-Rāzī (d. 606/1210) integrated philosophical arguments into Ash'arite theology: "Ibn Sīnā's proofs for divine existence and unity, properly modified, strengthen kalām arguments. We reject his specific conclusions about creation and knowledge while adopting his demonstrative method." Al-Ījī (d. 756/1355) in al-Mawāqif shows thorough engagement: "The philosophers' analysis of necessary existence provides useful tools for understanding divine attributes, provided we maintain revealed truths about divine freedom and knowledge."

The synthesis of Ibn Sīnā's philosophy with mysticism produced profound developments. While not explicitly Avicennan, Ibn 'Arabī's concept of "necessary existence" (wujūb al-wujūd) shows clear influence: "The Real (al-Ḥaqq) is necessary existence giving existence to all possibilities. But unlike Ibn Sīnā's abstract Necessary Existent, the Real is also the self-disclosing (mutajallī) source of all divine names." 'Abd al-Razzāq al-Qāshānī (d. 736/1335) explicitly synthesized: "Ibn Sīnā demonstrated intellectually what the mystics experience directly—that only One truly exists, and all else exists through It. The Necessary Existent of the philosophers is the Absolute Reality (al-ḥaqīqa al-muṭlaqa) of the 'ārifīn."

Ibn Sīnā's influence extends into modern Islamic philosophy through various channels. Muhammad Iqbal critically engaged with Ibn Sīnā: "Avicenna's static Necessary Existent needs reformation through the

Quranic conception of God as dynamic will. Yet his emphasis on divine transcendence and demonstration remains valuable." Contemporary Iranian philosophy, represented by thinkers like 'Allāmah Ṭabāṭabā'ī and Murtaḍā Muṭahharī, built extensively on Avicennan foundations while addressing traditional critiques, showing the tradition's continued vitality.

Beyond specific doctrines, Ibn Sīnā's methodological contributions endured across multiple dimensions of Islamic intellectual life. His attempt to demonstrate religious truths rationally became a permanent feature of Islamic philosophy through what might be called demonstrative theology. His careful distinctions between existence and essence, necessary and possible, provided permanent tools for theological discussion through technical precision. His integration of logic, physics, and metaphysics into theology set standards for systematic thinking through systematic comprehensiveness. His model of relating philosophical theology to natural science influenced Islamic approaches to science-religion dialogue through engagement with science.

Ibn Sīnā's concept of the Necessary Existent represents a monumental attempt to articulate divine transcendence through pure rational demonstration. His system pushed the principle "laysa kamithlihi shay'un" to radical conclusions—God as pure existence, absolutely simple, transcending all categories applicable to contingent beings. While his specific positions generated justified critiques, particularly regarding creation, divine knowledge, and religious doctrine, his fundamental insight remains profound: rational reflection on the nature of existence itself leads to recognition of a reality utterly transcending the contingent world. His technical contributions—the existence-essence distinction, the analysis of necessity and possibility, the logic of divine simplicity—permanently enriched Islamic intellectual discourse.

The varied reception of Ibn Sīnā's thought demonstrates Islamic tradition's capacity for critical engagement. Theologians adopted his tools while rejecting conclusions incompatible with revelation. Mystics found in his abstractions pointers to experiential realities. Later philosophers built on his foundations while addressing his limitations. Ibn Sīnā's legacy lies not in establishing philosophy's supremacy over revelation but in demonstrating that rigorous rational thought, properly pursued, confirms and deepens understanding of divine transcendence. His Necessary Existent, for all its abstract character, points to the same reality proclaimed in "laysa kamithlihi shay'un"—a reality so utterly unique that even calling It "existent" in the ordinary sense falls short.

In our contemporary context, where Muslims engage with various philosophical traditions, Ibn Sīnā's example remains instructive: fearless rational inquiry combined with genuine reverence for transcendent truth. His successes and failures alike teach that approaching the Incomparable through philosophy requires both intellectual rigor and recognition of reason's inherent limits before the One who transcends all categories—even those of necessary existence itself.

Chapter 11. Suhrawardi's Illuminationism: Light Metaphysics and Transcendence

Shihāb al-Dīn Yaḥyā ibn Ḥabash al-Suhrawardī (d. 587/1191), known as "Shaykh al-Ishrāq" (Master of Illumination), developed a revolutionary philosophical system that transformed Islamic approaches to divine transcendence. His "Ḥikmat al-Ishrāq" (Philosophy of Illumination) critiqued Peripatetic abstraction while offering a metaphysics of light that claimed to unite rational demonstration with mystical experience. This chapter examines how Suhrawardī's light metaphysics provided a unique articulation of the principle "laysa kamithlihi shay'un," preserving absolute divine transcendence while making it luminously present rather than abstractly distant.

Suhrawardī's Illuminationist philosophy emerged in a specific intellectual milieu shaped by both the achievements and perceived limitations of Avicennan philosophy, as well as by vibrant mystical traditions. By the late 6th/12th century, Avicennan philosophy dominated intellectual circles from Iran to Andalusia. However, several critiques had emerged. Al-Ghazālī had challenged the philosophers' claims to demonstrative certainty in metaphysics. Mystically inclined thinkers found Peripatetic philosophy overly abstract. As 'Ayn al-Quḍāt al-Hamadhānī (d. 525/1131), Suhrawardī's predecessor, wrote: "The philosophers speak of the Necessary Existent as if describing a mathematical theorem. Where is the Divine Beauty that ravishes hearts? Where is the Light that illuminates souls? Their god is a concept, not the Living Reality experienced by the lovers of God."

Born in Suhraward, northwestern Iran, around 549/1154, Suhrawardī studied both philosophy and Islamic sciences. His teacher Majd al-Dīn al-Jīlī introduced him to Avicennan philosophy, while Fakhr al-Dīn al-Mārdīnī guided his study of jurisprudence and theology. Suhrawardī himself describes his intellectual journey in Ḥikmat al-Ishrāq: "I first mastered the Peripatetic philosophy until I could navigate it better than its adherents. But I found it insufficient—it explained the what but not the why, the structure but not the life. Through divine grace and spiritual struggle, I was granted illumination (ishrāq) that revealed what discursive philosophy conceals."

Suhrawardī explicitly positioned his work as a grand synthesis. In the introduction to Ḥikmat al-Ishrāq, he writes: "This book revives the wisdom of the ancient Persian sages, which is the same wisdom Plato and the earlier Greek sages possessed, which agrees with the inner meaning of the Quran and the experience of the Sufi masters. This is not syncretism but recognition that divine wisdom has appeared in various forms." He identified several streams feeding into his synthesis, including ancient Persian wisdom and the light metaphysics of Zoroastrian sages, Platonic philosophy with its doctrine of Forms and imagery of light, Islamic revelation particularly the Light Verse (24:35), and mystical experience understood as direct tasting (dhawq) of spiritual realities.

Suhrawardī's life coincided with the Crusades and the rise of Saladin. He traveled extensively, reaching Aleppo where he gained influence at the court of al-Malik al-Ẓāhir, Saladin's son. However, his philosophical views and influence aroused opposition from conservative jurists. His execution at age thirty-six, ordered by Saladin reportedly at the jurists' insistence, reflects the tensions surrounding philosophical innovation. Yet his works survived and inaugurated a tradition that would profoundly influence Islamic thought, particularly in Persia and the Ottoman lands.

Suhrawardī's choice of light as the central metaphor for his metaphysics built upon rich precedents in Islamic thought, transforming scattered insights into systematic philosophy. The Quran employs light imagery extensively, most famously in the Light Verse: "Allah is the Light of the heavens and the earth. The parable of His light is as if there were a niche and within it a lamp: the lamp enclosed in glass: the glass as it were a brilliant star: lit from a blessed tree, an olive neither of the east nor of the west, whose oil is well-nigh luminous, though fire scarce touched it: Light upon Light! Allah guides to His Light whom He will." (24:35)

Early exegetes recognized this verse's metaphysical implications. Al-Ṭabarī records interpretations suggesting that Allah is the illuminator (munawwir) of the heavens and earth, that Allah is the guide (hādī) of the inhabitants of heaven and earth, and that Allah is the Light itself with all other lights being metaphorical. These early interpretations established light as a legitimate theological concept for understanding divine nature.

Muslim theologians had long explored light's metaphysical significance. Al-Ḥasan al-Baṣrī interpreted divine light as knowledge: "Allah's being Light means He is manifest to intellects as light is to eyes. Through Him all things are known, as through light all things are seen." Al-Māturīdī in his Ta'wīlāt developed this further: "Light has four characteristics that apply to Allah metaphorically: it is self-manifest, makes others manifest, is the condition for sight, and admits of degrees. Allah is self-evident, makes truth evident, is the condition for all knowledge, and relates to creatures in degrees."

Muslim philosophers before Suhrawardī had employed light metaphors with varying degrees of sophistication. Al-Kindī (d. 256/870) in Fī al-'Aql used light to explain intellection: "The Active Intellect relates to potential intellects as the sun to eyes—enabling actualization of inherent capacity." Ibn Sīnā occasionally used light imagery: "The Necessary Existent relates to possible existents as light to darkness—one is positive reality, the other mere privation." However, he generally preferred the metaphysically neutral language of existence.

Sufi masters extensively developed light symbolism in their descriptions of mystical experience. Al-Ḥallāj (d. 309/922) proclaimed: "I saw my Lord with the eye of my heart. He said, 'Who are you?' I said, 'I am You.' You are He who fills all place, but place does not know where You are. In my subsistence is my annihilation; in my annihilation, I remain. You are my light!" Al-Ghazālī's Mishkāt al-Anwār (The Niche of Lights) provided sophisticated analysis: "Lights are of different levels: sensory, imaginative, intellectual, and divine. Each higher light reveals the lower as darkness by comparison. The Real Light is Allah, and all other lights are metaphorical." Najm al-Dīn Kubrā (d. 618/1221) developed detailed phenomenology of spiritual lights: "The seeker witnesses lights of different colors—white, green, red, black—each indicating spiritual states and divine manifestations."

While building on these precedents, Suhrawardī transformed light from metaphor to metaphysical principle: "Previous thinkers used light as comparison (tashbīh) for spiritual realities. But light is not mere metaphor—

it is the fundamental reality. What we call existence, the Peripatetics' primary concept, is actually an abstraction from the concrete reality of light and its absence." This move from metaphorical to literal understanding of light as the basic constituent of reality marked Suhrawardī's revolutionary contribution.

Suhrawardī's system represents a unique synthesis that claimed to unite the certainty of philosophical demonstration with the immediacy of mystical experience. He began by identifying limitations in Avicennan philosophy through systematic critique. In al-Talwīḥāt, he argues concerning the problem of knowledge by presence: "Ibn Sīnā cannot explain self-knowledge. If the soul knows itself through a form or concept, then it knows the form, not itself. But we have immediate, non-conceptual knowledge of ourselves. This is knowledge by presence (al-'ilm al-ḥuḍūrī), which Peripatetic philosophy cannot accommodate."

He identified what he called the poverty of existence: "The Peripatetics make existence the primary concept, but existence is the most abstract and empty of notions. Light, by contrast, is the most concrete and evident reality—self-manifest and manifesting others." He also addressed the problem of individuation: "Peripatetics struggle to explain what individuates beings of the same species. But in the reality of light, each light has its own unique luminosity, requiring no external principle of individuation."

Suhrawardī developed a comprehensive metaphysics based on light that would become the foundation of his entire philosophical system. He established the fundamental distinction between light and darkness: "Reality consists of light (nūr) and darkness (ẓulma). Light is positive reality, self-manifest and manifesting. Darkness is pure privation, having no positive existence. What appears as darkness is merely the absence of light."

At the summit of this system stands the Light of Lights: "At the summit of reality is the Light of Lights (nūr al-anwār), absolutely pure Light with no darkness. This is what the Peripatetics call the Necessary Existent, but understood concretely rather than abstractly." He emphasizes this preserves transcendence: "The Light of Lights is utterly unlike all other lights. As the Quran says, 'laysa kamithlihi shay'un.' Other lights depend on It, while It depends on nothing. Other lights have some admixture of darkness; It is pure Light."

From the Light of Lights emanates a hierarchy that structures all reality. At the highest level are the immaterial lights (anwār mujarrada), pure intelligences without material attachment. Below these are the commanding lights (anwār qāhira), lights that rule over bodily spheres. Next come the managing lights (anwār mudabbira), comprising human and animal souls. Finally, at the lowest level are the accidental lights (anwār 'āriḍa), including physical lights and material manifestations. This hierarchical structure provided a comprehensive framework for understanding all of reality through the single principle of light.

Suhrawardī insisted that philosophical demonstration and mystical experience converge in the pursuit of wisdom: "The true philosopher (ḥakīm) must be both a discursive thinker (baḥḥāth) and an intuitive mystic (dhawqī). Discursive philosophy without intuition is empty; mysticism without philosophy is blind. The complete sage unites both." He describes the method in Ḥikmat al-Ishrāq as involving conceptual preparation through mastering logic and philosophy to clarify thinking, spiritual purification through undertaking ascetic practices to polish the soul's mirror, illuminative experience through receiving direct witnessing of light realities, and philosophical expression through articulating the experience in demonstrative form. This fourfold method integrated intellectual and spiritual development into a comprehensive path.

One of Suhrawardī's most influential contributions was the systematic articulation of the imaginal world (ālam al-mithāl): "Between the world of pure intelligences and the material world exists an intermediate realm—the world of suspended images (al-ṣuwar al-mu'allaqa). This is more real than the material world but less real than the intelligible world." This realm explains various phenomena including prophetic visions and dreams, the forms seen in mystical experience, the resurrection body, and the reality of symbols and myths. "In this realm, spirits are corporealized and bodies spiritualized. The abstract becomes concrete without becoming material. This is where meaning takes form."

Suhrawardī's epistemology centered on knowledge by presence as the highest form of knowing: "The highest knowledge is not conceptual but presential—the direct presence of the known to the knower without mediating forms. This is how we know ourselves, how God knows all things, and how the mystic knows God in illumination." He distinguished levels of such knowledge, beginning with self-knowledge understood as the soul's immediate awareness of itself, progressing to illuminative knowledge through direct witnessing of higher lights, and culminating in divine knowledge understood as God's immediate presence to all things as their Light. "The Peripatetics err in making all knowledge conceptual. But the most certain knowledge—our awareness of ourselves—is non-conceptual. This opens the path to understanding divine knowledge, which is pure presence."

Suhrawardī's execution did not end his influence; rather, his thought inaugurated a tradition that profoundly shaped subsequent Islamic philosophy, particularly in Persia and India. Shams al-Dīn al-Shahrazūrī (d. after 687/1288) wrote the first major commentary on Ḥikmat al-Ishrāq and compiled Suhrawardī's biography: "The Master achieved what no philosopher before him accomplished—uniting the path of demonstration (burhān) with the path of witnessing (mushāhada). His light metaphysics is not alternative to being but explains what being really is."

Quṭb al-Dīn al-Shīrāzī (d. 710/1311) produced the most influential commentary, integrating Illuminationism with Avicennan philosophy and astronomy: "Suhrawardī's critique of Ibn Sīnā should be understood as completion, not rejection. Light explains what existence describes abstractly. The Necessary Existent is the Light of Lights—the same reality approached differently."

The encounter between Illuminationism and Ibn 'Arabī's metaphysics produced creative syntheses that enriched both traditions. Ṣadr al-Dīn al-Qūnawī (d. 673/1274), Ibn 'Arabī's stepson, integrated both systems: "Suhrawardī's lights are Ibn 'Arabī's divine names in manifestation. The Light of Lights is the Absolute Reality (al-ḥaqq al-muṭlaq), and the hierarchy of lights represents the levels of divine self-disclosure." Dāwūd al-Qayṣarī (d. 751/1350) developed this synthesis further: "Light is existence viewed from its manifest aspect; existence is light viewed from its hidden aspect. Suhrawardī and Ibn 'Arabī describe the same reality from complementary perspectives."

The 11th/17th century witnessed Illuminationism's full integration into mainstream Islamic philosophy through the School of Isfahan. Mīr Dāmād (d. 1041/1631) incorporated Illuminationist insights while maintaining Peripatetic framework: "Suhrawardī correctly identified knowledge by presence as irreducible to conceptual knowledge. This insight must be incorporated into any complete philosophy."

Mullā Ṣadrā (d. 1050/1640) achieved the most comprehensive synthesis in his "Transcendent Philosophy": "Suhrawardī's great insight was the primacy of knowledge by presence. But he erred in making light, not existence, fundamental. Existence itself, properly understood, has all the characteristics Suhrawardī attributes to light—self-evidence, manifestation, and degrees of intensity." Mullā Ṣadrā incorporated key Illuminationist insights including the imaginal world as ontological realm, knowledge by presence as epistemological foundation, the unity of intellectual and spiritual perfection, and light symbolism for existence's self-manifestation. This synthesis demonstrated how Illuminationist insights could be integrated into a broader philosophical framework.

Illuminationist thought spread beyond Persia into Ottoman lands and India. In Ottoman territories, scholars like Ismā'īl Ḥaqqī Bursevī (d. 1137/1725) integrated Illuminationist concepts into Quranic commentary: "The Light Verse describes not metaphor but metaphysical reality. Creation is divine light in various degrees of luminosity and opacity." In India, the Mughal prince Dārā Shikōh (d. 1069/1659) found in Illuminationism a framework for understanding Hindu philosophy: "The Upanishadic 'Brahman' and Suhrawardī's 'Light of Lights' point to the same reality—the self-luminous source of all existence."

Illuminationist philosophy experienced revival in modern times through various channels. Henry Corbin introduced Suhrawardī to Western academia, emphasizing the imaginal world: "Suhrawardī provides resources for understanding symbolic consciousness in an age dominated by literalism and abstraction." Seyyed Hossein Nasr presents Illuminationism as perennial philosophy: "Suhrawardī's synthesis shows how discursive and intuitive knowledge unite in wisdom traditions worldwide." Contemporary Iranian philosophers like Mehdi Ha'iri Yazdi have developed Illuminationist epistemology: "Knowledge by presence provides solutions to contemporary philosophical problems about consciousness and self-knowledge."

Illuminationism's influence extends beyond technical philosophy into multiple dimensions of Islamic thought. In mystical philosophy, Suhrawardī provided vocabulary and concepts for articulating mystical experience philosophically, with terms like "imaginal world" and "knowledge by presence" becoming standard in Islamic mystical discourse. In aesthetic theory, light metaphysics influenced Islamic aesthetics, with beauty understood as the manifestation of light and art as capturing light in material forms. In hermeneutics, the concept of the imaginal world transformed scriptural interpretation, as symbolic narratives came to be understood as describing imaginal realities, neither purely literal nor merely allegorical. In cosmology, the hierarchy of lights provided an alternative to Aristotelian cosmology, influencing astronomical and cosmological speculation.

Suhrawardī's Illuminationist philosophy represents a unique approach to divine transcendence in Islamic thought. By making light rather than abstract existence the fundamental reality, he preserved the principle "laysa kamithlihi shay'un" while making divine transcendence luminously manifest rather than conceptually distant. His critique of Peripatetic philosophy was not wholesale rejection but creative transformation. Where Ibn Sīnā's Necessary Existent seemed abstract and remote, Suhrawardī's Light of Lights is immediately present as the source of all manifestation. Where Peripatetic epistemology struggled with self-knowledge and mystical experience, Illuminationist knowledge by presence provided coherent explanation.

The synthesis of philosophy and mysticism in Illuminationism offered a model for integrating intellectual rigor with spiritual experience. Suhrawardī showed that the highest philosophy culminates not in abstract concepts but in direct witnessing, and that mystical experience gains clarity through philosophical articulation. His introduction of the imaginal world as an ontological realm between the sensible and intelligible provided resources for understanding prophetic and mystical experience without reducing them to psychology or dismissing them as fantasy. This contribution continues to influence Islamic thought and offers resources for contemporary discussions about consciousness, imagination, and spiritual experience.

The later development of Illuminationist thought demonstrates its vitality and adaptability. Rather than remaining a historical curiosity, it continued to evolve, engaging with other philosophical schools and addressing new challenges. The integration with Ibn 'Arabī's thought and incorporation into Mullā Ṣadrā's synthesis show how Suhrawardī's insights became part of the broader Islamic philosophical tradition.

Suhrawardī's legacy lies not only in specific doctrines but in demonstrating that preserving divine transcendence need not result in philosophical abstraction or mystical obscurity. Through the metaphysics of light, the One who is "naught is like unto Him" becomes the most evident reality—self-manifest and manifesting all else, transcendent yet immediately present, beyond comprehension yet directly witnessed in illumination. In an age seeking integration of intellectual and spiritual approaches, Suhrawardī's

Illuminationism continues to offer profound resources for understanding divine transcendence.

Chapter 12. Mulla Sadra's Dynamic Metaphysics

Ṣadr al-Dīn Muḥammad ibn Ibrāhīm al-Shīrāzī (d. 1050/1640), known as Mullā Ṣadrā, represents the culmination of Islamic philosophical development in many respects. His "Transcendent Philosophy" (al-Ḥikma al-Muta'āliya) achieved a remarkable synthesis of Peripatetic philosophy, Illuminationist wisdom, mystical insight, and Shi'i theology, all while introducing revolutionary concepts that transformed understanding of divine transcendence. His doctrine of substantial motion provided a dynamic metaphysics that preserved the principle "laysa kamithlihi shay'un" while explaining how the Immutable relates to the changing world. This chapter examines how Mullā Ṣadrā's system emerged from earlier traditions, his revolutionary contributions, and his profound influence on subsequent Islamic thought.

Mullā Ṣadrā's philosophical system, which he termed "al-Ḥikma al-Muta'āliya" (The Transcendent Philosophy), emerged from creative engagement with multiple intellectual traditions that had developed over the preceding centuries. The Safavid period (907-1135/1501-1722) created unique conditions for philosophical development. The establishment of Shi'ism as the state religion, the patronage of learning, and the gathering of scholars in Isfahan produced an intellectual renaissance. Mullā Ṣadrā benefited from this environment while also experiencing its tensions.

Born in Shiraz around 979/1571, Mullā Ṣadrā studied in Isfahan, the Safavid capital, under two masters who embodied different philosophical approaches. Mīr Dāmād (d. 1041/1631), his primary teacher, represented sophisticated Avicennan philosophy with Illuminationist influences. He taught that "existence is a conceptual construct (i'tibārī) while quiddity is fundamental." This position, known as the "primacy of quiddity" (aṣālat al-māhiyya), dominated the philosophical establishment. Shaykh Bahā'ī (d. 1031/1621) embodied the integration of rational and transmitted sciences, showing how philosophy could harmonize with religious disciplines.

Mullā Ṣadrā explicitly acknowledged his debt to earlier thinkers while transforming their insights. In the introduction to al-Asfār al-Arba'a, he writes: "I have drunk from the springs of ancient wisdom—from the divine Plato and the great Aristotle among the Greeks, from the masterful Ibn Sīnā and the illuminated Suhrawardī among the Muslims, from the realized mystics who tasted reality rather than merely discussing it. But through divine grace, I was shown how these scattered jewels form a single necklace."

He identified specific contributions from each tradition that would shape his synthesis. From Ibn Sīnā, he drew the logical rigor, the necessity-possibility framework, and the systematic approach to metaphysics. However, he writes: "Ibn Sīnā glimpsed the primacy of existence but didn't fully grasp its implications." From Suhrawardī, he appropriated the critique of conceptual knowledge, the reality of knowledge by presence, and the gradational nature of reality. "Suhrawardī correctly saw that reality admits of degrees—his error was making light, not existence, the fundamental reality." From Ibn 'Arabī, he incorporated the experiential dimension of metaphysics and the dynamic nature of divine manifestation. "The greatest master showed that existence is not static but constantly renewed. But this insight needs philosophical articulation." From Shi'i theology, he drew the emphasis on divine justice, human perfectibility, and the role of the Imams as perfect humans. "The Imams represent the philosophical ideal of the Perfect Human (al-insān al-kāmil) who unites all levels of existence."

After initial success in Isfahan, Mullā Ṣadrā faced opposition from conservative scholars who viewed his synthesis as dangerous innovation. He retreated to Kahak, a village near Qom, where he spent years in contemplation and writing. This period proved crucial for his philosophical development. He later described this transformation: "In Kahak, through spiritual exercises and divine illumination, what I had known conceptually became presential experience. The primacy of existence changed from a philosophical position to a tasted reality."

Upon returning to Shiraz, where he taught until his death, Mullā Ṣadrā articulated his revolutionary synthesis. The "Transcendent Philosophy" transcended its predecessors by establishing existence as the sole reality with quiddities as mental constructs, introducing substantial motion that made change fundamental to created reality, uniting intellectual and experiential knowledge in a single system, and providing dynamic metaphysics that explained both permanence and change. He claimed this was not mere eclecticism: "Previous philosophers were like those describing an elephant in darkness—each grasped part of the truth. Through divine grace, the lights were turned on, revealing the whole elephant."

Mullā Ṣadrā's doctrine of substantial motion (al-ḥaraka al-jawhariyya) represents his most revolutionary contribution, transforming static metaphysics into dynamic philosophy while preserving divine transcendence. Classical philosophy, following Aristotle, maintained that motion occurs only in accidents such as quantity, quality, position, and place, while substance remains unchanging. This created theological problems concerning how the Immutable God relates to a changing world, how human souls develop and perfect themselves, and how bodily resurrection is possible. Ibn Sīnā had argued: "If substance changed, a thing would cease to be itself. A changing substance is a contradiction—it would be and not be simultaneously."

In al-Asfār, Mullā Ṣadrā argues: "The philosophers erred in making substance static. In reality, the material world is pure becoming—constantly renewed existence flowing from the Necessarily Existent. What we call 'substance' is not a fixed substratum but a continuous flow of existence manifesting as apparent stability." He provides detailed argumentation from multiple angles. From the nature of time, he reasons: "Time is the measure of motion. But if only accidents moved while substance remained static, we would have two times—one for changing accidents, another for permanent substance. This is absurd." From identity through change, he observes: "A child becomes an adult while remaining the same person. This identity-through-change requires substantial motion—the substance itself flows while maintaining continuity." From gradation of existence, he concludes: "Existence admits of degrees of intensity. A substance can intensify in its existence without ceasing to be itself, just as light can grow brighter while remaining light."

This doctrine resolved major theological issues across multiple domains.

Regarding divine transcendence, he argued: "God alone is absolutely immutable—pure permanent existence. All else is becoming. This emphasizes divine transcendence: 'laysa kamithlihi shay'un' because nothing shares His permanence." Regarding creation, he maintained: "Creation is not a single past event but continuous divine effusion (fayḍ). At each moment, God creates the world anew. The mystics' 'renewal of creation at each breath' receives philosophical explanation." Regarding human perfectibility, he explained: "The soul perfects itself through substantial motion, intensifying its existence through knowledge and virtue. This explains spiritual development without requiring additions to a static substance."

Critics asked: If everything changes substantially, how is anything permanent? Mullā Ṣadrā's sophisticated answer was: "Substantial motion doesn't mean chaos. There are different levels of stability." At the highest level stands absolute permanence, belonging to God alone who exists beyond all motion. Below this is intellectual permanence, characterizing immaterial intellects that are permanent in essence yet active in operation. The imaginal world exhibits its own form of permanence, where forms remain stable but not static. Natural permanence describes physical substances that appear stable while substantially flowing. Finally, accidental change represents surface changes that are most obvious but least fundamental. He uses the analogy of a river: "A river maintains identity while its water constantly flows. Similarly, substances maintain formal identity through material flux."

This doctrine transformed epistemology in profound ways: "If substance is dynamic, so is the knowing soul. Knowledge is not acquiring static forms but the soul's substantial transformation. In knowing, the soul becomes what it knows through substantial motion." This explains mystical experience: "The mystic doesn't just 'know about' God but undergoes substantial transformation toward divine perfection. This is why true knowledge transforms the knower."

Mullā Ṣadrā's genius lay not merely in synthesizing earlier traditions but in transforming them through creative integration. While predecessors debated existence versus quiddity, Mullā Ṣadrā established existence as the sole reality: "Existence is the sole reality; quiddities are mental constructs abstracting from existence's limitations. When we say 'human exists,' existence is real while 'humanity' is our conceptual grasp of a particular existential limitation."

This transformed earlier positions in multiple ways. Against Ibn Sīnā, he argued: "Ibn Sīnā correctly distinguished existence from quiddity but erred in making them parallel realities. Quiddity is how intellect grasps existence's limitations." Against Suhrawardī, he maintained: "Suhrawardī rightly saw existence as abstract concept, but only because he considered conceptual existence. Real existence is the most concrete reality—identical with light itself." In harmony with Ibn 'Arabī, he affirmed: "The mystics correctly proclaim 'all is God' meaning all existence is divine manifestation. But this needs philosophical precision to avoid pantheism."

Mullā Ṣadrā developed a sophisticated account of existence's gradation through his doctrine of tashkīk: "Existence is one reality admitting of infinite degrees—from the Necessary Existent's infinite intensity to prime matter's minimal existence. Differences between things are not quidditative but existential intensities." This resolved classical problems that had troubled earlier philosophers. Regarding unity and multiplicity, he explained: "Reality is one existence with many degrees. Unity and multiplicity are not contradictory but complementary aspects of tashkīk." Regarding divine simplicity and attributes, he argued: "God's attributes are not additions to His essence but aspects of His infinite existential intensity. In lower intensities, these aspects appear separate."

Mullā Ṣadrā resolved the classical problem of knowledge through a revolutionary insight: "In true knowledge, the intellect, the act of intellection, and the intelligible become one existence. This unity occurs through substantial motion—the intellect becomes the intelligible substantially, not accidentally." This applied at all levels of knowing. In human knowledge: "When truly knowing fire, the soul doesn't receive fire's 'form' but becomes fire at the intellectual level of existence." In divine knowledge: "God's self-knowledge is perfect identity of knower and known. His knowledge of others is their existence through Him."

Unlike thinkers who kept mysticism and philosophy separate, Mullā Ṣadrā integrated them into a comprehensive system: "The philosophers demonstrate what the mystics experience. The mystics experience what the philosophers demonstrate. Perfect wisdom unites demonstration (burhān) and witnessing (shuhūd)." He provided philosophical framework for mystical concepts that had previously lacked rigorous articulation. Fanā' (annihilation) he explained as: "The mystic's annihilation is recognizing that one's existence is not independent but a divine manifestation. This is philosophical truth, not mere experience." Baqā' (subsistence) he understood as: "Subsistence after annihilation is existing through divine existence consciously—knowing oneself as divine manifestation while maintaining servant-hood."

Mullā Ṣadrā philosophically articulated the mystical doctrine of the Perfect Human: "The Perfect Human is the complete manifestation of existence, uniting all its degrees—from material to divine. In him, the arc of descent and ascent meet. This is not mythology but metaphysical necessity." He identified this with Shi'i Imamology: "The Imams represent this perfection, uniting all existential degrees. Their knowledge encompasses all levels; their existence is the most intense after the divine."

Mullā Ṣadrā's influence on subsequent Islamic philosophy, particularly in Shi'i contexts, proved profound and enduring. His immediate students established the "School of Transcendent Philosophy" that would perpetuate and develop his insights. 'Abd al-Razzāq Lāhījī (d. 1072/1661) wrote influential commentaries defending substantial motion against critics: "Those who reject substantial motion haven't grasped existence's primacy. Once that's understood, substantial motion follows necessarily." Muḥsin Fayḍ Kāshānī (d. 1091/1680) integrated Mullā Ṣadrā's philosophy with Shi'i hadith interpretation: "The Imams' esoteric teachings accord perfectly with Transcendent Philosophy. What they expressed symbolically, philosophy demonstrates rationally."

Subsequent generations developed and refined his system with increasing sophistication. Qāḍī Sa'īd Qummī (d. 1103/1691) applied Sadrian principles to Quranic commentary: "The Quran's levels of meaning correspond to existence's degrees. Substantial motion explains how the same verse yields ever-deeper meanings." Mullā Hādī Sabzawārī (d. 1289/1873) systematized Transcendent Philosophy in his Sharḥ al-Manẓūma, which became the standard teaching text: "Mullā Ṣadrā completed what earlier philosophers began. After him, philosophy's foundations are established; only building remains."

Transcendent Philosophy became central to Shi'i intellectual tradition through multiple channels of influence. In seminary education, major Shi'i seminaries incorporated philosophical training based on Mullā Ṣadrā's works, with the Asfār becoming an advanced curriculum alongside jurisprudence and theology. In theological articulation, Shi'i theologians used Sadrian concepts to articulate doctrines, explaining the Imams' knowledge through knowledge by presence, bodily resurrection through substantial motion, and divine justice through existence's gradation. In mystical philosophy, Shi'i mysticism found a philosophical framework in Transcendent Philosophy, with the integration of philosophy, mysticism, and Shi'ism becoming characteristic of Persian Islamic thought.

Mullā Ṣadrā's influence extended into modern times through various figures and movements. 'Allāmah Ṭabāṭabā'ī (d. 1402/1981) defended and developed Transcendent Philosophy against modern challenges: "Mullā Ṣadrā provides resources for engaging Western philosophy while maintaining Islamic principles. His dynamic metaphysics anticipates process philosophy while preserving divine transcendence." Mehdi Ha'iri Yazdi (d. 1420/1999) brought Sadrian philosophy into dialogue with analytic philosophy: "Knowledge by presence solves problems in consciousness studies. Substantial motion offers alternatives to static substance metaphysics." Contemporary Iranian philosophy continues to teach Transcendent Philosophy as a living tradition, with universities in Iran treating it not as a historical curiosity but as a vital philosophical resource. Scholars like Gholamreza Aavani and Seyyed Mohammed Khamenei continue developing Sadrian insights for contemporary contexts.

Beyond Shi'i contexts, Mullā Ṣadrā influenced broader Islamic thought through multiple avenues. In comparative philosophy, his work facilitates dialogue between Islamic and Western philosophy, with concepts like substantial motion engaging process philosophy, while knowledge by presence addresses phenomenological concerns. In Islamic philosophy within the Western academy, scholars like Henry Corbin, Seyyed Hossein Nasr, and Oliver Leaman brought Mullā Ṣadrā to Western attention, recognizing him as a major world philosopher whose contributions transcend confessional boundaries. In contemporary Islamic thought more broadly, thinkers across Islamic traditions draw on Sadrian insights for addressing modern challenges ranging from consciousness studies to environmental philosophy.

Mullā Ṣadrā's Transcendent Philosophy represents a watershed in Islamic thought's approach to divine transcendence. By making existence dynamic through substantial motion while maintaining divine immutability, he preserved "laysa kamithlihi shay'un" in the most radical way—only God is truly permanent; all else is becoming. His integration of earlier philosophical traditions was not mere eclecticism but creative transformation. The primacy of existence provided the key that unlocked coherent synthesis of Peripatetic logic, Illuminationist intuition, and mystical experience. His system showed how rigorous philosophy could articulate mystical insight without reducing its mystery.

The doctrine of substantial motion revolutionized Islamic metaphysics, providing solutions to perennial problems while opening new philosophical horizons. It explained how the Immutable relates to change, how souls perfect themselves, how knowledge transforms knowers—all while emphasizing divine transcendence through contrast with creaturely becoming. His influence on Shi'i thought proved particularly profound, providing philosophical framework for theological doctrines and establishing a tradition that continues vibrantly today. The integration of philosophy with theology and mysticism in Shi'i contexts owes much to his synthesis.

Perhaps most significantly, Mullā Ṣadrā demonstrated that preserving divine transcendence requires not static but dynamic metaphysics. In a world of constant change, divine permanence stands out more clearly. His thought suggests that approaching the One who is "naught is like unto Him" requires recognizing reality's fundamental dynamism while affirming the One who alone transcends all motion.

For contemporary Islamic thought engaging with process philosophy, evolutionary theory, and dynamic worldviews, Mullā Ṣadrā provides crucial resources. His demonstration that change and permanence, unity and multiplicity, transcendence and immanence can be coherently integrated continues to inspire those seeking to articulate divine incomparability in philosophically sophisticated ways while remaining true to Islamic principles.

Chapter 13. The Unity of Being: Classical Formulations and Interpretations

Muḥyī al-Dīn Muḥammad ibn 'Alī ibn 'Arabī (d. 638/1240), known as al-Shaykh al-Akbar (the Greatest Master), articulated the doctrine of the Unity of Being (waḥdat al-wujūd) that would profoundly influence Islamic mystical theology. This teaching, which asserts that existence is one and that all multiplicity represents divine self-manifestation, raised fundamental questions about the relationship between divine transcendence and creation. How can the One who is "naught is like unto Him" be related to the manifest world without compromising divine incomparability? This chapter examines how Ibn 'Arabī's doctrine emerged from earlier mystical insights, its articulation in his major works, the clarifications provided by his school, and the complex reception it received from orthodox scholars.

The doctrine of the Unity of Being did not emerge in a vacuum but developed from centuries of Sufi reflection on divine unity and the nature of existence. Ibn 'Arabī synthesized and systematized insights that earlier mystics had expressed in various forms. The foundations for the Unity of Being appear in the earliest Sufi expressions. Al-Junayd (d. 298/910), the "Master of the Path," articulated crucial insights: "Tawḥīd is separating the eternal from the temporal." When asked about the mystic's ultimate realization, he stated: "The affirmation of a thing's existence while simultaneously affirming its non-existence—its existence through God, its non-existence through itself."

Al-Sarrāj (d. 378/988) explains in Kitāb al-Luma': "Al-Junayd meant that the realized one sees things as simultaneously existent and non-existent—

existent through divine manifestation, non-existent in themselves. This is not contradiction but the deepest truth." Al-Ḥallāj (d. 309/922) expressed similar insights more boldly: "I am the Real (anā al-Ḥaqq)" and "I saw my Lord with the eye of my heart. I said: 'Who are You?' He said: 'You.'" While controversial, these statements pointed toward the unity underlying apparent duality. Al-Qushayrī (d. 465/1074) interprets cautiously: "Al-Ḥallāj spoke from a state of overwhelming divine presence where consciousness of self was replaced by consciousness of God. His words describe experience, not theological doctrine."

Several key figures developed theological frameworks approaching the Unity of Being. Abū Ḥāmid al-Ghazālī (d. 505/1111) in Mishkāt al-Anwār approaches unity through light metaphysics: "Existence is light, non-existence is darkness. The Real is the Light of lights, and all existence derives from this one Light. Multiplicity is the variegation of the one Light through different receptacles." He carefully maintains transcendence: "Do not think this means God is everything or everything is God. Rather, everything is from God, through God, and has no independent existence apart from God. The servant remains servant, the Lord remains Lord."

'Ayn al-Quḍāt al-Hamadhānī (d. 525/1131) pushed further in Tamhīdāt: "Existence (wujūd) belongs only to God. What we call 'our existence' is borrowed, metaphorical. When mystics say 'Nothing exists but God,' they mean nothing has independent, real existence except the Real." Ibn Sabʿīn (d. 669/1270), though later than Ibn 'Arabī, represents parallel development: "The investigators speak of God and creation, but the realized see only God. Not that creation is God, but that creation's existence is God's existence manifested."

Muslim philosophers contributed concepts that Ibn 'Arabī would transform into his mystical metaphysics. Ibn Sīnā's distinction between necessary and possible existence provided a crucial framework. Ibn 'Arabī would argue that possible things have no existence of their own—their existence is the Necessary Existent's self-manifestation. Al-Suhrawardī's gradational ontology, with its idea that reality admits of degrees, influenced Ibn 'Arabī's understanding of existence's levels. However, where Suhrawardī spoke of light's gradations, Ibn 'Arabī would speak of existence's self-disclosure.

Several figures directly influenced Ibn 'Arabī's formulation. Ibn Barrajān (d. 536/1141) of Andalusia developed systematic mystical theology. Ibn

'Arabī acknowledges: "I benefited greatly from the works of Ibn Barrajān, particularly his understanding of divine names as relationships, not entities." Abū Madyan (d. 594/1197), whom Ibn 'Arabī never met but considered his spiritual master, taught insights that proved foundational: "Abū Madyan taught that 'He who knows himself knows his Lord' means recognizing one's non-existence before eternal existence. This opened the door to understanding waḥda." Ibn al-'Arīf (d. 536/1141) wrote in Maḥāsin al-Majālis: "The realized one witnesses that all actions emanate from God, all attributes belong to God, all existence is God's existence appearing in forms."

Ibn 'Arabī articulated the Unity of Being throughout his vast corpus, with certain passages becoming focal points for understanding and debate. The Fuṣūṣ al-Ḥikam (Bezels of Wisdom) contains Ibn 'Arabī's most influential statements on unity. In the chapter on Adam, he writes: "The Real willed to see His own essence in a comprehensive being that contained the entire divine order... The cosmos was like an unpolished mirror. It was the requirement of the divine name 'Light' that there be a mirror to reflect it."

Al-Qāshānī (d. 736/1335) comments: "The cosmos is God's self-manifestation, not something created 'alongside' Him. Creation is the exterior (ẓāhir) of the Real, while the Real is creation's interior (bāṭin). They are not two entities but two aspects." In the chapter on Seth, Ibn 'Arabī states: "Know that what is called 'other than the Real'—or the cosmos—relates to the Real as shadow to person. The cosmos is God's shadow." Dāwūd al-Qayṣarī (d. 751/1350) explains: "Shadow metaphor preserves both unity and distinction. The shadow is not the person yet has no existence without the person. Similarly, the cosmos is not God yet has no existence save through God."

In his magnum opus, the Futūḥāt al-Makkiyya, Ibn 'Arabī provides extensive exposition. A crucial passage states: "Existence is one reality (ḥaqīqa wāḥida). It accepts neither division nor multiplicity in its essence. What appears as multiplicity are relationships (nisab) and aspects (wujūh), not multiple existences. When we say 'the existence of Zayd' and 'the existence of 'Amr,' we speak of one existence in multiple loci of manifestation (maẓāhir)."

He emphasizes transcendence within unity: "Do not fall into the error of those who say 'All is God' (al-kull huwa Allāh). Rather, say 'All is through God' (al-kull bi-Allāh). The servant remains servant in his servanthood, the Lord remains Lord in His Lordship." This careful formulation demonstrates

Ibn 'Arabī's concern to preserve the Creator-creature distinction even while affirming existential unity.

Ibn 'Arabī frequently discusses the relationship between the Real (al-ḥaqq) and creation (al-khalq): "Al-ḥaqq is the inner dimension of al-khalq, and al-khalq is the outer dimension of al-ḥaqq. They are like the outside and inside of a garment—two aspects of one reality. Yet the Real remains transcendent (munazzah) in His essence while being the essence of manifestation." 'Abd al-Razzāq al-Qāshānī clarifies: "This doesn't mean creation is identical to the Creator. Rather, creation's existence is not its own but the Creator's existence delimited by possibilities (mumkināt). The limitation belongs to creation; the existence belongs to the Real."

One of Ibn 'Arabī's most characteristic expressions appears throughout his works in what became known as the "He/not He" formula: "So the cosmos is He and not He (huwa lā huwa). It is He from the perspective of existence, not He from the perspective of delimitation and form." Ṣadr al-Dīn al-Qūnawī (d. 673/1274), Ibn 'Arabī's stepson and chief disciple, explains: "This formula preserves both unity and transcendence. 'He' affirms that only divine existence is real. 'Not He' maintains the Creator-creature distinction. Both are true simultaneously."

The Akbarian tradition developed principles for interpreting these texts that would guide proper understanding and prevent misinterpretation. Sa'īd al-Dīn al-Farghānī (d. 695/1296) insists on contextual reading: "Never isolate statements about unity from their context. The Shaykh always balances unity with distinction, immanence with transcendence." Technical precision proves essential, as terms like wujūd (existence), ẓuhūr (manifestation), and tajallī (self-disclosure) have precise technical meanings that prevent pantheistic interpretation. The experiential basis of the doctrine must be recognized, as it describes mystical realization rather than philosophical speculation, with intellectual understanding alone missing the point. Finally, the orthodox framework within which the doctrine operates must be maintained, as the Unity of Being deepens understanding of tawḥīd rather than replacing it.

Ibn 'Arabī's immediate disciples and subsequent commentators clarified and systematized his teaching, addressing criticisms and preventing misunderstandings. Al-Qūnawī, Ibn 'Arabī's foremost interpreter, provided philosophical precision in works like Miftāḥ al-Ghayb: "The Unity of Being means that existence (wujūd) is one reality that manifests in infinite forms.

These forms are not 'parts' of existence but its self-determinations (ta'ayyunāt). Think of the ocean and its waves—the waves are not separate from the ocean yet maintain distinct forms."

He addresses the transcendence concern: "God's essence (dhāt) remains absolutely unknowable and transcendent. What manifests are the names and attributes, not the essence itself. The essence is eternally veiled even in manifestation." Akbarian commentators developed systematic accounts of existence's levels. 'Abd al-Karīm al-Jīlī (d. 826/1423) in al-Insān al-Kāmil outlines five levels of manifestation. At the highest level stands aḥadiyya (absolute unity), the pure essence beyond all relations. Below this is wāḥidiyya (unity of names), the essence with all names in undifferentiated unity. The level of arwāḥ (spirits) represents the first differentiation into immaterial beings. The imaginal realm of mithāl contains intermediate forms between spirit and matter. Finally, ajsām (bodies) represents full manifestation in material multiplicity. "At each level, the One Existence manifests differently while remaining one. Multiplicity is in manifestation, not in existence itself."

The school developed standard responses to common criticisms and misunderstandings. Against pantheism, al-Qāshānī writes: "Saying 'existence is one' differs radically from saying 'everything is God.' The first is tawḥīd's deepening; the second is kufr. We affirm that God alone truly exists while creatures exist through Him, not that creatures are God." Against determinism, al-Jīlī clarifies: "The Unity of Being doesn't negate human responsibility. Although our existence is divine manifestation, our choices remain ours. The Real manifests in us as free agents, not puppets." Against antinomianism, Ibn 'Arabī himself warned: "He who uses unity to justify abandoning the Law has neither understood unity nor the Law. The realized one is more scrupulous in observance, not less."

Later Akbarians developed precise formulations that would become standard in the tradition. Maḥmūd al-Qūnawī (d. 788/1386) distinguishes three aspects that must be maintained simultaneously: God's essence remains absolutely transcendent (tanzīh muṭlaq), existence belongs to God alone (waḥdat al-wujūd), and creatures possess relative existence (wujūd iḍāfī) through divine manifestation. 'Abd al-Ghanī al-Nābulusī (d. 1143/1731) synthesizes: "The Unity of Being is the metaphysical truth underlying the theological truth of tawḥīd. It doesn't replace kalām but deepens it. The theologian says 'Nothing is like God'; the 'ārif adds 'Nothing exists independently of God.'"

The Unity of Being generated diverse responses from orthodox scholars, ranging from fierce rejection to cautious accommodation to full integration. Initial critics focused on apparent contradictions with orthodox theology. Ibn Taymiyya (d. 728/1328) launched comprehensive critique: "The claim that existence is one contradicts the clear distinction between Creator and creation established by revelation. If creation is divine manifestation, then either God changes (which is impossible) or creation is eternal (which contradicts scripture)."

However, he distinguished between Ibn 'Arabī and extremist followers: "Ibn 'Arabī himself maintained the Law and spoke of mysteries beyond common understanding. But many claiming his authority use unity to justify heresy." Al-Taftāzānī (d. 792/1390) in his theological works warns: "Beware those who speak of waḥdat al-wujūd. If they mean that only God is necessarily existent while all else is contingent, this is orthodox. If they mean creation is actually God, this is unbelief."

More nuanced scholars engaged seriously with Akbarian thought. Ibn Kamāl Pāshā (d. 940/1534), Ottoman Shaykh al-Islam, wrote a treatise distinguishing three groups. True followers of Ibn 'Arabī who maintain transcendence within unity represent orthodox mystics. Those who understand unity as negating distinction are misguided. Those who claim identity between God and creation are unbelievers. This tripartite distinction enabled orthodox scholars to affirm legitimate expressions while rejecting extremist interpretations.

Al-Sha'rānī (d. 973/1565) defended Ibn 'Arabī while acknowledging concerns: "The Shaykh al-Akbar spoke for the elite who understand that unity of existence doesn't negate the servant-Lord relationship. Common people should focus on simpler formulations of tawḥīd." Many orthodox scholars found ways to incorporate Akbarian insights into mainstream theology. Zakariyyā al-Anṣārī (d. 926/1520), the Shaykh al-Islam of Egypt, stated: "Properly understood, waḥdat al-wujūd is the highest expression of tawḥīd. It means recognizing that only God possesses true existence while creation exists derivatively. This accords with Ash'arī theology."

Ibn Ḥajar al-Haytamī (d. 974/1567) provided guidelines for approaching problematic statements. When Ibn 'Arabī's statements seem problematic, one should first seek orthodox interpretation, consider the technical meaning of terms, remember he spoke from spiritual states, and if no acceptable interpretation exists, leave it to God. This hermeneutic of charity enabled orthodox scholars to engage constructively with Akbarian thought.

Many Sufi orders integrated the Unity of Being into their teaching. The Shādhiliyya, through Ibn 'Aṭā' Allah al-Iskandarī (d. 709/1309), incorporated Akbarian concepts: "Realizing that 'all is from God' (al-kull min Allah) is the beginning; realizing 'all is through God' (al-kull bi-Allah) is the path; realizing 'nothing exists save God' (lā mawjūd illā Allah) is the arrival." The Naqshbandiyya, despite their sobriety, engaged seriously through later figures like Aḥmad Sirhindī (d. 1034/1624): "The Unity of Being is a valid spiritual state (ḥāl) but not the ultimate station (maqām). Beyond it lies the Unity of Witnessing (waḥdat al-shuhūd) where unity is experienced while distinction is maintained."

Contemporary traditional scholars continue diverse approaches to the doctrine. Many accept waḥdat al-wujūd as legitimate mystical expression requiring proper understanding, with training in Ibn 'Arabī's works occurring in traditional institutions under careful guidance. Contextual teaching emphasizes that such doctrines suit advanced seekers grounded in sharī'a and 'aqīda, as premature exposure risks misunderstanding. Rather than theoretical debate, emphasis falls on practical spirituality, examining how understanding divine unity enhances worship and ethics.

The doctrine of the Unity of Being represents one of Islamic mysticism's most profound attempts to articulate the relationship between the One who is "naught is like unto Him" and the manifest world. Ibn 'Arabī's synthesis drew upon centuries of mystical insight while providing systematic expression that would influence Islamic thought for centuries. The doctrine preserves divine transcendence not by distancing God from creation but by denying creation any independent existence. If only God truly exists, then He remains utterly unique—"laysa kamithlihi shay'un" receives its deepest affirmation. Creation neither adds to nor limits divine reality but expresses it in delimited forms.

The Akbarian school's clarifications demonstrate Islam's capacity for sophisticated theological development. Through precise terminology, systematic exposition, and careful qualification, they articulated a metaphysics that claimed to deepen rather than compromise orthodox theology. Their success appears in the doctrine's widespread influence despite initial controversy. The varied orthodox responses—from rejection to accommodation to integration—reveal Islamic tradition's complex negotiation with mystical theology. That major orthodox figures found ways to incorporate Akbarian insights suggests the doctrine's compatibility with core Islamic principles when properly understood.

Perhaps most significantly, the Unity of Being shows how the principle of divine incomparability generates rather than stifles profound theological reflection. The attempt to understand how the Incomparable relates to creation produced one of Islamic thought's most sophisticated metaphysical systems—one that continues to inspire, challenge, and guide those seeking to understand the deepest mysteries of existence. The ongoing relevance appears in contemporary discussions where Muslims engage with non-dualist philosophies, process thought, and consciousness studies. The Unity of Being provides resources for such engagement while maintaining Islamic distinctiveness—affirming radical unity while preserving the Creator-creature distinction essential to Islamic worship and ethics.

Chapter 14. Divine Self-Disclosure in Akbarian Thought

The doctrine of divine self-disclosure (tajallī) stands at the heart of Ibn 'Arabī's mystical theology, providing the dynamic complement to the Unity of Being. While waḥdat al-wujūd describes the metaphysical structure of reality, tajallī explains how the One who is "naught is like unto Him" becomes manifest while remaining transcendent. This concept transforms the static philosophical notion of emanation into a living, perpetual process of divine self-revelation. This chapter examines how the concept of tajallī developed in earlier Sufi thought, Ibn 'Arabī's systematic elaboration, its relationship to previous mystical traditions, and how it preserves divine transcendence within immanence.

The notion of divine self-disclosure emerged early in Sufi thought as mystics sought to understand their experiences of divine presence and the relationship between the Hidden and the Manifest. The concept of tajallī finds its roots in scriptural sources that speak of divine manifestation. The Quran states: "By the Mount, and by a Book inscribed" (52:1-2), which commentators connected to Moses's experience at Mount Sinai. More directly: "And when Moses came to Our appointed time and his Lord spoke to him, he said, 'My Lord, show me that I may look at You.' He said, 'You will not see Me, but look at the mountain; if it remains in its place, then you will see Me.' But when his Lord manifested Himself (tajallā) to the mountain, He made it crumble to dust" (7:143).

Al-Qushayrī (d. 465/1074) comments in his Laṭā'if al-Ishārāt: "This verse establishes that divine tajallī is real but overwhelming. The mountain's destruction shows that nothing in creation can bear full divine disclosure in this world." A foundational hadith states: "Allah was in a cloud ('amā') with no air above or below it." Early Sufis understood this as indicating divine hiddenness before manifestation. Another crucial tradition: "Allah was and there was nothing with Him, and He is now as He was." This suggested that manifestation doesn't change divine reality.

The earliest Sufis developed initial understandings of divine self-disclosure that would provide foundations for later systematic development. Dhū al-Nūn al-Miṣrī (d. 245/859) spoke of tajallī in terms of divine attributes: "When the Real manifests His beauty (jamāl) to the heart, it expands with joy. When He manifests His majesty (jalāl), it contracts with awe. These are the tajallīyāt that educate the seeker." Al-Junayd (d. 298/910) provided crucial insight: "Tajallī is the lifting of the veil between the servant and his Lord, yet the veil is from the servant's side only. God is always manifest; it is we who are veiled by our own existence." Al-Niffarī (d. 354/965) in his Mawāqif describes intimate divine communications: "He stopped me and said: 'I manifest Myself to everything according to its capacity. To the intellect as truth, to the heart as light, to the secret (sirr) as Myself beyond attributes.'"

By the 5th/11th century, Sufis had developed more systematic approaches. Al-Qushayrī in his Risāla distinguishes types of tajallī according to their object and intensity. Tajallī of the attributes (ṣifāt) occurs when divine qualities become manifest in the servant. Tajallī of the names (asmā') involves divine names actualizing their effects. Tajallī of the essence (dhāt) is rare and overwhelming, usually leading to fanā'. He warns: "Each tajallī corresponds to the recipient's preparation. Seeking tajallī beyond one's capacity is spiritual presumption."

Al-Ghazālī (d. 505/1111) in Mishkāt al-Anwār develops light metaphysics of tajallī: "As the sun is always shining but clouds veil it variably, so the divine light perpetually radiates while recipients vary in their capacity to receive. Tajallī is not God changing but veils lifting." Rūzbihān Baqlī (d. 606/1209) in 'Abhar al-'Āshiqīn emphasizes beauty: "The cosmos exists because 'I was a Hidden Treasure and loved to be known.' All tajallī springs from divine love of self-disclosure. Beauty (jamāl) seeks contemplation; hence the universe."

Sufi theorists developed technical vocabulary around tajallī that would become standard in the tradition. Tajallī dhātī refers to essential self-disclosure, which is extremely rare. Tajallī ṣifātī designates attributive self-disclosure, which is more common. Tajallī afʿālī involves self-disclosure through divine acts. Tajallī khāṣṣ denotes particular disclosure to individuals, while tajallī 'āmm refers to general disclosure in creation. This terminology would provide Ibn 'Arabī with conceptual tools for his synthesis.

Ibn 'Arabī transformed scattered insights about tajallī into a comprehensive metaphysical system explaining the relationship between the One and the many, the Hidden and the Manifest. Ibn 'Arabī's entire system of tajallī centers on the hadith qudsī: "I was a Hidden Treasure (kanz makhfī) and I loved to be known (aḥbabtu an u'raf), so I created the creation in order that I might be known."

In the Fuṣūṣ al-Ḥikam, he provides extensive commentary: "This hadith contains the entire secret of existence. The treasure is the divine names in their state of non-manifestation. Love is the motive for manifestation. Creation is the locus of this manifestation. Knowledge is the purpose—but it is God knowing Himself through the medium of creation." He emphasizes that this is not about God gaining something He lacked: "How could He who knows all things seek knowledge? Rather, He sought the actualization of His knowledge in external forms. The difference is between eternal knowledge and its temporal manifestation."

Ibn 'Arabī develops the concept of the "Breath of the All-Merciful" (nafas al-Raḥmān) as the vehicle of tajallī: "The divine names were in a state of constriction (karb) seeking manifestation. The Breath of the All-Merciful relieved this constriction by bringing the cosmos into existence. This Breath is continuous—at each moment creation is renewed." 'Abd al-Razzāq al-Qāshānī explains: "The Breath is not air but the existentiating power that brings possibilities from non-existence to existence. It is called 'breath' because it flows out from the divine essence carrying the forms of the names."

Ibn 'Arabī systematizes tajallī into precise levels in works like Futūḥāt al-Makkiyya. The first level is the Most Holy Effusion (al-fayḍ al-aqdas): "This is the eternal self-disclosure of the Essence to Itself, revealing the infinite possibilities contained within divine knowledge. This is not yet creation but the eternal archetypes (a'yān thābita)." The second level is the Holy Effusion (al-fayḍ al-muqaddas): "This is the existentiation of the archetypes in external existence. The possibilities receive the dress of existence through the Breath of the All-Merciful." The third level comprises particular tajallīyāt: "Within manifest existence, tajallī continues perpetually. Each moment brings new self-disclosure. No tajallī ever repeats because divine infinity precludes repetition."

One of Ibn 'Arabī's most important doctrines is that divine self-disclosure never repeats: "He who claims to receive the same tajallī twice lies, for 'Each day He is upon some matter' (55:29). The divine infinity means that self-disclosure is always new. What seems like repetition is similarity, not identity." Ṣadr al-Dīn al-Qūnawī elaborates: "This explains constant change in creation. What appears stable is actually rapid renewal—like a swiftly spinning point appearing as a circle. Substantial motion is the philosophical expression of perpetual tajallī."

The Perfect Human (al-insān al-kāmil) holds special significance in the system of tajallī: "The Perfect Human is the most complete locus of divine self-disclosure, manifesting all divine names in balanced perfection. While each creature manifests some names, the Perfect Human manifests all, becoming the isthmus (barzakh) between the Absolute and creation." He identifies prophets and saints as approximating this perfection, with Muhammad as its complete realization: "The Muhammadan Reality (al-ḥaqīqa al-Muḥammadiyya) is the first determination of the Absolute, the logos through which all tajallī occurs."

Ibn 'Arabī distinguishes multiple types of self-disclosure according to their nature and intensity. Tajallī of the essence is overwhelming and rare, usually resulting in the recipient's annihilation (fanā'), as Moses requested but could not bear. Tajallī of the attributes is more common, involving experiencing divine qualities such as mercy, power, and knowledge in oneself or creation. Tajallī of the names is most accessible, involving seeing divine names at work in the world, such as the Provider in sustenance or the Guide in guidance. Tajallī of acts involves witnessing that all actions proceed from the One Actor, though mediated through creation.

Ibn 'Arabī's doctrine of tajallī, while revolutionary in its systematic comprehensiveness, built upon and synthesized earlier mystical traditions. Ibn 'Arabī explicitly acknowledges his debts: "What I present about tajallī is not innovation but clarification of what the masters always knew. Al-Junayd spoke of the pre-eternal covenant (mīthāq) where souls witnessed divine disclosure. Al-Ḥallāj experienced essential tajallī, hence his utterance. I merely provide the metaphysical framework."

He reinterprets earlier Sufi experiences through his system. On fanā' and baqā', he explains: "What Sufis call annihilation is the overwhelming effect of essential tajallī. Subsistence is learning to bear this disclosure while maintaining one's ontological level." On states and stations, he clarifies: "Spiritual states (aḥwāl) are temporary tajallīyāt, while stations (maqāmāt) are stabilized capacities to receive certain types of disclosure."

While critiquing philosophers, Ibn 'Arabī incorporated their insights into his synthesis. Regarding Neoplatonic emanation, he observes: "The philosophers speak of necessary emanation from the One. This contains truth but makes God subject to necessity. Tajallī is free self-disclosure motivated by love, not necessary overflow." Regarding Avicennan metaphysics, he notes: "Ibn Sīnā correctly distinguished Necessary and possible existence. But possibilities are not external to the Necessary—they are its infinite self-disclosures."

Ibn 'Arabī carefully related tajallī to theological concerns to demonstrate its compatibility with orthodoxy. Regarding creation ex nihilo, he argues: "Tajallī doesn't contradict creation from nothing. The 'nothing' is the non-existence of the fixed entities before receiving existence through divine disclosure." Regarding divine freedom, he maintains: "Each tajallī is a free divine act. That self-disclosure follows divine nature doesn't negate freedom—God freely is what He is."

Ibn 'Arabī's genius lay in synthesizing these elements: "The philosophers were right about the logical structure but missed the personal dimension. The theologians preserved divine freedom but couldn't explain the God-world relationship. The Sufis experienced the reality but lacked systematic expression. Through divine grace, I was shown how these perspectives unite in the doctrine of tajallī."

The most remarkable aspect of Ibn 'Arabī's doctrine is how it maintains absolute divine transcendence while affirming radical immanence. Ibn 'Arabī addresses the apparent contradiction: "How can the Transcendent (munazzah) become manifest? The answer is that He manifests while remaining transcendent. What manifests are the names and attributes, not the essence itself. The essence remains forever hidden even in its most complete disclosure." He uses the metaphor of the sun: "The sun's light fills the earth while the sun itself remains in the heavens. Similarly, divine tajallī fills creation while the divine essence remains transcendent."

A crucial principle is that manifestation itself veils: "The intensity of divine disclosure blinds creatures to the divine reality. They see the forms and miss the One manifesting in the forms. Thus God is 'nearer than the jugular vein' yet most are heedless." Al-Jīlī develops this: "The divine wisdom hides God through manifesting Him. If He remained purely transcendent, He might be known intellectually. By manifesting everywhere, He becomes hidden in plain sight."

Ibn 'Arabī describes how transcendence is preserved at each level of consciousness and realization. In ordinary consciousness, most see only the forms, maintaining practical dualism necessary for religious life, with divine transcendence preserved by the veils of phenomena. In mystical experience, the mystic sees through forms to the One manifesting, yet knows that what he witnesses is not the essence but its self-disclosure, with transcendence preserved by the inadequacy of any experience to encompass the Real. In metaphysical realization, the 'ārif understands that all tajallī is the Real's self-disclosure while the Real remains absolved of all relations (munazzah 'an al-nisab), with transcendence preserved by comprehending that comprehension is impossible.

The formula "He/not He" (huwa lā huwa) perfectly expresses tajallī's preservation of transcendence: "In every locus of manifestation, it is He who manifests—hence 'He.' Yet the locus is not identical to Him—hence 'not He.' The sun's reflection in water is the sun's light, not the sun itself." This principle operates at all levels of divine activity and presence. In divine acts, He acts yet through secondary causes. In divine attributes, His mercy manifests yet in creaturely form. In divine presence, He is present yet not contained.

This preservation of transcendence has practical consequences for religious life. For worship, knowing that all is tajallī doesn't diminish worship but perfects it, as the 'ārif worships more precisely because he knows both the immanence that makes worship possible and the transcendence that makes it necessary. For ethics, seeing divine disclosure in all doesn't justify all actions, since the divine names include the Misguider as well as the Guide, requiring discrimination (furqān) to recognize which tajallī to follow. For theology, orthodox theology is not replaced but deepened, as when theology says God is unlike creation, tajallī explains how, and when it affirms divine attributes, tajallī shows their operation.

Ibn 'Arabī concludes that the deepest preservation of transcendence lies in the mystery of tajallī itself: "Why does the Self-Sufficient manifest? Why does the Hidden Treasure seek to be known? This returns us to the divine love that seeks no cause beyond itself. The deepest transcendence is that God's self-disclosure springs from His nature, which remains ultimately unknowable." 'Abd al-Ghanī al-Nābulusī summarizes: "Tajallī is the solution to the problem of transcendence and immanence, yet it deepens the mystery. We understand better how God can be 'with us wherever we are' while being 'naught is like unto Him.' But the why remains with Him."

Ibn 'Arabī's doctrine of divine self-disclosure represents one of Islamic mysticism's most sophisticated attempts to explain how the Incomparable God relates to creation. By developing tajallī as a comprehensive metaphysical principle, he provided a dynamic understanding that preserves both divine transcendence and immanence. The systematic development from earlier Sufi insights shows Islamic thought's capacity for creative synthesis. What began as scattered mystical experiences and insights became a complete metaphysical system that could engage with philosophy while remaining rooted in spiritual realization.

The doctrine's genius lies in making manifestation itself the mode of transcendence. Rather than seeing immanence and transcendence as contradictory, tajallī reveals them as complementary aspects of one reality. God remains utterly transcendent precisely through being immanently present—hidden by His very manifestation. The influence of this doctrine extends far beyond technical mysticism. It provides resources for understanding religious diversity through different tajallīyāt to different recipients, natural theology through creation as divine self-disclosure, and spiritual psychology through the soul's capacity to receive tajallī. Contemporary discussions about divine action, religious experience, and the relationship between God and world continue to find Ibn 'Arabī's framework illuminating.

Most profoundly, the doctrine of tajallī demonstrates that approaching the One who is "naught is like unto Him" requires embracing paradox productively. The Hidden Treasure that loves to be known, the Manifest who remains Hidden, the Immanent who is absolutely Transcendent—these are not contradictions to be resolved but mysteries that deepen understanding. In showing how divine self-disclosure preserves divine incomparability, Ibn 'Arabī provided a framework that continues to guide those seeking to understand the deepest mysteries of existence.

Chapter 15. Complementary Opposites in Classical Mystical Theology

The recognition that the Divine Reality transcends and unites apparent opposites represents one of the most profound insights in Islamic mystical theology. While theologians struggled to explain how God could possess seemingly contradictory attributes—being simultaneously the Manifest and the Hidden, the First and the Last, the Constrictor and the Expander—Sufi mystics developed sophisticated frameworks for understanding these complementary opposites as essential aspects of divine perfection. This chapter examines how early Sufis recognized this principle through spiritual experience, how Ibn 'Arabī systematized it into comprehensive doctrine, how later commentators refined and clarified these insights, and how orthodox theology eventually found ways to integrate this understanding while maintaining traditional boundaries.

The mystical recognition that divine reality encompasses and transcends opposites emerged early in Sufi thought, rooted in both Quranic meditation and spiritual experience. The Quran itself presents divine names in complementary pairs that challenged linear thinking. The verse "He is the First and the Last, the Manifest and the Hidden" (57:3) became a cornerstone for mystical reflection. Early Sufis recognized that these were not contradictions but complementary aspects of divine perfection.

Al-Ḥasan al-Baṣrī (d. 110/728) offered an early insight that would echo through centuries: "How can the same essence be both First and Last, both Hidden and Manifest? This is possible only for Allah, who transcends the limitations that make these opposites for us. In Him, all perfections unite without contradiction." This fundamental recognition that divine transcendence allows for the unity of what appear to human minds as contradictory attributes would become a recurring theme in mystical theology.

Rābi'a al-'Adawiyya (d. 185/801) expressed this through her famous prayers that united fear and hope, distance and nearness: "O God, if I worship You from fear of Hell, burn me in Hell. If I worship You from hope of Paradise, exclude me from Paradise. But if I worship You for Your own sake, do not withhold from me Your eternal beauty." Her spiritual experience transcended the opposition between divine mercy and rigor, demonstrating how lived spiritual reality could encompass what appeared conceptually contradictory.

As Sufi thought matured, practitioners developed specific terminology to express the unity of opposites with increasing precision. Al-Junayd (d. 298/910) articulated what became a fundamental Sufi teaching regarding jam' and farq, gathering and separation. He described the spiritual path as involving three stages: farq, or separation, where the seeker sees creation as distinct from the Creator; jam', or gathering, where one sees only the Creator; and jam' al-jam', the gathering of gathering, where one sees the Creator in creation and creation in the Creator without confusion. He explained further that in farq, opposites remain opposite, in jam' opposites disappear entirely, while in jam' al-jam' opposites are recognized as complementary manifestations of the One.

The spiritual states of qabḍ and basṭ, contraction and expansion, corresponding to the divine names al-Qābiḍ and al-Bāsiṭ, were experienced as complementary rather than contradictory. Abū Sa'īd al-Kharrāz (d. 286/899) taught that the realized one experiences contraction and expansion simultaneously—contraction in his own existence, expansion in divine existence. These apparent opposites are one experience viewed from different angles, demonstrating how spiritual realization transforms the perception of opposition into one of complementarity.

By the fourth Islamic century, Sufis were developing more systematic understandings of this principle. Al-Niffarī (d. 354/965) in his Mawāqif received divine communications expressing paradoxical unity: "He stopped me and said: 'I am the Evident in My hiddenness and the Hidden in My evidence. I am the First in My lastness and the Last in My firstness. Opposites in creation are unities in Me.'" Such visionary communications provided experiential confirmation of what was becoming theological doctrine.

Abū Ṭālib al-Makkī (d. 386/996) in Qūt al-Qulūb systematically treated divine names in complementary pairs, establishing that each divine name has its counterpart, and perfection lies in understanding their unity. He explained that the Giver (al-Mu'ṭī) and the Withholder (al-Māni') are one divine act viewed from the perspective of giving or withholding, and that the servant must see both as divine mercy. This systematic pairing of divine names would become a standard feature of later mystical analysis.

Early Sufis consistently emphasized that understanding the unity of opposites came through experience rather than theoretical speculation. Al-Ḥallāj (d. 309/922) expressed this in his ecstatic poetry: "I am the One I love, and the One I love is I, We are two spirits dwelling in one body. If you see me, you see Him, And if you see Him, you see us both." While controversial, this expressed the mystical experience where lover and Beloved, servant and Lord, cease to be experienced as opposites. Al-Shiblī (d. 334/946) taught through paradox that the closest to Allah is the furthest from himself, while the furthest from Allah is the closest to himself, with distance and nearness uniting in the station of bewilderment.

Ibn 'Arabī transformed these scattered insights into a comprehensive metaphysical system where the unity of opposites became central to understanding divine reality and its relationship to creation. In the Fuṣūṣ al-Ḥikam, he establishes the fundamental principle: "Know that the Divine Names, which are seemingly opposed, are united in the Divine Essence. They are distinguished in their effects on the recipients, not in the One who is named. The Avenger (al-Muntaqim) and the Compassionate (al-Raḥīm) are one reality manifesting according to the preparedness of the locus."

He provides the philosophical framework through an illuminating analogy: "Opposition exists only in manifestation, not in the source. Like water that freezes into ice or evaporates into steam—apparently opposite states of the same reality. The Divine Reality similarly manifests in seemingly opposed modes while remaining one." This principle that opposition belongs to the realm of manifestation rather than essence becomes foundational for his entire system.

Ibn 'Arabī systematically analyzed how opposite names relate through four fundamental oppositions that structure divine self-manifestation. First, al-Awwal and al-Ākhir, the First and the Last, represent not temporal sequence but ontological relationship: "He is First in that all emerges from

Him, Last in that all returns to Him. These are not temporal descriptions but ontological—He is the Origin and the End simultaneously." Second, al-Ẓāhir and al-Bāṭin, the Manifest and the Hidden, express the paradox that "He is Manifest in that nothing is more evident than His effects, Hidden in that nothing is more concealed than His essence. Every manifestation increases His hiddenness." Third, al-Qābiḍ and al-Bāsiṭ, the Constrictor and the Expander, operate simultaneously—constricting in one aspect while expanding in another, with the heart's systole and diastole imaging this divine rhythm. Fourth, al-Mu'izz and al-Mudhill, the Honorer and the Abaser, demonstrate that honor and abasement are relative to the recipient's state, such that what appears as abasement may be the beginning of true honor.

His notion of barzakh, or isthmus, became crucial for understanding how opposites can be unified without confusion. He defines a barzakh as what separates and unites simultaneously, with the supreme barzakh being the Divine Reality itself—separating the Absolute from creation while uniting them. The Perfect Human functions as a barzakh between all opposites, uniting heaven and earth, spirit and body, Lord and servant. In Futūḥāt al-Makkiyya, he elaborates that every divine name has this barzakh nature, facing the Essence with its reality and facing creation with its properties. This explains how the One becomes many without division and the many remain one without confusion.

The concept of the Divine Breath provided Ibn 'Arabī with a dynamic understanding of how opposites emerge from and remain within unity. "The Breath of the All-Merciful is one, but it carries all the divine names—those of beauty and majesty, gentleness and rigor. As human breath carries different letters without ceasing to be one breath, the Divine Breath manifests opposite qualities while remaining one act." This dynamic understanding prevented static interpretation, for at each moment the breath renews creation, with what was manifestation becoming hiddenness and what was hidden becoming manifest. The opposites perpetually transform into each other without losing their essential unity.

Ibn 'Arabī's concept of al-insān al-kāmil, the Perfect Human, represents the ultimate embodiment of the unity of opposites in the created realm. "The Perfect Human gathers all opposites within himself. He is the slave in his servanthood and the lord in his vicegerency. He manifests divine rigor to those requiring discipline and divine mercy to those requiring compassion.

In him, all divine names find perfect balance." He identifies this supremely with the Prophet Muhammad: "The Muhammadan Reality encompasses all opposites—it is the first creation and the last prophet, the most hidden reality and the most manifest guide." Thus the Perfect Human becomes the hermeneutical key for understanding how divine opposites can exist in harmonious unity.

Ibn 'Arabī's insights generated extensive commentary that clarified, systematized, and sometimes reformed his teachings on complementary opposites. Ṣadr al-Dīn al-Qūnawī (d. 673/1274), Ibn 'Arabī's foremost disciple, provided philosophical precision in his Miftāḥ al-Ghayb, arguing that the opposition of divine names is not real but relational. He explains through analogy: "Consider knowledge and power—they seem different, but divine knowledge is creative and divine power is knowing. In the Essence, they are one; in relation to creation, they appear distinct." He developed the notion of universal and particular faces, whereby each name has a face turned toward the Essence where it unites with all names, and a face turned toward creation where it appears distinct. The realized one sees both faces simultaneously, comprehending both unity and distinction without contradiction.

'Abd al-Razzāq al-Qāshānī (d. 736/1335) in his commentary on the Fuṣūṣ provided systematic analysis through the metaphor of light and color. "The divine names are like colors in white light—united in their source, separated in manifestation. The prism of creation reveals the distinct colors without dividing the light itself. This is the secret of how the One who is 'naught is like unto Him' manifests infinite diversity." He clarified potential misunderstandings by emphasizing that when we say opposites unite in God, we do not mean He has contrary attributes in the way creatures might be sometimes angry and sometimes pleased. Rather, what appear as opposites to us are complementary perfections in Him, existing in a mode that transcends creaturely contradiction.

Dāwūd al-Qayṣarī (d. 751/1350) worked to integrate Akbarian insights with systematic theology, proposing a resolution to apparent tensions between mystical and theological discourse. "The theologians are correct that God cannot have truly contrary attributes. The mystics are correct that the divine names appear opposite. The resolution: these are not contrary attributes in the Essence but complementary relationships with creation." He developed important distinctions that would facilitate orthodox acceptance:

essential unity, whereby in the Essence all attributes are one; nominal distinction, whereby in divine knowledge names are distinguished; manifestational opposition, whereby in creation names appear opposed; and realized unity, whereby in mystical realization opposition resolves into complementarity. These distinctions allowed for multiple levels of truth without contradiction.

Sa'īd al-Dīn al-Farghānī (d. 695/1296) emphasized the practical spiritual implications of understanding the unity of opposites. "Understanding the unity of opposites transforms spiritual practice. When experiencing contraction (qabḍ), the seeker knows expansion (basṭ) is its hidden face. In spiritual poverty (faqr), he finds true wealth (ghinā). This prevents despair in difficulty and pride in ease." By grounding the metaphysical doctrine in spiritual psychology, al-Farghānī demonstrated its practical utility for the spiritual path, moving the teaching from abstract speculation to lived wisdom.

The mystical doctrine of complementary opposites required careful integration with orthodox theology to avoid charges of logical contradiction or theological innovation. Traditional theologians raised several substantive objections. Ibn Taymiyya (d. 728/1328) argued from the standpoint of logic: "To say God is simultaneously First and Last, Hidden and Manifest, violates the law of non-contradiction. These mystics abandon reason in favor of paradox." Some scholars considered the systematic treatment of divine opposites as bid'a, or innovation, arguing that earlier authorities had not approached divine names in this manner. Practical concerns also arose that emphasizing the unity of opposites might confuse ordinary believers about divine attributes, potentially undermining proper worship and theological understanding.

However, many orthodox scholars found ways to integrate these insights within traditional frameworks. Al-Sha'rānī (d. 973/1565) provided an influential synthesis in al-Yawāqīt wa-l-Jawāhir, arguing that "the apparent opposition of divine names is mentioned in the Quran itself. The mystics do not innovate but explain what scripture teaches. When properly understood, this deepens rather than contradicts theology." He established principles for orthodox integration that would gain wide acceptance: that opposites unite in the Essence but not in their effects, that this represents a mystery to be accepted rather than fully comprehended, that it does not negate the real distinction between divine acts, and that practical religious life must maintain necessary distinctions for proper worship and conduct.

Orthodox theologians developed frameworks to incorporate mystical insights while preserving theological boundaries. The distinction between essence and acts proved particularly fruitful. Zakariyyā al-Anṣārī (d. 926/1520) clarified: "In the Divine Essence, all attributes are one—this the mystics correctly emphasize. In divine acts, distinctions are real—this theology preserves. Both truths are necessary." This allowed for recognition of essential unity without eliminating the practical distinctions required for religious life and proper understanding of divine action in the world.

Ibn Ḥajar al-Haytamī (d. 974/1567) proposed a pedagogical framework based on levels of understanding. "There are three levels: the common people see opposites, the theologians understand their compatibility, the mystics experience their unity. Each level has its truth and necessity." This hierarchical model allowed different constituencies to maintain their respective perspectives without mutual contradiction, recognizing that deeper understanding builds upon rather than negates more elementary levels.

Orthodox integration came with important qualifications designed to safeguard transcendence and maintain proper religious practice. 'Abd al-Ghanī al-Nābulusī (d. 1143/1731) emphasized: "The unity of opposites in God does not mean He experiences opposition as creatures do. Rather, what are opposites for us are unified perfections for Him. This preserves 'laysa kamithlihi shay'un,'" the fundamental principle that nothing is like unto Him. Teachers stressed that recognizing ultimate unity does not eliminate practical distinctions in worship and spiritual etiquette. In worship, believers still seek the Beautiful names and seek refuge from the Majestic ones. Unity of opposites provides understanding but does not justify abandoning proper comportment, or adab, before the Divine.

The doctrine gradually entered various levels of Islamic education. Major theological commentaries began incorporating explanations of how divine opposites unite without contradiction. Sufi orders teaching within orthodox frameworks used the understanding of complementary opposites for spiritual development while maintaining sharī'a boundaries. Simplified versions even entered popular religious education, with teachers explaining that God's mercy and wrath are like the sun's light and heat—different effects of one reality. This multi-level integration ensured that the insight could benefit seekers at various stages of understanding without disrupting communal religious life.

The mystical understanding of complementary opposites in divine reality represents a profound development in Islamic thought. From early Sufi insights through Ibn 'Arabī's systematic articulation to later integration with orthodox theology, this doctrine demonstrates Islam's capacity for sophisticated theological development that preserves transcendence while explaining immanence. The key insight—that what appear as opposites in creation are unified perfections in the Creator—provides a framework for understanding numerous theological puzzles while maintaining the principle that "naught is like unto Him." By showing how the Divine Reality transcends the either-or logic that governs created existence, mystical theology opens space for a deeper understanding of tawḥīd.

The successful integration of this mystical insight into broader Islamic theology shows how experiential wisdom and intellectual rigor can complement each other. The doctrine of complementary opposites continues to provide resources for contemporary Islamic thought, offering ways to understand divine action that transcend simplistic anthropomorphism while remaining true to scriptural affirmations. Perhaps most significantly, this teaching demonstrates that approaching the Incomparable requires embracing modes of understanding that transcend ordinary logic without abandoning reason. The unity of opposites in the Divine—rigorously developed and carefully qualified—remains one of Islamic mysticism's most valuable contributions to the broader tradition's understanding of the One who encompasses all while transcending all.

Chapter 16. Perpetual Creation and Divine Transcendence

The doctrine of perpetual creation (al-khalq al-jadīd or tajdīd al-khalq) represents one of Islamic thought's most profound insights into the relationship between divine transcendence and the created order. Rather than viewing creation as a single past event, this teaching understands it as an ongoing divine act, with existence renewed at each moment. This dynamic understanding preserves divine transcendence by emphasizing that creation depends absolutely on God at every instant, while explaining the constant change observed in the phenomenal world. This chapter examines the scriptural foundations of this doctrine, its development through classical Islamic thinkers, Ibn 'Arabī's revolutionary synthesis, and its reception and influence in later Islamic thought.

The concept of perpetual creation finds deep roots in Islamic scripture, though its full implications would only be drawn out through centuries of reflection and spiritual insight. The Quran contains several verses that classical commentators understood as indicating continuous creation, with the most fundamental being the verse "Every day He is upon some matter (kulla yawmin huwa fī sha'n)" (55:29). This verse became the cornerstone for understanding divine creativity as ongoing rather than completed. Al-Ṭabarī (d. 310/923) records multiple early interpretations, noting that Ibn 'Abbās said: "Among His matters (shu'ūn) are that He gives life and causes death, creates and provides, lifts up and brings low. This indicates that divine creative activity never ceases." Al-Zamakhsharī (d. 538/1144) adds linguistic analysis, explaining that the phrase 'kulla yawmin,' or every day, uses 'yawm' not literally but to indicate perpetual continuity, meaning at every moment, every instant, without cessation.

The verse "Have they not considered how Allah begins creation and then repeats it?" (29:19) provided another key scriptural foundation. While often interpreted eschatologically as referring to resurrection, mystics saw deeper metaphysical meaning. Al-Qushayrī (d. 465/1074) comments that the repetition (i'āda) of creation is not only at resurrection but at each moment, with what we perceive as continuous existence being actually rapid renewal—like a flame that appears stable but consists of constantly new combustion. Similarly, the verse "Are We wearied by the first creation? Yet they are in doubt about a new creation (khalq jadīd)" (50:15) attracted mystical interpretation. Fakhr al-Dīn al-Rāzī (d. 606/1210) notes that while the apparent meaning concerns resurrection, the mystics understand this as indicating that creation is always 'new'—never the same at two successive moments.

Beyond these direct references, numerous verses implicitly support the doctrine through their depiction of divine sustaining activity. The verse "Allah holds the heavens and the earth lest they vanish; and if they should vanish, no one could hold them after Him" (35:41) proved particularly important. Ibn Kathīr (d. 774/1373) explains that this indicates creation requires continuous divine support, unlike a builder who can leave after construction is complete—Allah must perpetually maintain existence. The famous verse about divine command, "His command, when He intends a thing, is only that He says to it 'Be!' and it is" (36:82), also carried implications for perpetual creation. Al-Ghazālī interprets in Iḥyā' 'Ulūm al-Dīn that the present tense 'He says' (yaqūlu) indicates this is not a past event but ongoing, with Allah saying 'Be!' to each thing at each moment so that it continues to exist.

Hadith literature provided additional support for the doctrine. The tradition "Allah's mercy precedes His wrath" was understood by Sufi commentators in relation to the Divine Breath that perpetually creates. Al-Qāshānī explains that each breath contains mercy through creation and wrath through annihilation, with existence being perpetually created and annihilated in rapid succession. The famous hadith about Allah's descent to the lowest heaven each night was interpreted by some as indicating perpetual divine engagement with creation. Ibn 'Arabī notes that since it is always night somewhere on Earth, this descent is perpetual, symbolizing continuous divine creative presence. The tradition "Allah does not sleep, and it does not befit Him to sleep" (Muslim) also carried implications, with commentators observing that since sleep implies cessation of activity, Allah's sleeplessness indicates perpetual creative activity.

Early Quranic commentators recognized the profound implications of these verses. Mujāhid ibn Jabr (d. 104/722) commented on "Every day He is upon some matter" that this means He continuously creates, sustains, gives life, and causes death—His creative act never stops. Al-Ḥasan al-Baṣrī (d. 110/728) taught through vivid analogy: "Creation is not like a building that stands after the builder leaves. It's like light from a lamp—if the lamp is extinguished, the light instantly vanishes. Similarly, if Allah ceased His creative act for an instant, all would return to nothingness." This early recognition that existence depends on continuous divine action would profoundly shape later theological and mystical developments.

The doctrine of perpetual creation developed through contributions from theologians, philosophers, and mystics, each adding layers of sophistication to the fundamental insight. Among the Mu'tazilites, despite their later rejection on other theological grounds, their emphasis on divine justice contributed to understanding perpetual creation. Al-Jubbā'ī (d. 303/915) argued that if God created once and then ceased creating, He would be inactive—representing an imperfection. Divine perfection, he maintained, requires continuous activity. This argument, while embedded in broader Mu'tazilite theology, highlighted the relationship between divine perfection and ongoing creative action.

The Ash'arites developed the doctrine of continuous creation (khalq mustawmir) as part of their occasionalist metaphysics. Al-Bāqillānī (d. 403/1013) states in al-Tamhīd that accidents cannot persist for two moments, and since bodies are composed of accidents, they too require renewal at each instant. This renewal is God's continuous creation, making created things fundamentally dependent on divine action at every moment. Al-Juwaynī (d. 478/1085) refined this understanding in al-Irshād, explaining that what we call 'persistence' (baqā') is actually rapid re-creation. Like frames in motion creating the illusion of continuous movement, rapid re-creation creates the illusion of stable existence. This occasionalist framework, while philosophically distinct from later mystical formulations, established the theological legitimacy of understanding creation as ongoing divine act.

Muslim philosophers approached perpetual creation through different conceptual frameworks while arriving at complementary insights. Al-Kindī (d. 260/873) introduced the concept of "creation from nothing at each instant," arguing that true creation (ibdā') means bringing into existence without pre-existing matter. This occurs not once but continuously—otherwise things would have independent existence after their initial creation. Ibn Sīnā (d. 428/1037), while maintaining the doctrine of eternal creation, contributed the crucial insight of existential dependence. Possible beings depend on the Necessary Existent not just for coming-to-be but for continuing-to-be. Remove the cause, and the effect instantly ceases—like light depending on the sun. Al-Ghazālī's critique of the philosophers paradoxically strengthened the doctrine by clarifying its theological implications. The philosophers rightly see that contingent beings need continuous divine support, he argued, but their error is making this support necessary rather than freely willed. God freely chooses to recreate the world at each instant, preserving both divine freedom and creation's absolute dependence.

Sufis provided experiential confirmation of perpetual creation through direct mystical perception. Al-Junayd (d. 298/910) described his mystical experience: "In the state of fanā', I witnessed creation vanishing and returning with each divine glance. What seems stable to ordinary perception is actually flickering in and out of existence." Al-Niffarī (d. 354/965) records in Mawāqif a divine communication: "He stopped me and said: 'I manifest Myself anew at each instant. No two moments of manifestation are alike. Creation is My perpetual self-disclosure.'" Abū Yazīd al-Bisṭāmī (d. 261/875) exclaimed the apparently blasphemous "Glory be to me!" but explained when challenged that at that moment, he witnessed that only God truly exists, and all existence is His perpetual act. The 'me' that glorified was His existence in the mystic, revealing the radical divine immanence that perpetual creation implies.

By the fifth Islamic century, more systematic formulations of the doctrine emerged. Al-Qushayrī in his Risāla dedicates a section to "renewal of creation," teaching that the realized ones witness that the world is annihilated and recreated with each breath. This is not metaphor but metaphysical fact, with ordinary people prevented from seeing this reality only by the rapidity of renewal. Al-Ghazālī in Mishkāt al-Anwār provides a philosophical framework through the analogy of light. Existence is like light in that it must be continuously supplied. A shadow exists only while light is blocked; remove the obstruction, and the shadow instantly vanishes. Similarly, creation exists only through a continuous divine creative act, with no moment of independent subsistence.

Ibn 'Arabī transformed scattered insights about perpetual creation into a comprehensive metaphysical doctrine that would influence all subsequent Islamic mystical thought. Central to his synthesis is the concept of the "Breath of the All-Merciful" (nafas al-Raḥmān). In the Fuṣūṣ al-Ḥikam, he writes: "The universe is the words of God articulated through the Breath of the All-Merciful. Just as human speech requires continuous breath, the universe requires continuous divine breathing. Each breath brings new creation." He elaborates in Futūḥāt al-Makkiyya that with each divine breath, the universe is annihilated and recreated. What appears as one universe is actually countless universes succeeding each other with such rapidity that sensation cannot perceive the gap between annihilation and recreation.

Ibn 'Arabī provides a precise metaphysical framework for understanding this perpetual renewal. Everything in existence has two faces—a face toward nothingness ('adam) from which it came, and a face toward Being (wujūd) which gives it existence. At each moment, it returns to nothingness and re-emerges into being. This dual orientation explains both the transience and persistence of created things. Each divine name seeks manifestation, and the Breath carries these names into actuality. Since divine names are infinite and God never manifests the same name identically twice, creation is perpetually new. The fixed entities (a'yān thābita) in divine knowledge represent eternal possibilities, with perpetual creation being these possibilities continuously receiving the dress of existence through divine self-disclosure (tajallī).

He meticulously grounds this doctrine in scripture, providing Quranic warrant for what might otherwise appear as metaphysical speculation. On "Every day He is upon some matter," he explains that this is the clearest verse about perpetual creation, with 'every day' meaning every indivisible instant and 'upon some matter' meaning bringing new creation into existence. Regarding divine creativity, when God says 'Be!' this is not a single past command but a continuous address. At each moment, He says 'Be!' to each thing according to its appointed measure, making creation an ongoing dialogue between divine will and creaturely possibility.

Ibn 'Arabī draws out profound philosophical implications from this doctrine. The question of identity through change receives an elegant resolution: what maintains the apparent identity of things through perpetual recreation is that the fixed entity ('ayn thābita) remains constant in divine knowledge while its existence is renewed. Like a river maintaining its form while its water constantly changes, created things maintain identity through pattern rather than substantial continuity. The illusion of stability arises because ordinary perception sees stability when the renewal is faster than perception can grasp. Like a spinning firebrand appearing as a circle of light, rapid renewal appears as stable existence. Crucially, perpetual creation manifests divine freedom. At each moment, God could create differently. That He maintains similar patterns is from wisdom and mercy, not necessity—creation reflects divine choice at every instant.

Ibn 'Arabī insists this doctrine is not mere theory but reflects experiential reality accessible to the realized. The people of unveiling (kashf) witness perpetual creation directly. In certain spiritual states, the rapid flickering of existence becomes visible. This is terrifying for the unprepared but liberating for the realized, who discover their absolute dependence on divine creativity at each moment. He describes personal experience: "I was shown how existence is renewed with each breath. I saw the universe blinking in and out of existence like lightning flashes in a dark night. Only the Real remains constant." This grounding in spiritual experience distinguishes Ibn 'Arabī's treatment from purely philosophical or theological discussions, presenting perpetual creation as lived reality rather than abstract doctrine.

The doctrine of perpetual creation generated diverse responses and developments in later Islamic thought, ranging from philosophical elaboration through theological concern to practical spiritual application. Ṣadr al-Dīn al-Qūnawī (d. 673/1274) provided a philosophical elaboration that clarified the doctrine's implications. The Shaykh's doctrine of perpetual creation, he argued, solves ancient philosophical problems. It explains motion without requiring void, change without affecting divine immutability, and time as the measure of renewal rather than a container of events. He clarified potential misunderstandings by emphasizing that perpetual creation does not mean chaos. The divine wisdom maintains patterns and laws, creating similar but never identical forms. This explains both natural regularity and constant novelty, reconciling the appearance of natural law with metaphysical dynamism.

'Abd al-Razzāq al-Qāshānī (d. 736/1335) integrated the doctrine with Islamic philosophy more systematically. The philosophers' eternal creation and the theologians' temporal creation are reconciled in perpetual creation, he argued. Creation is eternal as a continuous act, temporal as renewed instances. This synthesis showed how apparently contradictory positions could be understood as partial perspectives on a more comprehensive truth, with perpetual creation providing the integrating framework.

Orthodox theological responses varied between concern and accommodation. Ibn Taymiyya (d. 728/1328) critiqued certain aspects while accepting others, distinguishing between what he considered orthodox and heterodox elements. That God continuously sustains creation is orthodox, he acknowledged. But claiming the substance itself is annihilated and recreated contradicts sensory evidence and stable natural laws. This critique reflected concern that the doctrine, taken literally, might undermine confidence in observable reality and natural causation. Al-Sha'rānī (d. 973/1565) provided an accommodating orthodox interpretation that would prove influential. Perpetual creation means God continuously sustains existence, not necessarily that substances are annihilated, he explained. The mystics speak of experiential reality, not necessarily physical fact. This interpretive flexibility allowed the doctrine to be accepted at different levels of understanding without requiring uniform literal acceptance.

Mullā Ṣadrā (d. 1050/1640) made perpetual creation central to his philosophical system, demonstrating its continued vitality in later Islamic thought. Trans-substantial motion (al-ḥaraka al-jawhariyya) is the philosophical expression of perpetual creation, he argued. Substance itself is in constant flux, continuously renewed by divine act. This solves the problem of how the Immutable relates to the changing without compromising divine transcendence. He integrated various streams of Islamic thought, showing how Ibn 'Arabī's perpetual creation, Avicenna's existential dependence, and Ash'arite occasionalism all point to the same truth—existence is dynamic divine act, not static fact.

Perpetual creation became standard teaching in many Sufi orders, integrated into practical spiritual pedagogy. Among the Shādhiliyya, Ibn 'Aṭā' Allah al-Iskandarī (d. 709/1309) writes in his Ḥikam: "You were not in existence yesterday to be annihilated today. Rather, you are perpetually in the process of being brought into existence. Understanding this brings humility and presence." The doctrine thus served practical spiritual purposes, cultivating awareness of absolute divine dependence and presence in the moment. In the Naqshbandiyya, Khwāja Bahā' al-Dīn Naqshband (d.

791/1389) made "awareness of breath" (hush dar dam) central to practice. Each breath contains death and resurrection, with inhaling being existence and exhaling being annihilation. The aware one witnesses perpetual creation in his own breathing, making the cosmic doctrine accessible through embodied practice.

Contemporary Muslim thinkers continue engaging with perpetual creation, finding in it resources for dialogue with modern thought. Muhammad Iqbal (d. 1357/1938) integrated it with modern philosophy, arguing that the doctrine of perpetual creation anticipates process philosophy. It shows reality as dynamic becoming rather than static being, consonant with modern physics' understanding of energy and change. Seyyed Hossein Nasr presents it as an Islamic contribution to perennial philosophy, arguing that perpetual creation reveals the metaphysical truth that existence is not self-subsistent but depends moment by moment on the Divine Principle. This teaching offers profound ecological and spiritual implications for the modern world, providing alternatives to mechanistic worldviews.

Modern Muslim thinkers note parallels between perpetual creation and contemporary science, observing that quantum mechanics reveals particles constantly appearing and disappearing, that matter at subatomic levels displays dynamic rather than static nature, and that energy must be continuously supplied to maintain structures. These parallels are noted not as proof but as consonance between revealed wisdom and observed nature, suggesting that traditional metaphysical insights may align with cutting-edge scientific understanding in unexpected ways.

The doctrine of perpetual creation represents a profound development in Islamic thought's understanding of divine transcendence and its relationship to creation. From Quranic verses speaking of continuous divine activity through philosophical and mystical elaborations to Ibn 'Arabī's comprehensive synthesis, this teaching reveals how Islamic thinkers grappled with fundamental questions about existence, time, and divine action. The doctrine preserves divine transcendence by emphasizing creation's absolute dependence on God at every moment. Nothing possesses independent existence; all things exist only through a continuous divine creative act. This makes the principle "laysa kamithlihi shay'un" even more profound—not only is nothing like God in attributes, but nothing shares His self-subsistent existence.

Ibn 'Arabī's synthesis, making perpetual creation central to Islamic mystical theology, provided a framework that influenced virtually all subsequent Islamic mystical thought. Whether accepted literally or interpreted metaphorically, the doctrine shaped understanding of divine-human relations, spiritual experience, and the nature of existence itself. The varied reception—from orthodox concern to philosophical integration to practical spiritual application—demonstrates Islamic thought's capacity for creative tension. Rather than requiring uniform acceptance, the doctrine generated productive dialogue that enriched multiple dimensions of Islamic intellectual life.

For contemporary Islamic thought, perpetual creation offers resources for engaging modern philosophical and scientific worldviews while maintaining traditional commitments. It provides a dynamic understanding of divine action that avoids both deism's distant God and pantheism's identification of God with nature. In showing how transcendence operates through immanence—how the utterly Other sustains all existence at each moment—the doctrine of perpetual creation continues to offer profound insights for those seeking to understand the deepest nature of reality.

Chapter 17. Sufi Approaches to Divine Transcendence

The Sufi tradition represents Islam's mystical dimension, where the principle "laysa kamithlihi shay'un" (naught is like unto Him) transforms from theological doctrine into lived spiritual reality. Through centuries of spiritual practice, teaching, and reflection, Sufis developed distinctive approaches to experiencing and expressing divine transcendence while maintaining orthodox boundaries. This chapter examines how early Sufi sayings articulated insights about divine incomparability, how classical manuals systematized these teachings, the crucial role of spiritual guidance in navigating transcendent experiences, and how the tradition preserved orthodox practice while pursuing mystical realization.

The earliest Sufis expressed their understanding of divine transcendence through pithy sayings, paradoxical utterances, and teaching stories that conveyed depths of meaning beyond systematic theology. The first generations established patterns of speaking about divine transcendence that would echo through centuries. Ḥasan al-Baṣrī (d. 110/728), often considered the foundational figure, taught that the root of all error is thinking you know Allah as you know created things. He who truly knows Allah knows that he does not know Him. The highest knowledge is knowing your inability to know. When asked about divine essence, he would say: "Do not think about the Essence of Allah, for you will never reach its reality. Instead, think about His blessings and signs, for these are doors to knowing what can be known of Him." This recognition that divine essence exceeds human comprehension while remaining knowable through signs and effects became foundational for the tradition.

Rābi'a al-'Adawiyya (d. 185/801) revolutionized understanding through her emphasis on pure love that transcends instrumental motivation. "Everyone serves You from fear of Hell or desire for Paradise, but I serve You for Yourself alone. You are transcendent beyond both reward and punishment, beyond what the seekers seek." Her famous prayer encapsulates transcendence through negation: "O God, if I worship You from fear of Hell, burn me in it. If I worship You from hope of Paradise, exclude me from it. But if I worship You for Your own sake, do not withhold from me Your eternal beauty." This shift from fear and hope to pure love for the Divine in itself represented a profound deepening of how transcendence was understood and approached.

The Baghdad masters developed sophisticated expressions of divine incomparability that balanced affirmation with negation. Ma'rūf al-Karkhī (d. 200/815) emphasized experiential transcendence, teaching that words are for those absent, but when the King is present, words become impertinence. Know that He transcends whatever you say about Him, but also whatever you experience of Him. This recognition that even mystical experience fails to comprehend divine reality prevented confusion between unveiling and ultimate knowledge. Bishr al-Ḥāfī (d. 227/842) taught through paradox that the closest to Allah are those who speak least about Him, not from ignorance but from knowing that every word falls short. Their silence is more eloquent than the eloquence of speakers. Sarī al-Saqaṭī (d. 253/867), uncle and teacher of al-Junayd, articulated key principles regarding levels of understanding. Tawḥīd has three levels: affirming His unity with the tongue—this is for the common people; affirming His unity in the heart—this is for the elite; witnessing that only He truly exists—this is for the elite of the elite.

Al-Junayd (d. 298/910), known as "Master of the Path," provided definitive formulations that would shape all subsequent Sufi discourse on transcendence. On the nature of tawḥīd, he taught that it is separating the Eternal from the temporal, recognizing that whatever enters your imagination, Allah is other than that. The images you form of Him are idols of the heart. His famous definition states: "Tawḥīd is the isolation of the Eternal from the temporal, and departing from your dwelling place, and separating from your peers, and forgetting what you know and don't know, and replacing all of this with the continuous invocation of the Real." On the limits of expression, he taught that when the tongues attempt to express His reality, they falter; when the intellects attempt to grasp Him, they return bewildered; when the birds of imagination attempt to fly in His sky, their wings break. This recognition of the failure of all human faculties before divine reality became a cornerstone of Sufi teaching.

Some early Sufis expressed transcendence through ecstatic utterances that pushed the boundaries of acceptable expression while revealing profound truths about divine-human relationship. Abū Yazīd al-Bisṭāmī (d. 261/875) exclaimed: "Glory be to me! How great is my station!" When questioned about this apparently blasphemous claim, he explained that this was not him speaking but He speaking through him. In that moment, the 'I' had vanished, and only He remained. Another of his sayings reveals the paradox of mystical vision: "I gazed at Him with the eye of certainty after He had turned me away from all that is other than Him. He illuminated me with His light, and showed me His wonders. He showed me His He-ness. I gazed at myself with His He-ness, and my light vanished in His light." Al-Ḥallāj (d. 309/922) famously declared "Anā al-Ḥaqq" (I am the Real), later explaining that when you see that only He exists, and your existence is borrowed from His, then the 'I' that speaks is not the created 'I' but the Creator speaking through His creation. These controversial utterances required careful interpretation to distinguish between claims of identity with God and expressions of self-annihilation in divine presence.

Early Sufis mastered paradoxical expression to convey what systematic discourse could not capture. Al-Shiblī (d. 334/946) taught that the Real is too mighty to be known and too merciful to leave us without knowledge. So He is known and unknown, near and far, evident and hidden—all at once. Al-Nūrī (d. 295/908) expressed the paradox of divine immanence and transcendence: "He manifests Himself to hearts while remaining hidden from eyes. He is closer than the jugular vein while being beyond all directions. This is the marvel that breaks intellects." Such paradoxical formulations acknowledged that divine reality exceeds the either-or logic that governs ordinary understanding.

Early Sufis often conveyed transcendence through teaching stories that operated on multiple levels. Dhū al-Nūn al-Miṣrī (d. 245/859) told this parable: "A man sought to see the king. After much effort, he was admitted to the palace. Room after room he passed, each more magnificent. Finally, he entered the throne room—but found it empty except for a mirror. Looking into it, he saw only himself. Then he understood: the King is not seen—He sees." Such stories communicated profound truths about the reversal of subject and object in divine knowledge, where the seeker discovers himself as the object of divine seeing rather than the subject who sees the Divine.

As Sufism developed, comprehensive manuals emerged that systematized earlier insights about divine transcendence into teachable doctrine and method. Abū Naṣr al-Sarrāj (d. 378/988) produced one of the earliest systematic manuals, Kitāb al-Luma'. On divine transcendence, he writes that the foundation of the Path is correct understanding of tawḥīd, which has levels. The tawḥīd of the common people involves negating partners from Allah. The tawḥīd of the elite involves negating attributes from the Essence. The tawḥīd of the elite of the elite involves negating all that is other than Him from existence. He systematizes approaches to incomparability by teaching that the seeker must pass through stations of transcendence: first, transcending creation through zuhd or renunciation; second, transcending the self through fanā' or annihilation; third, transcending transcendence itself through baqā' or subsistence in the Divine.

Abū Bakr al-Kalābādhī (d. 385/995) in Al-Ta'arruf li-madhhab ahl al-taṣawwuf provides doctrinal clarity regarding potentially controversial Sufi expressions. The Sufis agree that Allah is unlike His creation in every respect, he explains. They differ only in expression, not in meaning. When they speak of 'union' (ittiḥād), they mean unity of will, not unity of essence. When they speak of 'incarnation' (ḥulūl), they mean manifestation of attributes, not indwelling of essence. He addresses controversial expressions by explaining that when the masters speak paradoxically about the Real, understand that ordinary language fails before transcendent reality. Their expressions are fingers pointing at the moon, not descriptions of the moon itself. This hermeneutical principle allowed orthodox scholars to accept seemingly problematic utterances when properly contextualized.

'Abd al-Karīm al-Qushayrī's (d. 465/1074) Risāla became the most influential manual in the tradition. His treatment of transcendence is comprehensive, defining the reality of tawḥīd as witnessing the Real in His absolute uniqueness, free from all attributes that the imagination might conceive or the understanding might grasp. It is seeing that He alone possesses true existence, while all else exists through Him. He provides practical methodology, explaining that the path to realizing transcendence passes through three stages. Takhallī, or emptying, involves removing all attachments to creation. Taḥallī, or adorning, involves cultivating divine attributes within human limits. Tajallī, or unveiling, involves receiving direct witness of divine reality. On maintaining balance, he teaches that the realized one witnesses divine incomparability while maintaining the courtesy (adab) of servanthood. He sees that nothing resembles Allah while fulfilling the duties that recognize the Lord-servant relationship.

'Alī al-Hujwīrī (d. 465/1074) provides Persian-speaking audiences with comprehensive treatment in his Kashf al-Maḥjūb. Divine transcendence (tanzīh) is the first principle of gnosis (ma'rifa), he teaches, but there are errors in understanding it. Some make Him so transcendent He cannot be known at all. Some make Him so immanent they lose His transcendence. The correct path recognizes that He is transcendent in Essence while immanent in signs. He explains the mystical approach by teaching that the Sufi realizes transcendence not through negation alone but through direct tasting (dhawq). When the heart is polished through spiritual practice, it reflects divine lights while knowing the Light transcends all reflection.

Abū Ḥāmid al-Ghazālī (d. 505/1111) achieved masterful integration of theological, philosophical, and mystical perspectives across multiple works. In Iḥyā' 'Ulūm al-Dīn, he writes that the highest degree of tawḥīd is witnessing that there is none in existence save Allah, that He is the Real Existent, and that all else is metaphorical existence, shadow without independent reality. In Mishkāt al-Anwār, he presents divine transcendence as having levels corresponding to human faculties. To the senses, He is absolutely hidden. To the imagination, He is beyond all forms. To the intellect, He is beyond all concepts. To the spirit, He is witnessed but not comprehended. His synthesis of philosophy and mysticism acknowledges that the philosophers correctly emphasize His transcendence of material attributes, while the Sufis correctly emphasize His transcendence of even immaterial concepts. The complete knower unites both perspectives without contradiction.

Ibn 'Aṭā' Allah al-Iskandarī (d. 709/1309) distilled centuries of wisdom into aphorisms that made profound truths accessible. "Your distance from Him is that you do not witness Him, not that He is absent. For how can anything be absent when He is more manifest than everything?" This reversal of the problem suggests that absence lies in the perceiver rather than the perceived. "He is independent of needing a proof to prove Him. How can anything else prove Him when He is more evident than everything? He manifested everything, so how can He be hidden?" "The Real is too majestic to be witnessed by the senses, too holy to be grasped by thoughts, too subtle to be contained by imaginations." These succinct formulations captured the tradition's accumulated wisdom in memorable form.

The Sufi tradition recognized that approaching divine transcendence required careful guidance to avoid spiritual dangers and doctrinal errors. Classical sources emphasize the indispensability of qualified guidance in navigating the complexities of mystical experience. Al-Junayd stated categorically: "He who has no shaykh, his shaykh is Satan." This referred specifically to navigating transcendent experiences where self-delusion could easily masquerade as authentic unveiling. Abū Sa'īd ibn Abī al-Khayr (d. 440/1049) explained the necessity of guidance: "The shaykh is one who has traveled the path and knows its dangers. When the seeker experiences divine disclosure, only the guide can distinguish between authentic unveiling and self-delusion."

Spiritual guides performed several crucial functions regarding the experience and interpretation of transcendence. Before allowing disciples to pursue mystical experience, shaykhs ensured solid grounding in orthodox theology. Al-Qushayrī notes that the shaykh first establishes correct 'aqīda in the murid. Only when the disciple understands divine transcendence intellectually can he safely pursue experiential knowledge. This doctrinal grounding prevented mystical experiences from leading to heterodox conclusions. Guides provided frameworks for understanding mystical experiences that might otherwise be misinterpreted. Ibn 'Arabī writes: "When the disciple experiences fanā', the shaykh explains: 'You have not become God nor has God become you. Rather, your consciousness of self has been replaced by consciousness of God.'" This interpretive function distinguished between the phenomenology of experience and its metaphysical reality. Shaykhs prevented disciples from making claims beyond their station that could lead to scandal or spiritual harm. Al-Suhrawardī notes in 'Awārif al-Ma'ārif that when disciples experience divine disclosure, they may speak words of apparent unbelief. The shaykh contextualizes these utterances and prevents public scandal while helping the disciple integrate the experience appropriately.

Classical manuals outline progressive stages of development under guidance, with each stage requiring different approaches to divine transcendence. In initial stages, the focus is on purification and ethical development, with the shaykh assigning practices to weaken ego and strengthen divine consciousness. At intermediate stages, the disciple is introduced to contemplative practices. As al-Ghazālī describes, the shaykh gradually introduces practices of the heart—meditation on divine names, contemplation of divine acts, remembrance of divine presence. At advanced stages, direct encounter with transcendence becomes possible. Ibn 'Aṭā' Allah explains that when the disciple is prepared, the shaykh may guide him to practices that precipitate fanā', but always with careful monitoring and interpretation to ensure proper understanding and integration.

Spiritual guides employed various methods to convey transcendence beyond conceptual teaching. Rather than explaining transcendence conceptually, masters led disciples to experience it gradually through practices calibrated to their capacity. Najm al-Dīn Kubrā (d. 618/1221) developed a detailed phenomenology of spiritual lights corresponding to levels of realization, providing disciples with maps of interior experience. Masters used apparent contradictions to break conceptual limitations that might otherwise constrain understanding. When Bāyazīd's disciple asked about God, he replied: "Whatever you think, He is other than that. Whatever you imagine, He transcends that. Yet He is closer to you than your own self." Such paradoxical teaching forced disciples beyond reliance on conceptual frameworks. Specific practices cultivated awareness of transcendence through embodied spiritual discipline. Silent meditation (murāqaba) on divine incomparability, contemplation (tafakkur) on the limits of human comprehension, and invocation (dhikr) emphasizing divine transcendence provided concrete methods for approaching the transcendent reality.

The tradition developed multiple safeguards to ensure mystical experience remained orthodox and productive. Shaykhs distinguished authentic mystical experience from imagination through careful verification. Al-Shādhilī taught: "If you claim to witness the Real, I will test you: Has it increased your humility? Has it strengthened your adherence to sharī'a? Has it made you more compassionate? True vision of transcendence produces these fruits." This emphasis on ethical and behavioral effects prevented self-deception. Guides prevented spiritual pride that could arise from mystical experiences. When a disciple of al-Junayd claimed high realization, he sent him to the market saying: "Tell everyone you meet that you have achieved union with God." The disciple returned ashamed, understanding his error. This practical test revealed whether the experience had genuinely produced self-annihilation or had instead inflated the ego.

Shaykhs provided orthodox interpretation of mystical experiences that might otherwise be misunderstood. When disciples experienced unity, guides explained it as unity of witnessing (shuhūd), not unity of existence (wujūd) in the heretical sense. This hermeneutical function preserved doctrinal boundaries while honoring the reality of mystical experience.

Throughout its history, mainstream Sufism carefully preserved orthodox practice while pursuing mystical realization of divine transcendence. Classical Sufis articulated the inseparable relationship between law and reality, refusing any dichotomy between sharī'a and ḥaqīqa. Al-Junayd established the foundational principle: "Our way is bound by the Book and the Sunna. He who does not memorize the Quran, write hadith, and study fiqh is not to be followed in this matter of ours." This integration of legal learning with mystical pursuit prevented the path from becoming antinomian. Al-Qushayrī elaborated through architectural metaphor: "The sharī'a is the foundation, the ṭarīqa is the building, the ḥaqīqa is the inhabitant. A building without foundation collapses; a foundation without building serves no purpose; both without inhabitant remain empty." This organic unity meant that each aspect required the others for completeness.

Sufis developed multiple mechanisms to preserve orthodoxy while pursuing transcendent realization. Rather than diminishing practice, mystical realization intensified observance. Abū Sa'īd ibn Abī al-Khayr said: "Before realization, I prayed because it was commanded. After realization, I pray because I witness the One to whom I pray. The form is the same, but the reality transforms." This enhanced observance demonstrated that mystical knowledge deepened rather than replaced ritual practice. Sufis provided deeper meanings for ritual practices without changing their forms. On ritual prayer, Ibn 'Arabī writes: "The standing is the station of servanthood, the bowing is the station of awe, the prostration is the station of nothingness before the Real. Each position teaches transcendence." This esoteric interpretation enriched practice while maintaining its exoteric form intact. Mystical experience was verified through ethical transformation rather than extraordinary phenomena. Al-Muḥāsibī stressed: "He who claims knowledge of God while his character worsens is a liar. True ma'rifa produces beautiful character (ḥusn al-khuluq)." This ethical criterion prevented confusion between genuine realization and mere psychological states.

When some claimed mystical realization freed them from religious law, mainstream Sufis responded forcefully to protect the tradition's integrity. Al-Hujwīrī writes: "If anyone says that gnosis releases from religious obligation, he is an infidel. The more one knows Allah, the more scrupulous one becomes in obedience." This categorical rejection of antinomianism protected the tradition from those who would use mystical language to justify transgression. Al-Qushayrī warned: "Beware those who use spiritual states to justify abandoning prayer or committing sin. They are highway robbers on the path to God, not guides." Ibn 'Aṭā' Allah clarified the relationship through geometric metaphor: "The sharī'a is like the circumference of a circle, the ḥaqīqa like its center. You cannot reach the center except through the circumference, and reaching the center doesn't mean abandoning the circumference." This spatial metaphor effectively conveyed how depth and breadth must go together.

Sufi orders developed institutional mechanisms to preserve orthodoxy across generations. Authentic transmission through recognized lineages ensured preservation of both method and doctrine. Each order traced its initiatic chain (silsila) to the Prophet, emphasizing continuity with Islamic tradition rather than innovation. Orders established daily practices combining obligatory prayers performed in congregation, supererogatory prayers and fasting, dhikr sessions with specific formulas, and study of classical texts. This comprehensive regimen integrated mystical practice with broader Islamic observance. Many Sufi masters were also recognized scholars of jurisprudence, hadith, and theology, ensuring mysticism remained grounded in traditional sciences. This dual expertise meant mystical insight was always balanced by legal and theological knowledge.

Major figures exemplified the integration of transcendent realization with orthodox practice, demonstrating their compatibility. 'Abd al-Qādir al-Jīlānī (d. 561/1166) was simultaneously the greatest Sufi master of his era and a respected Ḥanbalī jurist. His works seamlessly integrate mystical insight with legal precision, showing no tension between the two domains. Abū al-Ḥasan al-Shādhilī (d. 656/1258) emphasized that his disciples should excel in both outward practice and inward realization. His litanies combine profound mystical content with strictly orthodox formulations, never sacrificing one for the other. Jalāl al-Dīn Rūmī (d. 672/1273), despite his ecstatic poetry, maintained regular teaching of jurisprudence and issued legal opinions. His son Sultan Walad reports that his father never missed a prayer, even in states of mystical rapture. These examples demonstrated that the highest mystical realization was perfectly compatible with, indeed reinforced by, meticulous observance of Islamic law.

The Sufi approach to divine transcendence represents a unique contribution to Islamic thought—transforming theological doctrine into lived spiritual reality while maintaining orthodox boundaries. Through evocative sayings, systematic manuals, careful guidance, and preserved practice, Sufis developed methodologies for experiencing the One who is "naught is like unto Him" while avoiding the pitfalls of incarnationism or antinomianism.

The early Sufis' paradoxical utterances and teaching stories conveyed truths about divine incomparability that systematic theology could not capture. Their expressions, born from direct experience rather than conceptual speculation, enriched Islamic discourse about transcendence with experiential wisdom. The classical manuals transformed these scattered insights into comprehensive systems, making the mystical path accessible while maintaining quality control. By systematizing stages, states, and stations, they provided roadmaps for seekers while preserving the ultimate mystery of divine reality.

The emphasis on spiritual guidance recognizes that approaching transcendent reality requires more than individual effort—it demands authorized transmission, interpretive framework, and protective boundaries. The shaykh-murid relationship ensured that mystical experience enriched rather than undermined Islamic faith and practice. Most significantly, mainstream Sufism's preservation of orthodox practice while pursuing mystical realization demonstrates that experiencing divine transcendence need not lead to abandoning religious form. Instead, the forms become vehicles for deeper realization, their inner dimensions revealed through spiritual insight.

This integral approach continues to offer resources for contemporary Muslims seeking experiential knowledge of divine reality while remaining faithful to tradition. The Sufi synthesis suggests that the deepest appreciation of "laysa kamithlihi shay'un" comes not through philosophical speculation alone but through transformative spiritual practice guided by inherited wisdom and protected by orthodox boundaries.

Chapter 18. Ecstatic Utterances (Shathiyyat) in Historical Context

The phenomenon of ecstatic utterances (shaṭaḥāt, singular shaṭḥ) represents one of the most controversial yet illuminating aspects of Islamic mysticism. These spontaneous expressions, emerging from overwhelming spiritual experience, often appeared to violate the fundamental principle that "naught is like unto Him" by suggesting unity or identity with the Divine. Yet their persistence throughout Islamic history, the sophisticated interpretive strategies developed to understand them, and their eventual accommodation within orthodox frameworks reveal profound insights about the nature of mystical language and experience. This chapter examines the historical emergence of shaṭaḥāt, the interpretive frameworks developed by classical scholars, the boundaries established by orthodox authorities, and the enduring lessons these utterances provide for understanding how human language struggles to express encounters with divine transcendence.

The emergence of ecstatic utterances in early Sufism reflected the intensity of spiritual experience among the first generations of Muslim mystics, who found ordinary language inadequate to express their encounters with divine reality. The term shaṭḥ originally meant "movement" or "agitation," particularly the overflowing of a boiling pot. Early Sufis adopted it to describe words that "overflow" from an overpowering spiritual state. Al-Sarrāj (d. 378/988) provides an early definition in Kitāb al-Luma', explaining that shaṭḥ is an expression that occurs from the gnostic in a state of spiritual intoxication (sukr) and overwhelming divine manifestation (ghalabat al-wārid). It is like water overflowing from a vessel filled beyond capacity—the mystic cannot contain what he experiences and it spills out in words.

Abū Yazīd al-Bisṭāmī (d. 261/875) produced numerous shaṭaḥāt that shocked his contemporaries, including the famous "Glory be to me! How great is my station!" (Subḥānī mā a'ẓama sha'nī!), "I am the Throne and the Footstool!", and "Moses desired to see God; I do not desire to see God; He desires to see me!" When questioned about these utterances, al-Bisṭāmī would often claim no memory of them or provide interpretations. Regarding "Glory be to me," he later explained that this was God speaking about Himself through him. He was not present in that moment—only He was present. This claim that the mystic was absent during the utterance would become a crucial element in later interpretive frameworks.

Al-Ḥallāj (d. 309/922) became the most famous and controversial utterer of shaṭaḥāt. His declarations "I am the Real/Truth" (Anā al-Ḥaqq), "There is nothing in my cloak except God," and "I am the One whom I love, and the One whom I love is I; We are two spirits dwelling in one body" challenged the boundaries of acceptable mystical expression. His execution, partly due to these utterances, created a watershed moment in Islamic mysticism, forcing later Sufis to develop careful frameworks for understanding and contextualizing such expressions. The tragedy of al-Ḥallāj demonstrated that mystical experience, however profound, required appropriate expression and interpretation to avoid fatal misunderstanding.

Early sources emphasize that shaṭaḥāt emerged from specific spiritual states that temporarily overwhelmed normal consciousness. In states of annihilation (fanā'), al-Junayd (d. 298/910) explained, when the mystic experiences true fanā', his individual consciousness is effaced. What remains speaks, and that is not he but He. The shaṭḥ is divine speech through a human tongue whose owner is absent. This understanding that the mystic's ordinary consciousness was suspended during shaṭaḥāt provided crucial interpretive leverage. Divine overwhelm (ghalaba) represented another context. Al-Qushayrī (d. 465/1074) notes that the shaṭḥ occurs when divine manifestation overwhelms human capacity. Like lightning that splits a tree, divine tajallī can split normal consciousness, and what emerges are these extraordinary words. The metaphor of spiritual intoxication (sukr) proved particularly important. Al-Hujwīrī (d. 465/1074) writes that as the physically intoxicated says things he would never say when sober, the spiritually intoxicated by divine love speaks words that sobriety would forbid.

The early Muslim community reacted to shaṭaḥāt with a mixture of reverence, confusion, and alarm. Jurists worried about apparent blasphemy, with some arguing that claiming divinity, even in spiritual states, violated fundamental Islamic doctrine and potentially warranted capital punishment. Theologians saw threats to divine transcendence, concerned that if mystics could claim identity with God, the absolute distinction between Creator and creation seemed compromised. The general population often misunderstood these utterances literally, leading to accusations of incarnationism (ḥulūl) or unificationism (ittiḥād). Within Sufi circles, responses varied. Some, like al-Junayd, urged silence about such experiences. Others defended the utterers while developing interpretive frameworks that would protect both the mystics and the tradition.

As shaṭaḥāt became an established phenomenon, Muslim scholars developed sophisticated strategies for interpreting these problematic utterances while preserving both mystical insight and orthodox doctrine. In Kitāb al-Luma', al-Sarrāj established interpretive principles that would influence all subsequent discussion. First, he distinguished state from station, explaining that shaṭḥ emerges from temporary states (aḥwāl), not permanent stations (maqāmāt). It reflects a momentary experience, not an achieved realization. Second, he emphasized the absence of the speaker, teaching that in true shaṭḥ, the speaker is absent. The individual consciousness is suspended, and what speaks is divine presence through human absence. Third, he insisted on the metaphorical nature of these expressions, explaining that they use the language of union metaphorically (majāzan), not literally (ḥaqīqatan). When al-Ḥallāj says 'I am the Real,' the 'I' has already vanished. These principles provided the foundation for all later interpretation.

Abū Bakr al-Kalābādhī (d. 385/995) in al-Ta'arruf provided theological grounding for understanding shaṭaḥāt within orthodox frameworks. The shaṭaḥāt do not indicate that the mystic becomes God or God becomes the mystic, he explained. Rather, they indicate the complete dominance of divine attributes over human attributes in the mystic's consciousness. The drop does not become the ocean; it realizes it was always part of the ocean. He established crucial distinctions that operated on multiple levels simultaneously. Ontologically, the mystic's essence remains created and distinct. Experientially, the mystic's consciousness may be overwhelmed by divine presence. Linguistically, human language lacks vocabulary for such experiences. These distinctions allowed for acknowledgment of profound mystical experience without compromising the fundamental ontological distinction between Creator and creature.

Al-Qushayrī dedicated a full section to shaṭaḥāt in his Risāla, providing the most influential classical treatment. He categorized different types of ecstatic utterances to facilitate interpretation. Shaṭḥ of description involves describing divine attributes as if one's own. Shaṭḥ of claim involves claiming stations beyond one's actual state. Shaṭḥ of unity involves expressing experiences of divine unity. When interpreting shaṭḥ, he taught, one must consider the speaker's known character and adherence to sharī'a, the specific spiritual state producing the utterance, the possibility of metaphorical rather than literal meaning, and the danger of taking ecstatic speech as sober doctrine. Al-Qushayrī strongly preferred the "sober" approach, teaching that the perfect ones are those who experience what the intoxicated experience but maintain outward composure. They taste the wine but show no signs of drunkenness. This preference for sobriety would become increasingly dominant in later Sufism.

In Kashf al-Maḥjūb, al-Hujwīrī provides systematic analysis that further refined interpretive strategies. Shaṭaḥāt fall into four categories, he explains. True shaṭḥ emerges from authentic overwhelm and requires interpretation. Pretentious shaṭḥ represents false claims from those seeking reputation. Imitative shaṭḥ involves copying masters without genuine experience. Satanic shaṭḥ consists of delusions mistaken for divine inspiration. He provides criteria for discrimination, teaching that true shaṭḥ is involuntary, produces humility afterward, and is accompanied by increased adherence to sharī'a. False shaṭḥ is deliberate, produces pride, and leads to laxity in practice. These criteria provided practical tools for spiritual directors to distinguish authentic experience from its counterfeits.

Ibn 'Arabī transformed understanding of shaṭaḥāt through his metaphysical system. The shaṭḥ is not error but premature disclosure, he taught. The mystic speaks a metaphysical truth—that only God truly exists—but speaks it in the wrong context, to the wrong audience, in the wrong language. The truth requires wrapping in appropriate expression. He distinguishes levels of truth that must be held simultaneously. Metaphysically, only God possesses real existence. Theologically, Creator and creation are distinct. Legally, claiming divinity is forbidden. Mystically, all levels are simultaneously valid. This sophisticated framework acknowledged that statements could be true at one level while problematic at another, requiring careful contextualization rather than simple acceptance or rejection.

Later scholars synthesized these approaches into comprehensive frameworks. 'Abd al-Ghanī al-Nābulusī (d. 1143/1731) summarizes centuries of interpretation: "The shaṭḥ is like lightning—illuminating for an instant realities normally hidden. But like lightning, it can blind those unprepared for its brilliance. The wise seek the illumination while protecting themselves and others from the blinding flash." This metaphor captured both the value and danger of ecstatic utterances, suggesting why they required careful management rather than either suppression or uncritical celebration.

The Islamic tradition's engagement with shaṭaḥāt reveals a complex process of negotiation between mystical experience and orthodox boundaries, resulting in sophisticated frameworks that preserved both. Initial orthodox reactions ranged from outright condemnation to cautious acceptance. The trial and execution of al-Ḥallāj in 309/922 marked a decisive moment. While political factors were involved, his shaṭaḥāt provided the legal pretext. The charges included claiming divinity through saying "Anā al-Ḥaqq," teaching the sufficiency of internal pilgrimage, and suggesting ritual prayer could be performed anywhere. Yet even his execution was controversial. Many scholars defended him, arguing his words were misunderstood or taken out of context. The martyrdom of al-Ḥallāj created a permanent reminder of the stakes involved in mystical expression.

As the leading Sufi authority, al-Junayd established a moderate position that would become mainstream: "These utterances are true for those who understand and poison for those who don't. Therefore, speak to people according to their understanding. Keep the secrets of lordship hidden." This became the dominant Sufi position—acknowledge the reality behind shaṭaḥāt while discouraging their public expression. The wisdom lay not in denying mystical experience but in recognizing that its communication required appropriate audience and context.

Orthodox scholars developed several strategies to accommodate shaṭaḥāt while maintaining boundaries. The principle of charitable interpretation, established by al-Ghazālī in Fayṣal al-Tafriqa, held that when a statement admits of both belief and unbelief interpretations, charity requires choosing the interpretation consistent with faith, especially when the speaker is known for piety. The state versus statement distinction proved equally important. Scholars distinguished between the spiritual state (ḥāl), which was potentially valid and from God; the verbal expression (qāl), which was potentially problematic and requiring interpretation; and the doctrinal claim (i'tiqād), which must conform to orthodox belief. This triple distinction allowed acknowledgment of authentic spiritual experience while maintaining doctrinal boundaries. The private-public divide provided another protective framework. Ibn 'Aṭā' Allah articulated that what occurs between the servant and his Lord in private is not subject to legal judgment. But what is expressed publicly must conform to sharī'a requirements.

Sufi orders developed institutional mechanisms for managing shaṭaḥāt that balanced spiritual freedom with communal coherence. Orders created safe spaces for ecstatic expression through private gatherings (khalwa) where shaṭaḥāt could occur without scandal, interpretation sessions where masters explained problematic utterances, and gradual preparation ensuring disciples understood context before exposure. Only qualified shaykhs could determine authenticity of shaṭaḥāt, provide orthodox interpretation, and decide what could be shared publicly. Advanced texts taught how to understand shaṭaḥāt through standard curriculum like al-Qushayrī's Risāla, commentaries on famous shaṭaḥāt providing orthodox readings, and warning literature highlighting dangers of imitation.

Despite accommodations, clear boundaries were maintained regarding what remained absolutely prohibited. Direct claims to divinity, denial of Creator-creature distinction, rejection of religious obligations, and teaching antinomian doctrines could not be accepted regardless of the spiritual state claimed. When shaṭaḥāt occurred, they must be involuntary rather than deliberate, followed by "return" to normal consciousness, accompanied by increased religious observance, and interpreted within orthodox frameworks. The tradition increasingly emphasized sobriety (ṣaḥw) over intoxication (sukr). Al-Qushayrī notes that the perfect ones experience what produces shaṭḥ in others but maintain perfect composure. This is superior to losing control. This preference for integration over dramatic expression reflected spiritual maturity.

Several historical examples illustrate successful accommodation of potentially problematic mystical expression. Ibn al-Fāriḍ (d. 632/1235) wrote poetry containing apparent shaṭaḥāt: "I am the one I love, and the one I love is I / We are two spirits dwelling in one body." Orthodox scholars accepted these as poetic metaphor rather than credal statement, expression of mystical experience rather than theological doctrine, and protected by the conventions of Arabic poetry. When al-Shādhilī (d. 656/1258) experienced states producing potential shaṭaḥāt, he would say: "O God, You know what my tongue would say if I allowed it. Accept the intention without the expression." This became a model for experiencing overwhelming states while maintaining orthodox expression, demonstrating that spiritual realization could be preserved without problematic articulation.

The historical phenomenon of shaṭaḥāt provides enduring lessons about the nature of mystical language and its relationship to transcendent experience. Shaṭaḥāt dramatically illustrate language's inadequacy before transcendent reality. When human consciousness encounters divine reality, ordinary language categories break down in experiential overflow. The shaṭḥ represents language pushed beyond its limits, struggling to express the inexpressible. The apparently contradictory nature of many shaṭaḥāt—claiming to be God while remaining human—functions as paradoxical pointer to realities that transcend either-or logic. They suggest experiences where normal distinctions temporarily dissolve without being ontologically erased. The tradition's recognition that shaṭaḥāt require metaphorical interpretation reveals that all language about ultimate reality is necessarily figurative, pointing beyond itself rather than capturing its object.

The controversy surrounding shaṭaḥāt highlights the social dimension of religious language. The same expression might illuminate the prepared and scandalize the unprepared, leading to emphasis on speaking according to the audience's capacity. The need for authoritative interpretation shows that mystical experience, while personal, requires communal frameworks for understanding and integration. The varying receptions of similar utterances reveals how social, political, and institutional factors shape the boundary between acceptable and unacceptable mystical expression. These observations demonstrate that religious language operates within social matrices that condition both its production and reception.

The phenomenon of shaṭaḥāt provides insights into mystical psychology. The temporary dissolution of self-consciousness that produces shaṭaḥāt illustrates the mystical teaching that the ego veils divine reality. When it dissolves, what remains speaks. The tradition's emphasis on "return" (rujū') after ecstatic states highlights the importance of integrating peak experiences with ongoing life rather than remaining suspended in extraordinary states. The preference for maintaining composure during intense spiritual states points to a sophisticated understanding of spiritual development that values integration over dramatic expression, suggesting that the highest realization maintains equilibrium rather than exhibiting extraordinary behavior.

The interpretation of shaṭaḥāt established hermeneutical principles applicable beyond mysticism. Understanding requires contextual reading that considers the speaker's overall character and teaching, the specific circumstances of utterance, the intended audience, and the broader framework of meaning. The recognition that the same statement might be metaphysically true, theologically problematic, legally unacceptable, and mystically profound provides a multiplex understanding that enriches Islamic hermeneutics generally. The principle of interpreting ambiguous statements in the best possible light, especially from those known for piety, provides a model for charitable religious discourse that seeks understanding before condemnation.

The lessons from shaṭaḥāt remain relevant for contemporary concerns. In interfaith dialogue, understanding how the Islamic tradition dealt with apparently blasphemous mystical utterances provides resources for understanding similar phenomena in other traditions without either dismissing or literalizing them. For the psychology of religion, the shaṭaḥ phenomenon offers data for understanding peak experiences, ego dissolution, and the relationship between consciousness and language. Regarding religious authority, the tradition's management of shaṭaḥāt illustrates how religious communities balance individual experience with communal norms, neither suppressing personal spirituality nor allowing it to undermine collective coherence. In mystical literature, recognizing the special nature of ecstatic utterance helps in reading mystical literature from any tradition, distinguishing poetic metaphor from doctrinal statement and appreciating the full range of mystical expression.

The phenomenon of ecstatic utterances in Islamic mysticism reveals the profound tension between transcendent experience and human expression. These spontaneous overflows of spiritual experience challenged fundamental Islamic teachings about divine transcendence while simultaneously pointing to the deepest truths of tawḥīd—that only God possesses true existence. The sophisticated interpretive strategies developed by classical scholars demonstrate Islam's capacity to preserve both mystical insight and orthodox doctrine. Rather than simply suppressing or uncritically accepting shaṭaḥāt, the tradition developed nuanced frameworks that acknowledged their experiential validity while maintaining necessary boundaries.

The orthodox accommodations achieved reveal a mature religious tradition capable of holding creative tension between order and ecstasy, law and spirit, sobriety and intoxication. The frameworks developed allowed mystics to explore the furthest reaches of spiritual experience while remaining within the broad tent of Islamic orthodoxy. Most significantly, the lessons derived from this historical phenomenon extend beyond Islamic mysticism. They illuminate universal questions about the relationship between experience and expression, the social nature of religious language, and the challenges of articulating encounters with transcendent reality. The Islamic tradition's engagement with shaṭaḥāt provides a model for how religious communities can honor profound spiritual experience while maintaining communal coherence and doctrinal integrity.

In an age where various forms of spiritual experience seek expression, the wisdom gained from centuries of Islamic engagement with ecstatic utterances remains profoundly relevant, offering insights into both the possibilities and limitations of human language in the face of divine mystery.

Chapter 19. Annihilation and Subsistence: Classical Formulations

The paired concepts of fanā' (annihilation) and baqā' (subsistence) represent perhaps the most distinctive and profound teachings in Islamic mysticism regarding the soul's journey toward divine reality. These terms describe the transformation of human consciousness when it encounters the Absolute—the "passing away" of the limited self and the "remaining" in divine presence. While apparently suggesting a dissolution of the fundamental distinction expressed in "laysa kamithlihi shay'un," classical formulations carefully preserved divine transcendence while articulating genuine mystical experience. This chapter examines the scriptural precedents for these concepts, their development in early Sufi thought, their systematic elaboration in classical manuals, and the orthodox interpretations and safeguards that prevented their misunderstanding.

While the technical terms fanā' and baqā' do not appear in their mystical sense in the Quran or hadith, Sufi thinkers identified numerous scriptural precedents that laid the foundation for these concepts. The Quran contains several passages that Sufis interpreted as indicating the annihilation of the ephemeral and subsistence of the eternal. Most fundamental is the verse "Everyone upon it [the earth] will perish (fān), and there will remain (yabqā) the Face of your Lord, Owner of Majesty and Honor" (55:26-27). This verse, using the very roots f-n-y and b-q-y, became central to Sufi understanding. Al-Qushayrī (d. 465/1074) comments that this teaches that all existence is perishing except the divine Face, with the mystic realizing this truth experientially—witnessing his own perishing nature and God's eternal subsistence. Al-Ghazālī elaborates in Iḥyā' 'Ulūm al-Dīn that the 'Face' that remains is not a physical face but the divine essence and attributes. Everything perishes in its independent existence while subsisting through divine existence.

The verse "Indeed we belong to Allah, and indeed to Him we are returning" (2:156) provided another crucial foundation. Early Sufis understood this not only as referring to physical death but as describing the spiritual return to the origin. Al-Junayd (d. 298/910) interpreted this return (rujū') to Allah as the fanā' from all that is other than Him. We return to the state before we were—existing in His knowledge without independent existence. The account of Moses and the mountain became the paradigmatic example of fanā'. When Moses asked to see God and the divine manifestation struck the mountain, causing it to crumble while Moses fell unconscious (7:143), this represented what happens to all contingent existence before divine manifestation. Al-Sarrāj (d. 378/988) explains that the mountain's crumbling represents what happens to all contingent existence before divine manifestation, while Moses's unconsciousness shows fanā' of human consciousness in divine presence.

Verses describing divine presence also pointed toward the necessity of self-effacement. "And He is with you wherever you are" (57:4) and "We are nearer to him than his jugular vein" (50:16) suggested that realizing divine presence required the effacement of the illusion of independent selfhood. Ibn 'Arabī notes the paradox: how can you be conscious of yourself when He is nearer than your self? True consciousness is consciousness of Him, requiring unconsciousness of independent self.

Several prophetic traditions provided foundations for understanding fanā' and baqā'. The hadith of voluntary devotions became central to understanding how human attributes could be "annihilated" in divine attributes: "My servant continues to draw near to Me with voluntary devotions until I love him. When I love him, I am his hearing with which he hears, his sight with which he sees, his hand with which he strikes, and his foot with which he walks" (Bukhārī). Al-Kalābādhī (d. 385/995) interprets this as not meaning God becomes the servant's limbs, but that the servant's actions become so aligned with divine will that only divine agency remains apparent. The hadith of divine jealousy indicated that true tawḥīd requires fanā' from all attachments: "Allah is jealous (yaghār), and Allah's jealousy is that His servant should not love anything except Him" (Muslim). Al-Qushayrī comments that divine jealousy demands that nothing remain in the heart except Him, achieved through fanā' from all that is other than Him.

The Prophet's prayer "O Allah, You are the First, so there is nothing before You; and You are the Last, so there is nothing after You; and You are the Manifest, so there is nothing above You; and You are the Hidden, so there is nothing beyond You" (Muslim) pointed toward the reality that only God truly exists. Al-Ghazālī notes that when nothing is before, after, above, or beyond Him, what remains for us? Only fanā' in His absolute reality. Early Quranic commentators recognized these mystical implications. Al-Ḥasan al-Baṣrī (d. 110/728) on "Everything perishes except His Face" taught that this verse has levels, with the apparent meaning referring to the Day of Judgment while the inner meaning is that at every moment, everything is perishing except what is for His Face. Ja'far al-Ṣādiq (d. 148/765) interpreted the verse about returning to Allah as having stages: returning from sins through repentance, returning from heedlessness through remembrance, and returning from seeing the self through fanā'.

The concepts of fanā' and baqā' evolved from scattered insights into systematic doctrine through the experiences and teachings of early Sufi masters. Rābi'a al-'Adawiyya (d. 185/801) expressed early insights without using technical terms when she said: "My existence is a sin with which no other sin can be compared." This pointed toward the need for fanā' of the self claiming independent existence. Ibrāhīm ibn Adham (d. 161/777) described stages of progressive annihilation: first, abandon the world through fanā' from worldly attachments; second, abandon the abandonment through fanā' from the act of abandoning; third, abandon all consciousness of abandonment through fanā' from fanā'.

The Baghdad masters developed the first systematic understanding of these concepts. Al-Muḥāsibī (d. 243/857) distinguished types of fanā' that would influence all later formulations. Fanā' of the attributes (ṣifāt) occurs when base qualities are replaced by praiseworthy ones. Fanā' of the actions (af'āl) happens when one sees all actions as from God. Fanā' of the essence (dhāt) represents the stage when consciousness of self vanishes entirely. Abū Yazīd al-Bisṭāmī (d. 261/875) provided experiential descriptions that conveyed the phenomenology of these states: "I gazed at Him with the eye of certainty after He had turned me away from all else. Then He illuminated me with His light, showed me His wonders and revealed to me His secrets. Then I gazed at myself with His eye, and my light vanished in His light, my might in His might." He also described baqā' in paradoxical terms: "After thirty years of spiritual practice, I looked and saw that He was my mirror—rather, I was my own mirror, for I was He and He was I." Such expressions required careful interpretation to preserve orthodox boundaries.

Al-Junayd (d. 298/910) provided the most influential early formulation, balancing mystical experience with theological sobriety. He defined fanā' as the passing away of vision of the actions through witnessing the Actor, then passing away of the attributes through witnessing the Described, then passing away of the essence through witnessing the Essence. He crucially added that true fanā' is followed by baqā'—subsistence in God. This is not the creature becoming the Creator, but the creature subsisting through the Creator while knowing the distinction. His famous definition captured the paradox with precision: "Fanā' is that you be His, without you, and that He be as He has always been." This preserved both mystical union and metaphysical distinction, establishing the framework all later Sufis would build upon.

Other early masters elaborated different aspects of the teaching. Al-Nūrī (d. 295/908) emphasized the experiential nature, teaching that fanā' cannot be learned from books or achieved through practices alone. It comes when God draws His servant to Himself, annihilating him from himself. Al-Shiblī (d. 334/946) added paradoxical depth by observing that fanā' is to perish from perceiving fanā'. If you are conscious of your annihilation, you are not annihilated. True fanā' has no self-awareness. Al-Wāsiṭī (d. 320/932) connected fanā' and baqā' as inseparable aspects of one reality: "Fanā' without baqā' is incompletion. Baqā' without fanā' is impossible. They are two faces of one reality—dying to the false self and living through the True Self."

As Sufism developed into a systematic discipline, major manuals provided comprehensive treatments of fanā' and baqā', establishing frameworks that would guide centuries of practice and understanding. Al-Sarrāj (d. 378/988) provided one of the earliest systematic treatments in Kitāb al-Luma', distinguishing three degrees of fanā'. The fanā' of the novice involves annihilation of blameworthy qualities. The fanā' of the intermediate involves annihilation of praiseworthy qualities through seeing them as from God. The fanā' of the realized involves annihilation of the consciousness of annihilation. He related these degrees to types of knowledge, teaching that knowledge of certainty ('ilm al-yaqīn) leads to fanā' from doubt, eye of certainty ('ayn al-yaqīn) leads to fanā' from self, and truth of certainty (ḥaqq al-yaqīn) leads to fanā' from all else. He provided crucial safeguards, insisting that he who claims fanā' while violating sharī'a is deluded. True fanā' increases observance of divine commands rather than decreasing it.

Al-Qushayrī's treatment in his Risāla became the standard reference for understanding these concepts. He provides a comprehensive definition: "Fanā' is the dropping away of the servant's attributes through the dominance of divine decree and the subsistence of divine attributes in place of human attributes." He distinguished multiple types of fanā' arranged in progressive order. Fanā' 'an al-ma'āṣī, or fanā' from sins, represents the beginning of the path. Fanā' 'an al-ghafla, or fanā' from heedlessness, constitutes the path itself. Fanā' 'an al-ṣifāt, or fanā' from attributes, represents approaching the goal. Fanā' 'an shuhūd al-fanā', or fanā' from witnessing annihilation, constitutes the goal itself. He emphasized the necessity of baqā', teaching that fanā' without baqā' is deficiency. The complete servant experiences fanā' of his human attributes and baqā' through divine attributes, while maintaining the sharī'a obligations that recognize servanthood. He warned against those who use fanā' to justify sin, claiming they have transcended good and evil. True fanā' makes one more scrupulous, not less.

Al-Hujwīrī provided analytical clarity in Kashf al-Maḥjūb through careful metaphysical distinctions. Fanā' does not mean the essence of the servant ceases to exist—this is impossible, for what God creates cannot become uncreated. Rather, it means the attributes and claims of the servant are annihilated. He distinguished three aspects of this experience. Fanā' of vision (mushāhada) involves seeing only God's acts. Fanā' of existence (wujūd) involves feeling only God's existence. Fanā' of knowledge (ma'rifa) involves knowing only through God's knowledge. Regarding the return, he taught that after fanā' comes baqā', which is not remaining as you were before, but remaining as you truly are—a servant whose existence and attributes are sustained by God.

Al-Ghazālī achieved masterful synthesis across multiple works, integrating philosophical precision with mystical insight. In Iḥyā' 'Ulūm al-Dīn, he taught that the path to God has two parts: journeying to God (sayr ilā Allah) which culminates in fanā', and journeying in God (sayr fī Allah) which is baqā'. The first removes veils; the second is endless exploration of divine perfections. He provided philosophical framework by explaining that existence belongs only to God. What we call our existence is like a loan that must be returned. Fanā' is recognizing this loan and returning it to its Owner. Baqā' is receiving it back as a trust, knowing its true Owner. He outlined practical method, teaching that fanā' is achieved through constant dhikr until only the Remembered remains, through contemplation until only the Contemplated exists, and through love until lover vanishes in Beloved. In Mishkāt al-Anwār, he presented levels of fanā' corresponding to the levels of light: fanā' from darkness through abandoning sin and ignorance, fanā' from sensory lights through transcending worldly attractions, fanā' from intellectual lights through moving beyond one's own understanding, and fanā' in the Light of lights.

Ibn 'Arabī transformed understanding through metaphysical precision that integrated mystical experience with philosophical rigor. Fanā' and baqā' are not sequential but simultaneous, he taught. At every moment, the servant is fānin or perishing in his temporality and bāqin or subsisting through divine permanence. Realization is becoming conscious of what always is. He distinguished levels of realization that progressively deepen this awareness. Fanā' of actions involves witnessing that there is no agent but God. Fanā' of attributes involves witnessing that there are no attributes but God's. Fanā' of essence involves witnessing that there is no existence but God's. He articulated the ultimate paradox: the highest fanā' is fanā' from fanā'—ceasing to be conscious of one's annihilation. And the highest baqā' is baqā' through fanā'—subsisting through the very annihilation of independent existence.

The potential for misunderstanding fanā' and baqā' as compromising the Creator-creature distinction led to careful orthodox interpretations and safeguards that preserved both mystical insight and theological boundaries. Orthodox scholars developed precise theological frameworks to prevent misunderstanding. Al-Ghazālī emphasizes that fanā' never means the servant's essence becomes the divine essence. Essences cannot transform into one another. Rather, the servant's consciousness is so overwhelmed by divine presence that he is unconscious of himself. Al-Qushayrī clarifies the crucial distinction between experience and ontology: "Fanā' is an experiential state (ḥāl wijdānī), not an ontological reality (ḥaqīqa wujūdiyya). The servant experiences absence of self-consciousness, not absence of self-existence." Ibn al-Jawzī (d. 597/1201) insists on the metaphorical nature of mystical language: "When Sufis speak of 'becoming God' through fanā', this is metaphorical like saying 'he became all ear' when listening intently. The expression indicates complete absorption, not literal transformation."

Orthodox authorities established clear boundaries regarding religious practice. Al-Sha'rānī (d. 973/1565) states categorically that anyone who claims fanā' exempts him from prayer, fasting, or moral obligations has neither achieved fanā' nor understood it. True fanā' produces meticulous observance. Authorities established behavioral criteria, insisting that genuine fanā' must result in increased humility rather than pride, greater compassion rather than indifference, stricter observance rather than laxity, and better character rather than antinomianism. Following al-Junayd, mainstream tradition emphasized the sobriety requirement: the perfect ones experience fanā' while maintaining outward sobriety. Losing control is imperfection; maintaining composure during overwhelming experience is completion.

Sufi orders developed institutional safeguards to ensure proper understanding and practice. Gradual preparation became essential, with orders establishing that fanā' should not be sought prematurely. Years of ethical purification, mastery of religious obligations, study of orthodox theology, and authorization from a qualified guide were required before practices leading to fanā' could be undertaken. Practices potentially leading to fanā' were carefully supervised through specific dhikr formulas at appropriate stages, limited periods of intense practice, regular assessment by the shaykh, and integration periods between intense experiences. Interpretive authority was carefully controlled, with only authorized shaykhs able to confirm authentic fanā' experiences, provide orthodox interpretation, authorize disciples to guide others, and determine readiness for advanced practices.

Orthodox scholars addressed frequent errors and misunderstandings. Against monistic interpretations that understood fanā' as proving only God exists, authorities clarified that fanā' reveals only God possesses independent existence. Creation exists dependently, not independently, but it does exist. Against claims of divine incarnation, they insisted that in fanā', divine attributes manifest through the servant, not divine essence in the servant. Light shines through glass without becoming glass. Against antinomian abandonment of religious law, they emphasized that the Prophet, the most perfect in fanā' and baqā', was the most scrupulous in sharī'a. Lesser beings claiming exemption prove their delusion.

Mainstream scholars provided positive orthodox formulations that integrated mystical experience with theological precision. Al-Sha'rānī's synthesis explains fanā' as the realization of our essential poverty (faqr) before God's essential wealth (ghinā), with baqā' being subsisting through His strength while knowing our weakness. Ibn 'Aṭā' Allah's practical approach defines fanā' as being absent from creation through presence with the Creator, with baqā' being returning to creation with the Creator, serving Him through serving them. Al-Nābulusī's metaphysical precision presents fanā' as the experimental realization of the theological truth that God alone is necessarily existent, with baqā' being living this truth while fulfilling the duties of contingent existence.

The classical formulations of fanā' and baqā' represent one of Islamic mysticism's most sophisticated contributions to understanding the relationship between divine transcendence and human spiritual experience. These concepts articulate how the soul can experience the reality that "naught is like unto Him" without compromising the fundamental distinction between Creator and creation. From Quranic verses about perishing and remaining through prophetic traditions about divine nearness, early Muslims recognized scriptural precedents for these profound spiritual realities. The development through early Sufi thought shows how raw experience gradually became refined understanding, culminating in al-Junayd's balanced formulation that preserved both mystical depth and theological sobriety.

The systematic treatments in classical manuals transformed personal insights into teachable doctrine, providing maps for seekers while warning of pitfalls. These works show remarkable sophistication in distinguishing experiential states from ontological claims, preserving orthodox theology while validating profound spiritual experience. The orthodox interpretations and safeguards demonstrate Islam's capacity to integrate potentially controversial mystical teachings within acceptable frameworks. By insisting that true fanā' enhances rather than eliminates religious observance, by requiring qualified guidance, and by maintaining clear theological boundaries, the tradition created space for profound mystical experience within orthodox Islam.

Perhaps most significantly, the teaching of fanā' and baqā' provides a lived resolution to the apparent paradox of divine transcendence and immanence. Through fanā', the mystic experientially realizes divine transcendence by witnessing the utter dependence of all existence. Through baqā', he lives this realization while maintaining the servant-Lord relationship essential to Islamic worship. This classical formulation continues to offer profound insights for contemporary seekers, providing a framework for understanding ego-transcendence that avoids both the nihilism of mere annihilation and the inflation of claiming divinity. In showing how human consciousness can be transformed by encountering the One who is "naught is like unto Him," while remaining within the boundaries of orthodox belief and practice, the tradition of fanā' and baqā' represents one of Islam's most sophisticated and enduring contributions to the world's mystical heritage.

Chapter 20. Divine Love in Classical Sufi Literature

Divine love (maḥabba, 'ishq, ḥubb) occupies a central position in Islamic mysticism, transforming the understanding of divine transcendence from abstract theological principle into lived experiential reality. While maintaining that "naught is like unto Him," Sufi literature developed sophisticated frameworks for understanding how love bridges the gulf between the Incomparable Divine and human hearts. This chapter examines how Quranic and prophetic sources established foundations for divine love, how early Sufis expressed this love in revolutionary ways, how classical texts systematized the stations and states of love, and how this potentially controversial teaching was integrated with Islamic law and theology.

The Quran and hadith literature provide rich foundations for understanding divine love, though early mystics would draw out implications that went far beyond surface readings. The Quran speaks of divine love in multiple contexts, establishing different dimensions that Sufis would later elaborate. The verse of mutual love stands as foundational: "O you who believe! Whoever among you turns back from his religion, Allah will bring a people whom He loves and who love Him (yuḥibbuhum wa yuḥibbūnahu)" (5:54). Al-Qushayrī (d. 465/1074) comments in his Laṭā'if al-Ishārāt that this verse establishes the reality of mutual love between God and servants. Divine love is not metaphorical but real, though its reality differs from human love as His essence differs from ours.

The Quran mentions both those whom Allah loves and those He does not love, establishing conditional and unconditional dimensions. Allah loves those who do good (2:195), those who are patient (3:146), while He does not love the oppressors (3:57). Al-Ghazālī explains in Iḥyā' 'Ulūm al-Dīn that divine love has levels. His general love encompasses all existence—else nothing would exist. His special love is for those who embody beautiful qualities. His elect love is for those who love Him for Himself alone. The verse of following became particularly central to Sufi understanding: "Say: If you love Allah, then follow me; Allah will love you and forgive your sins" (3:31). This verse, known as āyat al-ikhtibār or the verse of testing, provided the entire structure of the path. Al-Junayd (d. 298/910) taught that this verse contains the entire path: claim of love, test through following, divine response with love, and ultimate forgiveness—union through love.

Verses about divine beauty and human form also contributed to understanding love's foundations. "He is the one who shapes you in the wombs as He wills" (3:6) and "We have certainly created man in the best form" (95:4) suggested deeper meanings. Ibn 'Arabī connects divine beauty to love by observing that God created humans in the best form because the Lover (al-Muḥibb) naturally creates the beloved beautifully. Creation itself is an act of divine love expressing itself.

The hadith literature provides crucial foundations, particularly one sacred hadith that became central to all Sufi discussions of divine love: "I was a Hidden Treasure and I loved to be known (aḥbabtu an u'raf), so I created creation in order that I might be known." Though debated by hadith scholars regarding its authenticity, this tradition's influence on Sufi thought was immense. Al-Ghazālī comments that this hadith reveals love as the motive for creation itself. The cosmos exists because divine love sought an object—though He needs no object, love's nature is to overflow. The hadith of divine rejoicing provided another key insight: "Allah rejoices more at His servant's repentance than one of you who finds his lost camel in the desert" (Bukhārī and Muslim). Rābi'a al-'Adawiyya (d. 185/801) reflected that if He rejoices at our return, what of His state when we dwell constantly in His presence through love? This joy is not need but the Beloved's pleasure in the lover's arrival.

The hadith of voluntary devotions established the progressive nature of divine love: "My servant continues to draw near to Me with voluntary works until I love him..." (Bukhārī). Al-Sarrāj (d. 378/988) analyzes the process revealed in this tradition. Note the progression: first the servant loves through voluntary devotions, then God responds with love, then transformation occurs—the servant hears and sees through divine attributes.

Early Quranic commentators recognized love's centrality in scripture. Al-Ḥasan al-Baṣrī (d. 110/728) on "whom He loves and who love Him" taught that their love for Him is preferring Him over all else, while His love for them is drawing them near and removing veils. But His love is eternal while theirs is temporal—He loved them before they loved Him. Ja'far al-Ṣādiq (d. 148/765) taught that there are three types of love: the common people love God for His favors, the elect love Him for His beauty, the elect of the elect love Him for Himself with no cause. Muqātil ibn Sulaymān (d. 150/767) interpreted God's love as meaning He wills good for them, draws them near, and accepts their works. It is not like human love with need and emotion.

The early Sufis transformed love from theological concept to lived reality, often through expressions that challenged conventional understanding. Rābi'a al-'Adawiyya revolutionized Islamic spirituality by making divine love central. Her famous prayer encapsulates disinterested love: "O God, if I worship You from fear of Hell, burn me in Hell. If I worship You from hope of Paradise, exclude me from Paradise. But if I worship You for Your own sake, do not withhold from me Your eternal beauty." She explained that she has two loves for Him—a selfish love and a love worthy of Him. The selfish love is her remembrance of Him excluding all else. The worthy love is when He lifts the veils so she sees Him. No praise to her for either—praise belongs to Him for both. Her emphasis on love's exclusivity appeared radical. When asked about Satan, she replied that her love for the Real leaves no room to hate Satan. When asked about the Prophet, she said she loves him, but love of the Creator has so occupied her that no room remains for loving the created. She defined love as existence itself, declaring that she exists in two states: presence and absence. When He is present, she is absent. When she is present, He is veiled. Love is when only presence remains—His.

The Baghdad school developed these insights with greater systematization. Sarī al-Saqaṭī (d. 253/867) defined stages, teaching that love has three degrees: common love, which comes from divine favors; elite love, which comes from witnessing divine attributes; elect love, which comes from divine self-disclosure to the heart. Al-Muḥāsibī (d. 243/857) provided psychological analysis, explaining that love transforms the lover—his qualities become the Beloved's qualities, his will becomes the Beloved's will, his existence becomes a mirror reflecting the Beloved. Al-Junayd's synthesis balanced sobriety with love, teaching that love is the replacement of the lover's qualities with the Beloved's qualities. But this is not incarnation—it is the polishing of the mirror until only the Beloved's reflection appears.

Ecstatic expressions pushed language to its limits in attempting to convey love's overwhelming reality. Abū Yazīd al-Bisṭāmī (d. 261/875) exclaimed: "Your love makes lovers wander lost. Your face makes the beautiful ugly by comparison. Your perfect nature makes the wise appear fools. Your creatures are veiled from You by You—what veils You who have no veil?" Al-Ḥallāj (d. 309/922) expressed love through apparent paradox: "I am whom I love, and whom I love is I, We are two spirits dwelling in one body. If you see me, you see Him, And if you see Him, you see us both." He explained that love annihilates the lover in the Beloved until no trace of the lover remains. What speaks then is love itself, not the lover. Al-Nūrī (d. 295/908) demonstrated love dramatically by throwing himself into the Tigris, crying: "If I am truthful in my love, let the water not touch me!" Witnesses reported he walked on water. He explained that love makes the impossible possible.

Early theoretical frameworks emerged to organize these intense experiences. Dhū al-Nūn al-Miṣrī (d. 245/859) distinguished types of love: love of gratitude (maḥabbat al-shukr) arising from blessings, love of contemplation (maḥabbat al-naẓar) arising from beauty, and love of correspondence (maḥabbat al-munāsaba) arising from affinity. Al-Shiblī (d. 334/946) emphasized love's transformative power, teaching that love is a fire that burns everything except the Beloved's will. When it burns you, you think you exist. When it consumes you, you realize only He exists.

As Sufism developed systematic literature, divine love received comprehensive treatment in major manuals. Al-Sarrāj provided early systematic analysis in Kitāb al-Luma', defining love (maḥabba) as the heart's inclination toward what corresponds to it. Divine love is the heart's inclination toward God through witnessing His beauty, perfection, and favor. He distinguished degrees of love, with the love of the common arising from blessings and favors, the love of the sincere arising from proximity and intimacy, and the love of the gnostics arising from essential correspondence. He identified signs of love as preferring the Beloved's choice over one's own, remembering the Beloved constantly, and finding pleasure in solitude with the Beloved.

In analyzing Sufi doctrine, al-Kalābādhī (d. 385/995) addressed theological concerns in his Ta'arruf. The Sufis affirm real love between God and servants while maintaining divine transcendence, he explained. God's love is not need or emotion but will and favor. The servant's love is not mere obedience but total absorption in the Beloved. He addressed the controversial term 'ishq or passionate love, noting that some Sufis use 'ishq for divine love while theologians object that 'ishq implies excess. The Sufis respond that in loving the Infinite, no excess is possible.

Al-Qushayrī's section on love in his Risāla became definitive for the tradition. His comprehensive definition states that maḥabba is a state (ḥāl) that overcomes the heart when contemplating the Beloved's perfection. It produces preference for the Beloved over the self, correspondence with the Beloved's will, and yearning for constant nearness. He outlined the progression of love through stages. Mawadda or affection represents the seed of love. Khulla or intimate friendship occurs when love permeates. Maḥabba or love proper manifests when the heart is conquered. 'Ishq or passionate love emerges when love overwhelms reason. Hayamān or bewilderment occurs when the lover is lost. He maintained theological precision by distinguishing between divine and human love. God's love for servants is His willing good for them, drawing them near, and manifesting His attributes in them. It is eternal, without cause, without change. The servant's love is temporal, caused by divine love, constantly changing in intensity.

Al-Hujwīrī provided analytical treatment in Kashf al-Maḥjūb, distinguishing different approaches to love. The sobriety school, following al-Junayd, emphasizes love with composure. Love disciplines the lover, teaching courtesy (adab) with the Beloved. The perfect lover shows no outward sign, containing the fire within. The intoxication school, following al-Bisṭāmī, emphasizes overwhelming love. Love annihilates the lover's attributes, leaving only the Beloved. The lover cannot help but express what overwhelms him. His resolution acknowledges that both are correct for their practitioners. Sobriety suits those of strong constitution; intoxication overtakes those of sensitive nature. The Beloved accepts both.

Al-Ghazālī achieved masterful synthesis in the Iḥyā', dedicating the entire Book of Love to the topic. His philosophical foundation establishes that love is inclination toward what gives pleasure. Since knowing God is the highest pleasure for those capable of it, loving God is natural for the gnostics. The mystery is not that some love Him but that any could fail to love Him. He identifies five causes why humans love: self-love and what preserves the self, love for benefactors, love for beauty, love for hidden affinity, and love for the good in itself. All five causes reach perfection in God alone. He is our true Self, ultimate Benefactor, absolute Beauty, original Source, and pure Good. He distinguishes degrees of realization, with love of God's favors representing the beginning, love of God's attributes constituting the path, love of God's essence marking the goal, and love transcending subject-object representing the end.

Ibn 'Arabī transformed understanding through metaphysical precision. Love is a divine attribute, he teaches. Love is the cause of existence. The Hidden Treasure loved to be known—this love brought forth creation. Every movement in existence is a movement of love, though veiled by various forms. Regarding the unity of lover and beloved, he explains that in reality, God is both Lover and Beloved. He loves Himself through the medium of creation. We are the apparatus through which divine love knows itself. He distinguishes levels of love: natural love is every thing's love for its perfection, spiritual love is the soul's love for its Source, divine love is God's love for His own perfection manifest in creation, and essential love is the reality that these are all one love.

The centrality of love in Sufi teaching required careful integration with Islamic law and theology to avoid antinomian or heretical implications. Theological concerns arose regarding the nature of divine love, with orthodox theologians worried about anthropomorphism in attributing love to God. Al-Ash'arī established that God's love is His will to reward and draw near. It is not emotion or need as in creatures. Al-Māturīdī added that divine love is eternal and unchanging, unlike human love which begins and fluctuates. Sufis accepted these formulations while adding that what theologians describe abstractly, they experience concretely. Both descriptions are true and necessary.

The possibility of loving God faced philosophical objections, with some arguing humans could only love what they perceive sensually. Al-Ghazālī responded that humans love abstract realities—justice, knowledge, virtue. How much more can they love the Source of all perfection? The heart has perception beyond the senses. The 'ishq controversy sparked significant debate. Opponents argued that 'ishq implies excess and irrationality inappropriate for the divine-human relationship. Proponents like Aḥmad Ghazālī responded that in loving the Infinite, no amount is excess. 'Ishq expresses love's overwhelming nature better than calmer terms.

Sufis carefully related love to sharī'a obligations to demonstrate their compatibility. Al-Qushayrī taught that law provides the form while love provides the spirit. Prayer without love is mere movement; with love, it becomes intimate conversation. Love enhances rather than replaces obedience. Ibn 'Aṭā' Allah stated that the lover finds ease in what seems difficult to others. Night prayers are not burden but joy for one who loves the Beloved. Sufis mapped love onto legal categories to show its orthodox integration. Farḍ or obligatory love represents basic love arising from faith. Mandūb or recommended love manifests as increased love through devotions. Mubāḥ or permissible love appears in expressions of love in poetry and song. Makrūh or disliked love involves excessive public display. Ḥarām or forbidden is claiming divine love while violating law.

Orthodox scholars established boundaries against deviation. Against incarnationism, they insisted that love does not mean the lover becomes the Beloved. Al-Ghazālī clarifies that union (wuṣla) means lifting of veils, not fusion of essences. Against antinomianism, they emphasized that love increases rather than decreases adherence to law. Al-Sha'rānī insists that anyone claiming love exempts from religious duties understands neither love nor law. Against exclusivism, while emphasizing love's centrality, scholars maintained balance. Ibn al-Qayyim notes that love without fear leads to false security; fear without love leads to despair. The complete servant combines both.

Sufi orders developed practices integrating love with orthodox practice. Dhikr of divine names, especially al-Wadūd (the Loving) and al-Ḥabīb (the Beloved), reinforced love within orthodox invocation. Love poetry in devotion used permitted poetic expression while maintaining proper belief. Rules included clear statement that the Beloved is God, not a human; avoiding expressions suggesting equality; and maintaining metaphorical interpretation. Communal practices included samā' or sacred audition sessions where love poetry was sung, but within strict guidelines requiring qualified leadership, proper intention, no mixed gatherings, and no excessive movement.

Several major synthetic works successfully integrated love with orthodox theology. Al-Daylamī's 'Aṭf al-Alif provided a comprehensive treatise on divine love acceptable to theologians while profound for mystics. Ibn al-Qayyim's Madārij al-Sālikīn, though critical of some Sufi excesses, provides magnificent treatment of divine love within strict orthodoxy. Al-Sha'rānī's Lawāqiḥ al-Anwār demonstrates how the greatest expressions of divine love emerge from, rather than transcend, meticulous adherence to sharī'a.

Divine love in classical Sufi literature represents one of Islamic mysticism's greatest contributions to religious thought—transforming the relationship with the Transcendent from dutiful obedience to passionate engagement while maintaining essential boundaries. The scriptural foundations in Quran and hadith provided legitimacy for what might otherwise seem dangerously intimate language about the Divine who is "naught is like unto Him." Early Sufi expressions, particularly through Rābi'a's revolutionary focus on pure love, shifted Islamic spirituality's center of gravity. Love became not merely one station among many but the very heart of the path, the motive for creation, and the means of return. The sometimes shocking expressions of early mystics pushed language to its limits in attempting to convey love's overwhelming reality.

The systematic treatments in classical manuals achieved remarkable sophistication, analyzing love's types, degrees, causes, and effects with precision while preserving its essential mystery. These works demonstrate Islam's capacity to combine intellectual rigor with emotional depth, philosophical analysis with poetic expression. Perhaps most impressively, the tradition successfully integrated this potentially antinomian teaching with orthodox law and theology. By carefully distinguishing divine from human love, establishing clear boundaries against deviation, and showing how true love enhances rather than abolishes religious observance, classical scholars created space for profound mystical experience within orthodox Islam.

The treatment of divine love in classical Sufi literature continues to offer invaluable insights. It shows how the utterly Transcendent can be passionately loved without compromising divine incomparability, how law and love can reinforce rather than oppose each other, and how the deepest mystical experiences can find expression within traditional frameworks. In an age often characterized by either cold rationalism or unchecked emotionalism, the classical Sufi synthesis of rigorous theology with burning love provides a model of integrated spirituality that remains profoundly relevant.

Chapter 21. Modern Muslim Philosophers on Divine Transcendence

The encounter between Islamic thought and modernity has produced profound reflections on divine transcendence, as Muslim philosophers sought to articulate the principle "laysa kamithlihi shay'un" in dialogue with contemporary philosophical movements, scientific worldviews, and global intellectual currents. This chapter examines how major modern Muslim thinkers have engaged with divine transcendence, focusing on Muhammad Iqbal's revolutionary dynamic theology, Seyyed Hossein Nasr's perennialist approach, Fazlur Rahman's hermeneutical methodology, and the ways contemporary debates continue to draw upon classical resources while addressing uniquely modern challenges.

Muhammad Iqbal (1877-1938), philosopher-poet of the Indian subcontinent, revolutionized Islamic thought about divine transcendence by reconceptualizing God as pure duration, creative will, and dynamic becoming rather than static perfection. His The Reconstruction of Religious Thought in Islam begins with a fundamental critique of both classical Islamic philosophy and modern Western thought. "The classical systems, with their emphasis on divine immutability, have created a God so transcendent as to be irrelevant to the living, changing world. They sought to honor God by placing Him beyond time and change, but in doing so, they made Him a prisoner of human logic."

Iqbal specifically critiqued what he saw as the Greek influence on Muslim thought, arguing that Muslim philosophers, in their admiration for Aristotle, adopted a view of perfection as complete actualization, leaving no room for divine creativity or genuine novelty. He challenged the concept of static transcendence by observing that the God of traditional theology, absolutely complete and unchanging, cannot account for a dynamic universe or respond to free human actions. Even the Sufis, despite their profound insights, faced his criticism. He argued that mystics like Ibn 'Arabī, while offering valuable perspectives, reduced temporal existence to mere appearance, failing to give proper weight to the reality of becoming.

Iqbal proposed understanding God as the Ultimate Ego or Self, a radical reconceptualization grounded in his reading of both Islamic sources and contemporary philosophy. "The Ultimate Reality is a rationally directed creative life. To interpret this life as an ego is not to fashion God after man's image. It is to acknowledge that consciousness, purpose, and will—freed from human limitations—provide our best model for understanding divine nature." This framework involved several key aspects that transformed traditional understandings.

Drawing on Bergson while going beyond him, Iqbal developed the concept of pure duration as essential to understanding divine being. "Divine time is not serial time but pure duration—a continuous creative flow in which past, present, and future interpenetrate. God's eternity is not timelessness but intensive infinity of creative duration." This allowed him to articulate divine transcendence in temporal rather than atemporal terms. His notion of dynamic perfection challenged classical formulations directly: "We must distinguish between the perfection of death—complete, finished, static—and the perfection of life—ever-creative, ever-responsive, ever-new. God's perfection is of the second type, inclusive of change as the expression of inexhaustible creativity." His concept of inclusive transcendence sought to overcome the separation between God and world that he saw in traditional theology. "Divine transcendence does not mean God is separate from the world but that He includes it while infinitely exceeding it. The universe is His self-revelation, not His limitation."

Iqbal argued that his dynamic theology was more faithful to the Quran than classical philosophy had been. "The Quran presents God as 'every day in a new state' (55:29), responding to prayers, creating continuously, guiding history. This living God of religious experience, not the abstract Necessary

Existent of the philosophers, is the true Islamic conception." He reinterpreted key Quranic concepts to support this vision. Khalq became not a past event but continuous creation. Amr represented not static decree but dynamic creative command. Qadr was understood not as fixed predestination but as the self-imposed limits of divine creativity, allowing for genuine creaturely freedom and participation in the creative process.

Iqbal's most radical insight concerned human vicegerency (khilafa) and its relationship to divine transcendence. "The human ego is God's co-worker, participating in divine creativity. This does not compromise divine transcendence but fulfills it—God is so transcendent that He can create genuine others who freely participate in His creative work." This led to his famous declaration about human becoming: "The ultimate aim of the ego is not to see something but to be something. It is in the ego's effort to be something that he discovers his final opportunity to sharpen his objectivity and acquire a more fundamental 'I see' which includes the 'I am.'" This emphasis on human creative participation represented a dramatic departure from traditional formulations emphasizing creaturely dependence and passivity.

Iqbal's dynamic theology generated both enthusiasm and concern among Muslim intellectuals. Supporters praised his revitalization of divine relevance for modern life, his successful integration with modern thought, and his emphasis on human dignity and creativity as reflecting rather than threatening divine transcendence. Critics worried about apparent process theology elements that might compromise divine aseity, potential compromise of divine transcendence through making God subject to temporal becoming, and significant departure from traditional formulations that had sustained Islamic theology for centuries. Despite these concerns, his influence remains profound, inspiring subsequent thinkers seeking to articulate divine transcendence in dialogue with process thought, evolutionary theory, and contemporary physics.

Seyyed Hossein Nasr (b. 1933) represents a radically different approach from Iqbal, defending traditional metaphysics and divine transcendence through the lens of perennial philosophy. Nasr situates Islamic understanding of divine transcendence within universal metaphysics, arguing that "the doctrine of divine transcendence—expressed in Islam as 'laysa kamithlihi shay'un'—represents not merely an Islamic teaching but a universal truth recognized in all authentic traditions. The Absolute transcends all manifestation while being the source of all that exists." His perennialist framework rests on core principles including metaphysical transparency, whereby traditional civilizations possessed metaphysical knowledge now largely lost; universal doctrine, whereby all traditions point to the same transcendent Reality; and levels of reality, whereby existence comprises multiple levels from the material to the Divine.

Against modern reductionism and revisionist interpretations, Nasr vigorously defends classical Islamic formulations of transcendence. "The traditional Islamic doctrine of divine transcendence—as articulated by figures from al-Ghazālī to Ibn 'Arabī to Mullā Ṣadrā—represents not outdated philosophy but timeless wisdom. Modern attempts to make God more 'relevant' by compromising transcendence actually diminish both God and humanity." He argues forcefully against process theology, insisting that making God subject to becoming compromises the very meaning of divinity. The Immutable can be the source of change without being subject to it. He challenges modernist reinterpretation by asserting that efforts to demythologize reveal not intellectual sophistication but spiritual impoverishment, with traditional formulations preserving mysteries reason cannot penetrate. He advocates for integral tradition, emphasizing that divine transcendence must be understood within the total Islamic tradition—theology, philosophy, mysticism, and law forming an integral whole.

Nasr proposes "sacred science" as a framework for understanding divine transcendence in relation to creation, fundamentally challenging the assumptions of modern scientific materialism. "Modern science, by limiting itself to the quantitative and horizontal, cannot perceive vertical causation—how the transcendent Divine Principle continuously creates and sustains lower levels of existence. Sacred science recognizes both dimensions." This involves understanding nature through symbolic cosmology as divine theophany rather than mere matter, recognizing a hierarchy of being with multiple levels linking matter to Spirit, and developing qualitative science that includes spiritual significance alongside quantitative measurement.

Nasr emphasizes Sufism's crucial role in preserving experiential knowledge of transcendence beyond mere doctrinal formulation. "While theologians preserved the doctrine and philosophers the demonstrations, Sufis maintained the living experience of divine transcendence. Through spiritual practice, they verify that He who is 'beyond all' can be 'nearer than the jugular vein.'" He highlights Ibn 'Arabī's synthesis as representing the highest expression of divine transcendence, arguing that the Shaykh al-Akbar's doctrine of wahdat al-wujūd, properly understood, demonstrates that God alone truly exists. He emphasizes the continuing tradition, noting that living Sufi masters continue to guide souls to direct experience of the Transcendent, proving this is not mere history but present reality.

Nasr draws ecological conclusions from divine transcendence that give his traditional metaphysics contemporary urgency. "Environmental crisis stems from forgetting divine transcendence. When nature is seen as mere matter rather than divine manifestation, exploitation follows. Recovering traditional metaphysics is essential for environmental healing." This connection between metaphysics and ecology has made his work influential beyond strictly philosophical circles.

Nasr's perennialism has generated significant debate within contemporary Islamic thought. Critics argue that over-emphasis on tradition may stifle legitimate development needed to address genuinely new challenges, that perennialism might compromise Islamic uniqueness by emphasizing commonality with other traditions, and that there is insufficient direct engagement with modern philosophy on its own terms. Supporters value his vigorous defense of traditional metaphysics against reductionist alternatives, his integration of Islamic thought with other wisdom traditions, and his practical environmental applications of transcendence doctrine. His work represents the most sustained contemporary defense of traditional Islamic metaphysics in dialogue with modernity.

Fazlur Rahman (1919-1988) developed a distinctive approach emphasizing the Quran's ethical thrust while maintaining divine transcendence through sophisticated hermeneutics. His double movement theory seeks to preserve transcendence while ensuring contemporary relevance through careful methodology. "First movement: From the present situation to Quranic times—understanding the original context, the problems addressed, the solutions offered. Second movement: From those specific solutions to general principles, then from general principles to contemporary application." This method profoundly affects understanding of transcendence by requiring attention to historical context, whereby statements about God must be understood in their original context without being limited to it; emphasizing ethical dimensions, whereby divine transcendence serves not abstract theology but concrete ethical guidance; and enabling dynamic application, whereby the principle 'laysa kamithlihi shay'un' must be reapplied in each era's conceptual framework.

Rahman critiqued aspects of classical theology while respecting the tradition's achievements. "Medieval theology, under Greek influence, often made God so transcendent as to be irrelevant to moral struggle. The Quran's God is transcendent yet intimately concerned with human moral development." He specifically challenged Ash'arite occasionalism, arguing that denying natural causation to preserve divine power actually diminishes God's wisdom in creating an ordered universe. He found philosophical abstraction problematic, observing that the philosophers' Necessary Existent, while intellectually satisfying, lacks the personal dimension essential to religious life. He also cautioned against mystical excesses, noting that some Sufi formulations compromise the Creator-creature distinction essential to Islamic ethics.

Rahman emphasized recovering the Quran's integral worldview as the foundation for authentic Islamic thought about transcendence. "The Quran presents God as transcendent yet actively involved—creating, guiding, judging. This living transcendence, not philosophical abstraction, should guide Islamic thought." Key elements of this Quranic vision include taqwā or God-consciousness as the goal, whereby theoretical knowledge of divine transcendence serves the development of lived consciousness rather than being an end in itself; social justice grounded in the recognition that divine transcendence establishes human equality since all are equally creatures before the Creator; and historical engagement, whereby God's transcendence includes His action in history through guidance and human response rather than detached observation.

Rahman addressed contemporary issues through his hermeneutical lens with considerable sophistication. Regarding science and religion, he argued that divine transcendence means God works through natural laws, not against them, so that evolution and other scientific theories pose no threat when transcendence is properly understood. On religious pluralism, he maintained that God's transcendence means no human formulation fully captures divine reality, allowing respectful dialogue while maintaining Islamic distinctiveness. Concerning gender justice, he argued that traditional applications often reflected social contexts rather than eternal principles, with divine transcendence grounding human dignity regardless of gender.

Rahman's approach sparked significant discussion and continues to influence contemporary Islamic thought. Supporters appreciate his ethical emphasis in theology, which prevents transcendence from becoming abstract speculation; his sophisticated hermeneutics that allow engagement with modernity without abandoning tradition; and his serious engagement with modernity's genuine challenges. Critics worry about potential historicism that might relativize revealed truth, insufficient appreciation of tradition's accumulated wisdom, and rationalist tendencies that might undervalue mystical and experiential dimensions. Despite these concerns, his hermeneutical methodology has proven influential among those seeking to maintain Islamic authenticity while addressing contemporary questions.

Contemporary Muslim philosophers continue engaging divine transcendence while drawing on classical resources to address modern challenges in creative and sophisticated ways. Major contemporary issues demonstrate both the vitality of Islamic philosophical reflection and its continued relevance to pressing questions. The question of divine action in nature poses particular challenges. How does the transcendent God act in a law-governed universe understood through modern science? Nidhal Guessoum argues that divine transcendence means God acts through natural laws rather than violating them, with classical occasionalism needing updating rather than abandoning. Ibrahim Kalin proposes that Ibn 'Arabī's doctrine of perpetual creation, understood through contemporary physics, shows how divine action and natural law coincide without contradiction.

Religious diversity presents theological challenges requiring careful navigation. How does divine transcendence relate to religious pluralism in an interconnected world? Abdolkarim Soroush suggests that divine transcendence means revelation itself is larger than any single reception, so that multiple religions may reflect divine self-disclosure to different communities. Aref Ali Nayed responds that while divine transcendence exceeds human understanding, the Quran's finality remains, with transcendence allowing appreciation of others without compromising Islamic truth. This debate exemplifies how classical concepts of transcendence inform contemporary theological questions about religious diversity.

Feminist theology raises questions about how divine transcendence relates to gender justice and the critique of patriarchal religious structures.

Amina Wadud argues that divine transcendence means God is beyond gender, with masculine pronouns being a linguistic convention rather than theological truth. This insight liberates both theology and society from false limitations. Asma Barlas adds that the principle 'laysa kamithlihi shay'un' undermines all human hierarchies claimed in God's name, making divine transcendence radically egalitarian in its implications. These arguments demonstrate how traditional doctrines can support progressive social conclusions when properly understood.

Contemporary engagement with modern philosophy shows Muslim thinkers actively participating in global philosophical conversations while drawing on Islamic resources. Responding to post-modern challenges, Mohamed Aziz Lahbabi engaged Heidegger by arguing that Islamic 'laysa kamithlihi shay'un' anticipates post-modern critique of onto-theology while maintaining positive divine reality. Abdurrahman Taha develops a "trusteeship paradigm" whereby divine transcendence grounds human responsibility rather than nihilism, with post-modern critique clearing space for authentic Islamic thought. Within analytic philosophy, Shabbir Akhtar employs contemporary tools to defend divine transcendence using modal logic, presenting God as a necessary being transcending possible worlds while grounding them. Oliver Leaman examines religious language, noting that classical Islamic discussions of divine names anticipate contemporary philosophy of religious language, with ta'wīl providing a sophisticated theory of metaphor.

Scientific engagement demonstrates the continued relevance of transcendence doctrine to questions arising from contemporary physics and consciousness studies. Regarding quantum physics, Bruno Guiderdoni notes that quantum indeterminacy allows room for divine action without violating natural law, with classical Ash'arite occasionalism finding unexpected support. Mehdi Golshani argues that divine transcendence means science studies God's habitual action rather than limitations on divine power, so that no scientific discovery can challenge properly understood transcendence. In consciousness studies, Alparslan Açıkgenç proposes that Ibn Sīnā's theory of divine and human intellect, updated with neuroscience, shows how transcendent reality interfaces with human consciousness without reducing either to the other.

Contemporary thinkers increasingly mine classical tradition for resources to address modern questions. The revival of Mullā Ṣadrā shows philosophers like Mohammed Rustom demonstrating how Ṣadrā's dynamic metaphysics addresses process theology concerns while maintaining transcendence. Ibn 'Arabī's contemporary relevance appears in work by scholars like William Chittick, who demonstrates how the Shaykh's analysis of the "God of beliefs" illuminates religious diversity while maintaining truth claims. Ghazālī's balance attracts scholars like Mustafa Abu Sway, who argues that Ghazālī's synthesis of reason, revelation, and experience provides a model for contemporary integration. Rūmī's wisdom receives attention from scholars like Omid Safi, who shows how Rūmī's poetic theology captures transcendence's experiential dimension often lost in philosophical discourse.

Emerging syntheses draw on classical resources while addressing contemporary needs. Neo-traditionalism, represented by scholars like Abdal Hakim Murad, argues for renewed appreciation of traditional theology, insisting that classical formulations need appreciation rather than revision since their sophistication exceeds modern alternatives. Progressive Islam, articulated by thinkers like Khaled Abou El Fadl, maintains that divine transcendence relativizes all human authority, with classical principles supporting contemporary justice movements. Ecological theology, developed by scholars including Seyyed Hossein Nasr and Ibrahim Özdemir, demonstrates how divine transcendence grounds environmental ethics, with nature as divine sign requiring protection rather than exploitation.

Modern Muslim engagement with divine transcendence reveals both continuity and development within Islamic thought. From Iqbal's revolutionary reconstruction through Nasr's traditional defense to Rahman's hermeneutical approach, each thinker grapples with articulating "laysa kamithlihi shay'un" in contemporary context while remaining faithful to Islamic sources and concerns. Iqbal's dynamic theology, while controversial, opened new possibilities for understanding divine transcendence as creative and responsive rather than static and distant. His influence continues among those seeking to engage process thought and evolutionary worldviews while maintaining Islamic identity and commitment to divine sovereignty.

Nasr's perennialist approach provides vigorous defense of traditional formulations while demonstrating their universal significance and contemporary relevance. His work shows how classical Islamic metaphysics remains viable and vital in addressing modern challenges, from environmental crisis to the fragmentation of knowledge. Rahman's hermeneutical method offers tools for maintaining divine transcendence while ensuring ethical relevance and contemporary application. His influence appears among those emphasizing Quranic ethics and contextual interpretation as the path forward for Islamic thought.

Contemporary debates reveal how classical resources continue providing insight for uniquely modern challenges. Whether addressing scientific discoveries, religious pluralism, or gender justice, Muslim thinkers draw creatively on tradition while developing new applications that extend rather than abandon inherited wisdom. The diversity of approaches—from neo-traditionalist to progressive—demonstrates Islamic thought's vitality in engaging divine transcendence. Rather than offering a single answer, the tradition provides rich resources for continued reflection on the One who remains "naught is like unto Him" while being "closer than the jugular vein."

This ongoing engagement suggests that divine transcendence remains not merely historical doctrine but living reality requiring fresh articulation in each generation. The principle "laysa kamithlihi shay'un" continues challenging and inspiring Muslim philosophers to develop understanding adequate to both inherited wisdom and contemporary experience. The conversation between classical resources and modern questions enriches both, demonstrating that authentic tradition is not preservation of dead forms but creative engagement with perennial truths in ever-new contexts.

Chapter 22. Islamic Responses to Modern Philosophical Challenges

The encounter between Islamic thought and modern philosophy has generated profound challenges to traditional understandings of divine transcendence. From process theology's dynamic deity to postmodernism's critique of metaphysics, contemporary philosophical movements question classical formulations of "laysa kamithlihi shay'un." This chapter examines how Muslim thinkers have engaged these challenges, drawing on classical resources while developing creative responses that maintain Islamic authenticity while addressing contemporary concerns.

Process theology, emerging from Alfred North Whitehead's philosophy, presents a fundamental challenge to classical Islamic theism by proposing a God who evolves with creation. Muslim responses have ranged from outright rejection to creative appropriation. Process theology's core claims directly challenge traditional Islamic theology on multiple fronts. The concept of divine becoming asserts that God is "in process," experiencing temporal development alongside creation. Charles Hartshorne argues that a God who cannot change cannot love, since love requires real relationship, and real relationship requires mutual affecting. This contradicts the Quranic principle "Every day He is upon some matter" (55:29) as traditionally interpreted—not that God changes, but that His unchanging will manifests differently across time without alteration in the divine essence itself.

Process theology's dipolar theism distinguishes God's "primordial nature," which is eternal and absolute, from His "consequent nature," which is temporal and responsive to creaturely actions. Islamic theology traditionally maintains divine simplicity as essential to divine perfection. As al-Ghazālī states, any composition in God implies dependence on parts, contradicting necessary existence. The distinction between primordial and consequent natures suggests a composite deity fundamentally at odds with classical Islamic formulations. Process theology's panentheism holds that the world exists "in" God as His body or experience, though God exceeds the world. This challenges the Creator-creation distinction fundamental to Islamic tawḥīd. Ibn Taymiyya warned that any doctrine making creation part of God violates the principle 'laysa kamithlihi shay'un,' compromising the absolute distinction between divine and creaturely being.

Some scholars argue that Muhammad Iqbal anticipated process thought in significant ways, though with crucial differences. Iqbal writes in his Reconstruction of Religious Thought in Islam that the Ultimate Ego exists in pure duration wherein change ceases to be a succession of varying attitudes, and reveals its true character as continuous creation. His emphasis on creative evolution presents God's life as continuous creative activity, with knowledge interpreted as a kind of intimate awareness of the creative flow of life. His concept of human partnership suggests that the ultimate aim of the ego is not to see something but to be something, to participate in the creative life of God. However, Iqbal maintains critical differences from process theology. God's perfection includes dynamism but does not lack completion. Change represents God's free creativity rather than metaphysical necessity. Transcendence remains absolute despite immanence. Contemporary scholar Mustansir Mir notes that Iqbal's God is dynamic yet transcendent, creative yet complete—avoiding process theology's limitations while embracing its insights.

Seyyed Hossein Nasr provides a comprehensive traditional critique of process theology from the perspective of perennial philosophy. He identifies fundamental metaphysical errors, arguing that process theology commits the fundamental error of subjecting the Absolute to becoming. This destroys the very meaning of divinity—that which transcends all limitation, including temporal limitation. On the question of perfection, he argues that process theologians equate perfection with static completion and then reject it. But traditional perfection is infinite plenitude containing all possibilities, including the appearance of change while remaining changeless. He identifies a category mistake in the entire enterprise, suggesting that applying temporal categories to the Eternal resembles asking 'What is north of the North Pole?' The question contains category confusion that invalidates the inquiry.

Nasr proposes understanding divine action through traditional metaphysics as an alternative to process theology. God is pure Being, containing all possibilities without becoming or developing. Creation is divine self-disclosure rather than divine change, manifesting potentialities without altering the divine essence. Time measures created change, not divine becoming, belonging to the created order rather than divine reality. Perpetual creation gives dynamism without divine process, providing the temporal unfolding process theologians seek without compromising transcendence.

Some Muslim thinkers find limited value in process insights when carefully circumscribed. Muzaffar Iqbal suggests that process theology correctly emphasizes divine-world relationship but errs in compromising divine transcendence. Islamic occasionalism provides better framework—God continuously creates without Himself changing, maintaining dynamic relationship while preserving absolute transcendence. Ibrahim Kalin proposes that Ibn 'Arabī's doctrine of perpetual creation (al-khalq al-jadīd) anticipates process concerns while maintaining divine transcendence. Each moment brings new divine self-disclosure without divine change, providing temporal novelty without compromising eternal perfection. Mohamed Aziz Lahbabi developed "Islamic personalism" partially engaging process thought by presenting God as supreme Person rather than abstract Being, affirming real divine-human relationship, maintaining historical engagement without temporal limitation, and articulating dynamic transcendence rather than static remoteness.

Contemporary Muslims develop synthetic positions attempting to preserve process theology's insights while avoiding its theological problems. Dynamic traditionalism accepts dynamism in divine action while rejecting divine becoming, holding that God's eternal will includes temporal unfolding, divine knowledge encompasses without experiencing temporal succession, real relationship exists without mutual dependence, and transcendence operates through immanence rather than despite it. Reformulated occasionalism uses process insights to revitalize Ash'arite positions by understanding continuous creation as divine-world interface, natural laws as divine habits rather than limitations on divine power, human freedom within divine sovereignty through secondary causation, and temporal effects flowing from eternal causes without requiring divine temporality.

Postmodern philosophy's critique of metaphysics, grand narratives, and transcendent truth claims poses different challenges requiring distinctive Islamic responses. Key postmodern critiques affect Islamic theology in fundamental ways. Derrida's deconstruction of metaphysics argues that all metaphysics involves "logocentrism" and assumptions about "presence" that mask difference and deferral. This challenges Islamic claims about divine reality by questioning whether "laysa kamithlihi shay'un" can meaningfully refer if all language involves différance and perpetual deferral of meaning. Foucault's analysis of the power-knowledge nexus links truth claims to power structures, questioning whether Islamic theology genuinely describes divine reality or merely legitimates social arrangements and political authority.

Lyotard's proclamation of the end of grand narratives declares that modernity's grand narratives have lost credibility in the postmodern condition. Islam presents perhaps the grandest narrative imaginable—from pre-eternal covenant through prophetic history to eternal afterlife—making it a prime target for postmodern skepticism. Postmodern critique of transcendence suspects that transcendence claims mask immanent power plays, with divine transcendence viewed as projection legitimating earthly authority rather than genuine metaphysical truth. These challenges require sophisticated responses that neither simply dismiss postmodern insights nor capitulate to postmodern relativism.

Abdolkarim Soroush engages postmodern insights while maintaining Islamic commitment through his theory of the contraction and expansion of religious knowledge. He advocates hermeneutical humility, acknowledging that revelation is divine but understanding is human. All interpretation involves human limitation, cultural conditioning, and potential error. This includes his own views, preventing any human interpreter from claiming final authority. His distinction between religious knowledge as human construction and religion itself holds that we must distinguish religion itself (dīn) from religious knowledge ('ilm-i dīnī). The former is divine and perfect; the latter is human and fallible. This distinction allows for critical examination of interpretations without undermining revelation itself.

Soroush embraces pluralism within Islam, arguing that no single interpretation exhausts divine intent. Multiple readings create productive conversation rather than relativistic chaos, with diversity of interpretation reflecting the inexhaustibility of divine meaning. He articulates transcendence through absence, suggesting that God's transcendence appears precisely in the inability of any human system to capture divine reality. Postmodernism helps theology by preventing idolatry of concepts, clearing space for authentic encounter with the transcendent. Critics worry Soroush concedes too much, undermining Islamic truth claims through excessive epistemological humility. Supporters see necessary recognition of human limitation that actually strengthens rather than weakens faith by distinguishing human fallibility from divine perfection.

Mohamed Arkoun applied contemporary critical theory to Islamic thought with radical thoroughness. His critique of the "unthought" argues that Islamic tradition contains vast unexamined assumptions never critically scrutinized. Modern philosophy helps uncover these hidden premises, making genuine theological progress possible. His logospheric analysis notes that the Quran emerged in oral culture but was transformed by writing. This transformation affects how we understand divine speech, with shifts from oral to written to print to digital each reshaping interpretive possibilities. His concept of the imaginaire holds that religious imagination constructs meaningful worlds. Recognizing construction does not negate truth but clarifies human contribution to meaning-making. His applied Islamology moves beyond both orientalism and apologetics to critical engagement with tradition, refusing both hostile external critique and uncritical internal defense.

Arkoun maintained Muslim identity while radically questioning traditional assumptions, creating space for new thinking that some found liberating and others found threatening. His work demonstrates how postmodern critical tools can be applied to Islamic materials without requiring abandonment of Islamic commitment, though the extent to which his positions remain recognizably Islamic remains contested.

Tariq Ramadan represents confident traditional engagement with postmodernity rather than anxious defensiveness. His call for radical reform insists that Muslims need not defensive response but radical reform—returning to sources while engaging contemporary reality without fear or compromise. On universal values, he argues that Islamic principles provide universal ethics for postmodern world. Divine transcendence grounds human dignity beyond cultural relativism, offering alternatives to both universalist imperialism and relativist nihilism. His critical traditionalism acknowledges postmodern insights about power and interpretation while maintaining that objective truth exists—even if our grasp remains partial and perspectives multiple. His applied ethics focus on practical ethics rather than abstract metaphysics, showing Islamic values' contemporary relevance through concrete engagement with social issues.

Islamic responses to specific postmodern critiques demonstrate the tradition's resourcefulness in addressing contemporary challenges. Responding to deconstruction, Muslims note that language's limitations were acknowledged in classical tradition through formulations like "He is above what they describe." Apophatic theology functions as indigenous deconstruction, with the via negativa recognizing language's inadequacy. Divine names function as traces rather than presence, pointing toward rather than capturing divine reality. The tradition of ta'wīl represents perpetual interpretation, acknowledging that no reading achieves finality. Responding to the power-knowledge nexus, Muslims point to prophetic critique of power throughout Islamic history, distinction between divine truth and human authority preventing simple identification of theological claims with political interests, resources within the tradition for criticizing religious establishment when it becomes oppressive, and transcendence functioning as critique of all earthly power including religious authority.

Responding to the proclaimed end of grand narratives, Muslims note that Islamic narrative includes its own critique through Quranic emphasis on divine mystery. Multiple levels of meaning prevent closure, with legal, ethical, mystical, and philosophical readings coexisting. Emphasis on mystery within revelation preserves openness despite comprehensive narrative. Local applications of universal principles allow diversity within unity. Responding to critique of transcendence, Muslims present transcendence as liberation from human systems rather than legitimation of them. Divine incomparability undermines human pretensions to absolute authority. Mystical experience transcends conceptual capture, providing check against purely political readings. Ethical transcendence appears in social critique, with prophets consistently challenging established powers in God's name.

Muslim thinkers increasingly discover that classical Islamic thought anticipated many modern philosophical concerns and provides sophisticated resources for addressing them. The medieval debate between Ash'arites and Mu'tazilites about divine names anticipated nominalist-realist controversies in interesting ways. Ash'arites held that names are mental constructs indicating real divine attributes without being identical to those attributes. Mu'tazilites argued that names are human constructions with no separate reality beyond linguistic convention. Ibn 'Arabī proposed that names are relationships between Real and creation, neither purely mental nor purely objective. This debate's contemporary relevance appears in addressing linguistic philosophy and social construction without falling into either naive realism or total relativism.

Sufi texts provided detailed phenomenological accounts of religious experience centuries before modern phenomenology emerged. Al-Ghazālī's analysis of certainty (yaqīn) levels distinguishes knowledge of certainty ('ilm al-yaqīn), eye of certainty ('ayn al-yaqīn), and truth of certainty (ḥaqq al-yaqīn) as phenomenologically distinct modes of knowing. Ibn 'Arabī's mapping of states of consciousness provides detailed cartography of mystical experience. Al-Suhrawardī's illumination phenomenology offers sophisticated analysis of mystical cognition. Careful distinction between experience and interpretation prevents conflating psychological states with metaphysical claims. Contemporary application provides resources for consciousness studies and religious experience analysis informed by classical precision.

Classical tafsīr demonstrated hermeneutical sophistication anticipating modern interpretive theory. Recognition of multiple meaning levels through ẓāhir (apparent) and bāṭin (hidden) senses acknowledges textual polysemy. Contextual interpretation through asbāb al-nuzūl (occasions of revelation) recognizes historical situatedness of textual meaning. Intertextual reading through the principle that al-Qur'ān yufassiru ba'ḍuhu ba'ḍan (the Quran interprets parts of itself) develops holistic hermeneutics. Recognition that reader's spiritual state affects understanding acknowledges interpreter's role in meaning-constitution. Modern relevance appears in anticipating reader-response theory and hermeneutical circles without falling into pure subjectivism.

Islamic thought developed sophisticated dialectics providing methodological resources for contemporary engagement. Kalām methodology employs thesis-antithesis-synthesis patterns in theological argumentation. Sufi coincidentia oppositorum in divine names recognizes productive tensions in divine attributes. Legal reasoning balances competing principles through sophisticated casuistry. Recognition of productive tensions embraces complexity without requiring premature resolution.

Application addresses dialectical philosophies and complexity thinking with indigenous Islamic resources.

Classical texts often maintained deliberate ambiguity providing resources for engaging postmodern suspicion of closure. Mutashābihāt verses in the Quran remain deliberately unclear, resisting definitive interpretation. Multiple valid interpretations are recognized through the principle of wujūh al-qirā'āt. Apophatic moments interrupt kataphatic theology, preventing conceptual idolatry. Recognition of mystery within system preserves openness despite systematic elaboration. Relevance appears in responding to postmodern suspicion of systematic closure without abandoning systematic thought entirely.

Islamic thought emphasized practical wisdom providing resources for pragmatist engagement. Maqāṣid al-sharī'a (purposes of law) focuses on objectives rather than mere formal compliance. Maṣlaḥa (public interest) considerations allow contextual application. Contextual fatwa variation recognizes legitimate diversity in application. Theory-practice integration prevents abstract speculation divorced from lived reality. Contemporary use addresses pragmatist philosophy and applied ethics through indigenous practical reasoning traditions.

Specific classical concepts provide particularly rich resources for contemporary engagement. Ibn 'Arabī's concept of barzakh (isthmus) offers resources for thinking about liminality and in-between states. It describes reality between other realities, neither one nor the other. It employs neither/nor and both/and logic transcending binary oppositions. It functions as boundary that connects while separating, allowing relationship without fusion. Application extends to various philosophical problems involving boundaries, transitions, and intermediate states. The concept of tajdīd (renewal) offers resources for thinking about tradition and innovation. It maintains tradition's contemporary relevance through periodic renewal. It affirms change within continuity rather than requiring choice between them. It enables creative reinterpretation without abandoning tradition. It balances conservation and innovation, preserving while transforming.

The concept of khilāfa (vicegerency) provides resources for theological anthropology and environmental ethics. It articulates dignified humanism without anthropocentrism, grounding human significance in divine trust rather than autonomous assertion. It provides environmental ethics grounding through stewardship rather than domination. It offers political theology resources emphasizing responsibility over mere rights. It connects individual and cosmic responsibility in an integrated vision of human vocation.

Examining specific instances where Muslim thinkers creatively employed traditional resources for contemporary challenges reveals patterns and possibilities for ongoing engagement. Osman Bakar's work on science and transcendence addresses the challenge that modern science's methodological naturalism seems to exclude transcendence from legitimate inquiry. Drawing on al-Ghazālī's classification of sciences and their relationships, Bakar develops a creative response. Sciences study divine āyāt (signs) in nature, making scientific inquiry potentially sacred activity. Different sciences access different reality levels without hierarchical dismissal. Hierarchy of sciences reflects reality hierarchy without reducing higher to lower. Science becomes a sacred activity when properly oriented toward ultimate purposes. Bakar writes that Islamic science views nature as theophany. Modern science's power comes from focusing on one reality level. Its limitation comes from absolutizing that level. The innovation involves using traditional science classification to contextualize modern science without rejecting its achievements or methods.

Khaled Abou El Fadl's work on Islamic law and human rights addresses the challenge that modern human rights discourse seems to require autonomous human dignity independent of divine grounding. Drawing on maqāṣid al-sharī'a and human vicegerency concepts, he develops a creative response. Human dignity is rooted in divine breath rather than autonomous assertion. Rights function as divine trusts (amānāt) rather than mere human constructions. Legal purposes include human flourishing as an essential objective. Dynamic interpretation allows contemporary contexts to be addressed. Abou El Fadl argues that divine sovereignty does not negate human rights but grounds them more firmly than secular philosophy. Vicegerency creates inviolable human dignity that cannot be revoked by human authority. The innovation involves retrieving classical concepts to engage contemporary discourse while maintaining theological grounding that secular rights theory lacks.

Ingrid Mattson's work on gender and authority addresses feminist critique of male religious authority as patriarchal imposition. Drawing on Quranic emphasis on spiritual equality and historical female scholars often written out of tradition, she develops a creative response. Recovery of women's scholarly traditions demonstrates that female authority is not innovation but retrieval. Distinguishing cultural patriarchy from revelation prevents conflating social custom with divine command. Applying hermeneutical principles consistently reveals gender bias in interpretation. Developing inclusive institutions realizes tradition's egalitarian potential. Mattson demonstrates that the tradition contains resources for gender justice obscured by cultural overlay. Divine transcendence relativizes all human authority, including gendered authority claims lacking genuine religious warrant. The innovation involves using traditional principles to critique traditional practices, demonstrating that authentic tradition can be self-correcting.

Timothy Winter's work on aesthetics and modernity addresses the challenge of modern architecture's departure from traditional forms in ways that seem to abandon sacred dimensions. Drawing on Islamic aesthetic principles and philosophy of beauty, he develops a creative response. Beauty as a divine name requires manifestation in human creation. Traditional principles rather than mere forms provide continuity. Contemporary materials can embody eternal patterns through creative application. Sacred space in the modern context remains possible through principled design. Winter, known as Abdal Hakim Murad, writes that traditional aesthetics embody metaphysical principles. Contemporary Islamic architecture must manifest these principles in new forms, not merely copy historical styles that may be contextually inappropriate. The innovation involves extracting principles from forms for contemporary application, allowing continuity without mere repetition.

Ebrahim Moosa's work on bioethics addresses the challenge of modern biotechnology, raising unprecedented ethical questions without direct precedent in classical sources. Drawing on uṣūl al-fiqh methodology and ethical objectives, he develops a creative response. Analogical reasoning applies to new situations through sophisticated qiyās. Purposes take priority over literal precedents when contexts change dramatically. Consultation with scientific experts integrates technical and normative considerations. Collective ijtihād addresses complex issues requiring diverse expertise. Moosa proposes that classical legal theory provides sophisticated tools for addressing utterly new situations. The tradition is more flexible than either traditionalists or modernists often realize, containing methodological resources rather than merely substantive precedents. The innovation involves demonstrating classical methodology's contemporary relevance through actual application to bioethical questions.

These cases reveal consistent patterns in effective creative response to modern challenges. Deep traditional knowledge is essential, with effective response requiring genuine mastery of classical sources rather than superficial acquaintance. Sympathetic understanding of contemporary challenges prevents dismissive responses that fail to engage genuine difficulties. Creative application moves beyond mechanical application to innovative deployment of traditional resources. Maintaining core principles ensures that innovation occurs in application rather than compromising fundamental commitments. Practical focus addresses lived challenges rather than merely theoretical questions, ensuring relevance to actual Muslim communities.

Islamic responses to modern philosophical challenges demonstrate the tradition's vitality and resources. Rather than simply defending against contemporary thought, Muslim thinkers increasingly engage creatively, discovering classical anticipations of modern concerns and developing innovative applications of traditional principles. The engagement with process theology reveals that while Islam cannot accept a God who becomes or develops, it possesses resources for addressing process concerns about divine-world relationship through concepts like perpetual creation and dynamic divine action that maintains transcendent perfection while avoiding static remoteness.

Postmodern critiques, rather than simply threatening Islamic claims, often help recover indigenous critical resources within the tradition. Classical concepts of interpretation, mystery, and the limits of language provide sophisticated frameworks for engaging postmodern insights while maintaining commitment to transcendent truth. The recognition that divine reality exceeds human comprehension provides space for epistemological humility without collapsing into relativism. The recovery of classical resources shows that medieval Muslim thinkers often demonstrated remarkable philosophical sophistication, anticipating many supposedly modern concerns. Their dialectical thinking, hermeneutical awareness, and practical wisdom offer tools for contemporary engagement that neither uncritically accept nor defensively reject modern philosophy.

The case studies examined demonstrate that creative traditional response is not only possible but already occurring across diverse fields. From science to law to gender to aesthetics to bioethics, Muslim thinkers show how classical principles can address unprecedented contemporary challenges when applied with intelligence and creativity. The key insight emerging is that "laysa kamithlihi shay'un" provides not obstacle but resource for philosophical engagement. Divine incomparability means no human system—whether classical or modern—can claim to exhaust divine reality. This creates space for creative thought while maintaining authentic Islamic commitment to transcendent truth.

As Muslims continue engaging contemporary philosophy, the pattern of creative traditional response offers a promising way forward. Neither uncritical acceptance of modern philosophy nor defensive rejection serves the tradition well. Instead, deep engagement that takes both classical Islam and contemporary thought seriously, while maintaining core commitments to divine transcendence and revelation, provides the most fruitful path. The principle that "naught is like unto Him" thus serves not as conversation-stopper but as invitation to humility, creativity, and continued exploration. In engaging modern philosophical challenges through classical resources, Muslims demonstrate that authentic tradition is living tradition—ever ancient, ever new, addressing contemporary questions through eternal wisdom.

Chapter 23. Addressing Common Objections: A Response to Potential Concerns

This study of divine transcendence in Islamic intellectual history, with its emphasis on complementary opposites, perpetual creation, and mystical insights, may raise legitimate concerns among readers committed to orthodox Islamic belief and practice. This section directly addresses potential objections, acknowledging their validity while demonstrating how the patterns identified emerge from, rather than impose upon, the authentic Islamic tradition.

Perhaps the most serious concern readers might raise is whether systematically analyzing "patterns of transcendence" constitutes blameworthy innovation (bid'a) in religion. The objection might be stated thus: "This work appears to introduce new frameworks and terminology not found in classical sources. The Prophet ﷺ warned that 'every innovation is misguidance.' How is identifying 'patterns of complementary opposites' or 'systematic approaches to transcendence' different from the philosophical innovations that classical scholars condemned?" This concern reflects praiseworthy caution regarding religious innovation and deserves careful response.

The distinction between praiseworthy systematization and blameworthy innovation has clear precedent in Islamic scholarship. Imam al-Shāfi'ī systematized legal methodology (uṣūl al-fiqh) using categories not explicitly found in earlier sources. Al-Ash'arī developed systematic theology using Greek logical tools to defend traditional beliefs. Al-Ghazālī organized spiritual stages in ways previous Sufis had not articulated. Ibn Khaldūn identified patterns in history that earlier historians had not explicitly formulated. Each faced similar accusations of innovation, yet are now recognized as having served the tradition by providing a systematic understanding of realities already present in the sources.

This study explicitly grounds every significant claim in primary sources. The "patterns" identified are not imposed foreign frameworks but emerge from careful observation of what classical scholars actually wrote. When we note that Muslim thinkers consistently "preserved mystery within affirmation," we are describing rather than prescribing, observing a recurring approach rather than inventing a novel one. The Prophet's condemnation of innovation specifically concerns matters of worship ('ibādāt) and core beliefs ('aqā'id). Scholarly analysis and systematization of existing religious expressions fall under permissible intellectual activity (ijtihād fikrī). As Ibn Rajab al-Ḥanbalī clarifies in Jāmi' al-'Ulūm wa'l-Ḥikam: "Innovation that is condemned is that which has no basis in the Sharī'a. As for organizing and clarifying what exists in the sources, this is praiseworthy, like the scholars' compilation of grammar, rhetoric, and the sciences of hadith."

The mystical expressions analyzed here—fanā', baqā', tajallī—are not innovations of this study but established concepts with centuries of orthodox commentary. We merely observe how different scholars approached these realities, noting patterns in their approaches without claiming to have discovered something entirely new. Identifying patterns serves a practical religious benefit. Understanding how classical scholars navigated the tension between divine transcendence and immanence helps contemporary Muslims maintain authentic faith while engaging modern challenges. This is not innovation but a renewed understanding of inherited wisdom, making accessible what was always present in the tradition.

A second major concern involves the selection and interpretation of sources, particularly the extensive use of Sufi and philosophical texts. The objection might be formulated: "This study seems to privilege Sufi and philosophical sources over straightforward theological texts. By focusing on Ibn 'Arabī, al-Ghazālī's mystical works, and philosophical treatises, doesn't this present a skewed picture of Islamic thought? The majority of Muslims throughout history have followed simpler, more direct understandings of divine transcendence." This important objection deserves acknowledgment and careful response.

The selection of sources reflects the study's specific focus on how Muslim intellectuals grappled with the philosophical and mystical implications of divine transcendence. Just as a study of Islamic law would naturally focus on legal texts, examining theological complexity requires engaging those who most deeply explored such complexity. The work includes extensive treatment of mainstream theological sources across multiple chapters examining Ash'arī and Māturīdī theology, with Ḥanbalī perspectives receiving attention through Ibn Taymiyya and others. Orthodox creeds like those of al-Ṭaḥāwī and al-Nasafī are cited throughout, while mainstream exegetes like al-Ṭabarī, al-Qurṭubī, and Ibn Kathīr feature prominently in discussions of Quranic interpretation.

The emphasis on certain thinkers reflects their historical influence, not personal preference. Al-Ghazālī's works shaped centuries of Islamic thought across all schools. Ibn 'Arabī's ideas, whether accepted or rejected, demanded a response from subsequent scholars. These are not marginal figures but central to Islamic intellectual history, with their influence extending far beyond mystical circles into mainstream theology, jurisprudence, and exegesis. The study acknowledges diverse approaches and disagreements, noting Ibn Taymiyya's critiques of Ibn 'Arabī, orthodox concerns about philosophical methods, and debates within each school. This is not selective reading but comprehensive engagement with the tradition's diversity.

Focusing on sophisticated treatments serves contemporary needs. Modern Muslims face philosophical challenges requiring more than simple affirmation. Understanding how classical scholars developed nuanced approaches helps address contemporary questions while remaining orthodox, providing resources that both honor the tradition and speak to present concerns. The "simple faith" of the masses often contained profound wisdom. When we quote Rābi'a al-'Adawiyya or early Sufi sayings, we engage this wisdom expressed in accessible forms. Theological sophistication and simple devotion are complementary rather than contradictory, with each serving different needs and audiences within the comprehensive Islamic tradition.

A third concern involves whether the patterns identified align with orthodox Sunni theology or subtly promote heterodox ideas. The objection might be stated: "By emphasizing concepts like 'perpetual creation,' 'complementary opposites,' and mystical union, this study seems to blur important theological boundaries. Orthodox Sunni theology maintains clear distinctions between Creator and creation, affirms divine attributes without paradox, and rejects any hint of unificationism (ittiḥād) or incarnationism (ḥulūl)." This crucial concern about theological orthodoxy requires detailed clarification.

Every concept examined includes orthodox interpretations and safeguards carefully documented throughout the study. On perpetual creation, we show how mainstream Ash'arites like al-Bāqillānī and al-Juwaynī taught continuous divine sustenance of creation. This is not heterodox innovation but classical occasionalism expressed dynamically, with God's continuous creative act maintaining existence at every moment. On complementary opposites, we demonstrate how orthodox scholars from al-Ghazālī to al-Rāzī explained divine names that appear opposite. The resolution—that divine perfection transcends human logical limitations—is impeccably orthodox, acknowledging divine simplicity while recognizing that human language struggles to express transcendent reality. On mystical experience, we consistently note orthodox boundaries: fanā' is experiential rather than ontological, divine love maintains the servant-Lord distinction, and tajallī represents self-disclosure rather than incarnation.

We explicitly document orthodox critiques and concerns throughout, including Ibn Taymiyya's warnings about monistic interpretations that compromise divine transcendence, al-Taftāzānī's clarifications about divine attributes maintaining theological precision, orthodox Sufi masters' rejection of antinomian interpretations that would use mystical experience to justify abandoning religious law, and the execution of al-Ḥallāj as a warning about boundaries that cannot be crossed. The patterns identified operate within, not against, orthodox frameworks. Preserving mystery acknowledges human limitations before divine reality—a fundamentally orthodox position. Experiencing transcendence through spiritual practice follows the prophetic example. Maintaining creative tension between accessibility and incomparability reflects the Quranic balance between emphasizing divine nearness and divine transcendence.

Major orthodox authorities validated these approaches, demonstrating their legitimacy within the tradition. Al-Ghazālī was called "Proof of Islam" (Ḥujjat al-Islām) by his contemporaries and successors. Ibn 'Aṭā' Allah belonged to the orthodox Shādhilī order known for combining mystical insight with strict sharī'a observance. Al-Qushayrī wrote his Risāla specifically to defend Sufism's orthodoxy against charges of deviation. Even Ibn 'Arabī, despite controversy, influenced mainstream Ottoman theology and received endorsement from significant orthodox scholars. Orthodoxy itself contains diversity, with the Ash'arī, Māturīdī, and Atharī schools differing on significant points while remaining within Sunni orthodoxy. Similarly, the mystical expressions examined represent legitimate diversity within orthodox bounds rather than departure from them.

This study serves orthodox theology by showing its depth and sophistication. Rather than reducing Islam to simplistic formulas that cannot address genuine intellectual challenges, we demonstrate how orthodox scholars developed profound insights while maintaining core commitments. This strengthens rather than weakens orthodox theology's credibility, showing that traditional Islamic thought possesses the resources to address sophisticated questions without compromising fundamental principles.

The final major concern involves whether these theological patterns have problematic implications for religious practice. The objection might be formulated: "Emphasis on mystical experience, perpetual creation, and transcendent mystery might lead people to neglect concrete religious obligations. If everything is divine self-disclosure, if opposites are unified in God, if reality is constantly renewed, what happens to fixed prayers, clear prohibitions, and unchanging law?" This practical concern touches the heart of religious life and deserves comprehensive response.

The entire tradition emphasized that authentic mystical understanding increases rather than decreases religious observance. Al-Junayd insisted that genuine Sufism is "bound by Quran and Sunna," refusing to recognize as authentic any spiritual path that deviates from revealed guidance. Al-Ghazālī's mystical realization led to more meticulous practice rather than less, with his personal scrupulousness regarding religious obligations increasing after his mystical experiences. Ibn 'Arabī maintained strict adherence to Sharī'a throughout his life despite his profound mystical insights, demonstrating that the highest spiritual realization requires rather than exempts from legal observance. Every authentic Sufi order requires complete fulfillment of religious obligations as the foundation for spiritual progress, with masters refusing to accept students who neglect basic religious duties.

We document numerous statements warning against antinomian

misinterpretation, including al-Qushayrī's unequivocal assertion: "Anyone who claims spiritual realization exempts from religious law has neither realization nor understanding of law." This consistent emphasis throughout the tradition demonstrates that the patterns identified support rather than undermine religious practice.

The patterns identified actually strengthen religious practice when properly understood. Recognizing God's continuous creative act in perpetual creation makes each prayer a fresh encounter rather than mere repetition, investing ritual with renewed meaning. Understanding divine mercy and rigor as complementary opposites brings balanced practice—hope without complacency, fear without despair—that avoids both extremes of presumption and desperation. Acknowledging what transcends understanding through preserving mystery brings humility to worship, preventing the arrogance that claims complete comprehension of divine reality.

Classical authorities addressed the concern about antinomianism directly when it arose. When some claimed mystical experience freed them from law, orthodox mystics responded forcefully. Al-Hujwīrī taught that "Sharī'a is the root, ṭarīqa the branch, ḥaqīqa the fruit. No fruit without root and branch," emphasizing the inseparability of law and spiritual reality. Ibn 'Aṭā' Allah explained that "the Sharī'a is the circumference, ḥaqīqa the center. You cannot reach the center except through the circumference," using spatial metaphor to show how depth and breadth must go together. Al-Sha'rānī declared categorically: "Whoever abandons the Sharī'a has abandoned the path to God," leaving no room for antinomian interpretation.

The relationship between transcendent understanding and practical law is complementary rather than contradictory. Law provides the form that mystical experience fills with meaning, preventing spiritual experience from becoming formless and antinomian. Transcendent awareness prevents law from becoming mere formalism, investing external observance with internal reality. Understanding divine incomparability brings proper intention to worship, ensuring that ritual serves divine pleasure rather than social convention or personal benefit. Recognizing perpetual creation makes each moment's obligation fresh rather than stale, renewing commitment through awareness that existence itself is divine gift requiring grateful response.

Historical evidence supports this complementarity between profound theology and meticulous practice. The great mystics were often the most legally scrupulous. 'Abd al-Qādir al-Jīlānī was simultaneously the supreme mystic of his era and a respected Ḥanbalī jurist issuing legal opinions. Al-Sha'rānī wrote extensively on both mysticism and legal obligations, demonstrating their integration in a single religious life. Aḥmad Zarrūq formulated detailed principles keeping mysticism within legal bounds, ensuring that spiritual insight served rather than undermined religious law. These exemplary figures show that the deepest mystical realization and the most careful legal observance reinforce rather than oppose each other.

This study explicitly maintains that patterns of transcendence operate within, not beyond, revealed law. The divine incomparability that transcends human categories established those very categories for human guidance. As the tradition consistently taught, the same God who is utterly transcendent mercifully provided clear guidance for human life. The mystery that exceeds comprehension does not negate the clarity that enables practice. Divine transcendence and divine guidance are complementary attributes of the One who is both "nearer than the jugular vein" and "naught is like unto Him."

These responses to potential objections aim not to dismiss legitimate concerns but to demonstrate how this study emerges from and serves authentic Islamic tradition. The patterns identified—preserving mystery within affirmation, experiencing transcendence through practice, maintaining creative tensions—are not foreign impositions but careful observations of how Muslim scholars actually approached divine incomparability across centuries and contexts. The concern about innovation reflects praiseworthy caution that has protected Islamic tradition from corrupting influences. Yet that same tradition shows remarkable creativity in expressing eternal truths for new generations. This study follows that precedent—not innovating in fundamentals but providing fresh perspective on inherited wisdom, making accessible what was always present though perhaps not previously articulated in precisely this manner.

The question of sources and orthodoxy reminds us that Islamic tradition contains legitimate diversity within essential unity. By examining this diversity comprehensively, we serve contemporary Muslims who must navigate similar diversity while maintaining authentic faith. The tradition's richness should be celebrated rather than reduced, with different voices and approaches enriching rather than fragmenting the whole. The practical implications demonstrate that profound theology and meticulous practice reinforce each other rather than existing in tension. Understanding divine transcendence deeply leads not to antinomian abandon but to more meaningful observance of divine commands, with intellectual insight deepening rather than replacing devotional commitment.

Ultimately, studying how classical Muslims approached "laysa kamithlihi shay'un" serves the living tradition. In an age of both aggressive secularism and simplistic fundamentalism, understanding our intellectual heritage's sophistication helps Muslims maintain authentic faith while engaging contemporary challenges. This is not innovation but renewal (tajdīd)—making eternal wisdom speak to present needs while changing neither the wisdom nor the essential needs it addresses. The tradition has always renewed itself through the retrieval and reapplication of foundational principles, with each generation discovering fresh dimensions in inherited truth.

Chapter 24. Conclusion: Patterns of Transcendence in Islamic Intellectual History

As this study draws to a close, we return to the fundamental principle that has guided our exploration: "laysa kamithlihi shay'un"—naught is like unto Him. Through examining fourteen centuries of Islamic intellectual engagement with divine transcendence, from Quranic foundations through contemporary applications, certain patterns have emerged that reveal both the consistency and creativity with which Muslim thinkers have approached the ultimate mystery of divine reality. This conclusion synthesizes our findings, assesses their contribution to contemporary understanding, suggests directions for future research, and reflects on the enduring relevance of classical wisdom for modern challenges.

Throughout Islamic intellectual history, the most consistent pattern has been the simultaneous affirmation of positive knowledge about God while preserving ultimate divine mystery. From the earliest Quranic exegetes who wrestled with anthropomorphic verses to contemporary philosophers engaging process thought, Muslim thinkers have maintained that authentic theology must both say and unsay, reveal and conceal, affirm and negate. This fundamental pattern of preserving mystery within affirmation manifests across all schools and periods. The Mu'tazilites affirmed divine justice while insisting it transcends human concepts of justice, refusing to reduce divine attributes to creaturely analogues. The Ash'arites developed the "bilā kayf" formula—affirming divine attributes without claiming to understand their modality—as a sophisticated response to anthropomorphism that neither denies divine qualities nor presumes to comprehend them. The philosophers demonstrated divine existence through rigorous proofs while maintaining that the divine essence remains ultimately unknowable, with rational demonstration pointing toward what exceeds rational grasp. The Sufis experienced divine presence in overwhelming immediacy while insisting that the experience itself veils the Experienced, preventing confusion between the unveiling and the ultimately veiled reality. This is not a contradiction but sophisticated recognition that approaching the Incomparable requires a dialectical method that prevents both agnostic emptiness and anthropomorphic presumption.

A second major pattern involves maintaining creative tension between divine transcendence (tanzīh) and divine immanence (tashbīh). Rather than resolving this tension through one-sided emphasis, the tradition's greatest thinkers held both poles simultaneously in productive balance. Al-Ghazālī insisted God is utterly beyond creation while being "closer than the jugular vein," refusing to sacrifice either transcendence or intimacy. Ibn 'Arabī developed elaborate metaphysics showing how the Absolutely Transcendent manifests in all existence without becoming identified with existence, articulating how the One can be both utterly other and present in every particularity. Mullā Ṣadrā demonstrated how the Immutable God relates to the changing world through perpetual creation, providing sophisticated frameworks for understanding divine action that maintains both transcendence and engagement. This tension proves productive rather than problematic, generating insights impossible from either pole alone. It reflects the Quranic presentation of a God who is simultaneously "beyond all" and "with you wherever you are," with both poles essential to authentic understanding.

Islamic thought consistently demonstrates that approaching divine transcendence requires both rigorous rational analysis and recognition of reason's limits, integrating rational and super-rational approaches in ways that avoid both rationalist reductionism and anti-intellectual mysticism. This pattern appears in early theologians who used reason to establish what reason cannot comprehend, employing logical demonstration to show demonstration's necessary boundaries. Philosophers employed demonstration to show demonstration's limitations, using reason to point beyond itself toward realities exceeding rational categories. Mystics provided rational frameworks for super-rational experiences, refusing to abandon intellectual rigor even when describing states that transcend ordinary consciousness. Contemporary thinkers engage modern philosophy while maintaining traditional commitments, demonstrating that authentic tradition can think with modernity without being reduced to it. The tradition thus avoids both the rationalism that reduces mystery to logic and the anti-rationalism that abandons intellectual rigor. Instead, it employs reason as a ladder that, having served its purpose, points beyond itself toward realities requiring modes of knowledge transcending discursive thought.

Across all schools, we find recognition that a true understanding of divine transcendence requires more than conceptual knowledge. The theologian's meditative reflection on divine names provides knowledge that transforms consciousness, not merely information to be catalogued. The philosopher's intellectual intuition of necessary existence represents direct apprehension rather than merely a syllogistic conclusion. The mystic's direct tasting (dhawq) of divine presence gives certainty exceeding demonstrative proof. The jurist's humble service, recognizing divine command, embodies rather than merely conceptualizes transcendence. The tradition insists that "laysa kamithlihi shay'un" must be experienced and not merely understood, with experiential knowledge (ma'rifa) complementing rather than replacing conceptual knowledge ('ilm). This experiential dimension prevents theology from becoming a mere academic exercise while grounding mysticism in sound doctrine, ensuring that neither intellectual sophistication nor spiritual experience becomes divorced from the other.

Perhaps most remarkably, the tradition demonstrates continuous creativity in expressing divine transcendence for new contexts while maintaining essential continuity. Each generation has found fresh language and frameworks suited to their particular challenges and intellectual horizons. Philosophical vocabulary enriched theological expression, providing precision that served rather than subverted traditional teachings. Mystical insight deepened philosophical understanding, revealing experiential dimensions that pure rationalism missed. Legal precision grounded mystical enthusiasm, preventing spiritual experience from degenerating into antinomian license. Contemporary engagement revitalizes classical insights, showing their continued relevance for addressing modern questions. This pattern of renewal within tradition shows that approaching the Eternal requires both unchanging commitment to fundamental principles and ever-new expression suited to changing contexts. Authentic tradition thus proves neither static repetition nor arbitrary innovation but creative fidelity to eternal truth.

This study reveals that many contemporary debates rest on false dichotomies foreign to classical Islamic thought, with the recovery of classical patterns offering ways beyond these unproductive oppositions. The supposed conflict between reason and revelation dissolves when we recognize how the tradition shows these as complementary rather than conflicting. Reason prepares for revelation by establishing foundational truths and clearing away intellectual obstacles. Revelation guides reason by providing truths exceeding unaided rational capacity. Both serve the journey toward Truth without either claiming autonomy from or reduction to the other. The supposed opposition between law and spirituality proves equally foreign to classical sensibilities. Rather than opposing external law and internal spirituality, classical Islam integrated them in organic unity. Law provides the form that spirituality fills with meaning, preventing formless enthusiasm. Spirituality gives life to law's structure, preventing dead formalism. Neither can function properly without the other.

The engagement between philosophy (falsafa) and theology (kalām), despite genuine tensions and disagreements, enriched both rather than requiring a choice between them. Philosophical rigor served theological expression by providing conceptual precision and logical structure. Theological commitment grounded philosophical speculation by preventing reason from claiming autonomy from revelation. The productive dialogue between these disciplines demonstrates that apparent conflicts often mask deeper complementarity. The dichotomy between tradition and innovation also dissolves under examination. The patterns identified show tradition as living and creative rather than static repetition. Authentic tradition continuously renews itself while maintaining essential identity, with each generation discovering fresh dimensions in inherited truth without abandoning that truth's core. Innovation that serves tradition differs fundamentally from innovation that subverts it, with the former representing creative fidelity rather than unfaithfulness.

The classical patterns provide unexpected resources for addressing modern challenges that might seem far removed from medieval concerns. Regarding religious pluralism, the recognition that divine transcendence exceeds all human formulation—including Islamic—provides grounds for respectful dialogue while maintaining conviction. The tradition of seeing truth in other traditions while affirming Islamic finality offers nuanced approaches beyond both relativism that denies distinctive truth claims and exclusivism that refuses to acknowledge others' insights. This sophisticated balance allows genuine engagement without requiring either abandonment of Islamic commitments or refusal to learn from others.

The perpetual creation doctrine and sophisticated discussions of divine action in nature anticipate and address modern scientific understandings in surprising ways. The tradition's comfort with mystery and multilevel causation provides frameworks for science-religion dialogue that avoid both concordism that forces artificial harmony and conflict that requires choosing between science and faith. Classical discussions of how the transcendent God acts in the world through continuous creation offer resources for understanding divine action in a universe governed by natural law without requiring violations of that law.

Classical Islamic apophatic theology, recognition of language's limits, and sophisticated hermeneutics anticipate postmodern insights while maintaining commitment to transcendent truth. The tradition offers resources for engaging contemporary philosophy without capitulating to nihilism or relativism. The recognition that human language struggles to capture divine reality, that all theological formulations remain inadequate to their object, and that multiple valid interpretations can coexist without relativizing truth provides indigenous Islamic resources for addressing postmodern concerns without abandoning traditional commitments.

The principle that divine transcendence relativizes all human authority—including gendered authority—provides Islamic grounds for justice movements addressing contemporary concerns. The recovery of women's voices in the tradition, from Rābi'a al-'Adawiyya through female scholars and mystics whose contributions have often been marginalized, enriches contemporary understanding while demonstrating that gender justice finds support within rather than against authentic tradition. Divine incomparability undermines human pretensions to absolute authority regardless of the forms those pretensions take.

This study contributes methodological insights for Islamic studies that may prove as valuable as its substantive findings. Moving beyond chronicling individual thinkers to identifying patterns reveals the tradition's underlying coherence amid surface diversity. This approach illuminates connections that studies focusing only on individual figures or specific periods miss, showing how apparently disparate thinkers participate in shared patterns of thought. Examining theology, philosophy, mysticism, and law together reveals their essential interconnection rather than treating them as autonomous domains. Artificial disciplinary boundaries obscure the tradition's holistic nature, with the greatest thinkers typically working across these supposedly separate fields. Tracing concepts across centuries through diachronic analysis shows how ideas develop while maintaining identity, revealing both continuity and change in Islamic thought. This long-term perspective prevents both antiquarianism that treats ideas as static and presentism that ignores historical depth. Demonstrating classical resources for contemporary challenges shows Islamic intellectual heritage as living wisdom rather than museum artifacts, with relevance extending beyond historical interest to present application.

This study reveals vast unexplored territories inviting future investigation. Thousands of manuscripts on divine transcendence remain unedited and unstudied in libraries worldwide. Critical editions and translations of these texts would significantly enrich understanding, potentially revealing thinkers and ideas that challenge or nuance current narratives. Studies of how different cultural contexts affected the expression of divine transcendence in African, Southeast Asian, and Central Asian traditions would reveal new patterns and variations. The tradition's remarkable capacity for cultural adaptation while maintaining essential identity deserves systematic study that most existing scholarship has not provided.

Recovering women's theological voices throughout Islamic history remains a crucial work barely begun. Their perspectives on divine transcendence often emphasized different aspects than male scholars, with distinctive insights shaped by different social locations and spiritual concerns. A systematic study of female scholars, mystics, and theologians across Islamic history would significantly nuance current understanding while demonstrating that women's contributions extend far beyond the few celebrated figures typically mentioned. This study focused necessarily on major schools and figures whose influence shaped the tradition's development. Examining lesser-known movements and thinkers would nuance understanding by revealing diversity that dominant narratives obscure, showing roads not taken and alternative articulations of fundamental principles.

Systematic comparison with other traditions would prove fruitful for both Islamic self-understanding and broader religious studies. Examining how Islamic patterns of transcendence relate to Jewish and Christian approaches would illuminate both commonalities rooted in shared Abrahamic heritage and distinctive features reflecting each tradition's particular revelations and historical developments. Such a comparison could enrich all three traditions' self-understanding while facilitating more sophisticated interfaith dialogue. Comparing Islamic approaches with Hindu, Buddhist, and Daoist concepts of ultimate reality would illuminate both similarities, suggesting universal human concerns and distinctive features reflecting different metaphysical commitments. Such comparison guards against both the universalism that erases difference and the particularism that refuses cross-cultural learning.

How do Islamic patterns relate to indigenous concepts of the sacred across diverse cultures where Islam has taken root? Such investigation could enrich both traditions' self-understanding while revealing how universal principles find local expression. Systematic engagement between Islamic transcendence and contemporary secular philosophy—from phenomenology through cognitive science to analytic philosophy—awaits development. While individual Muslim thinkers have engaged these movements, comprehensive systematic study comparing classical Islamic and contemporary secular approaches to ultimate reality, consciousness, and meaning remains largely undone. Such work could demonstrate Islam's continued relevance to cutting-edge philosophical questions while showing how traditional wisdom addresses supposedly novel concerns.

Several areas demand further development for contemporary application. How does divine transcendence ground environmental ethics in Islamic terms? The relationship between tawḥīd and ecology needs systematic development showing how recognition of the Creator's transcendence shapes proper relationship with creation. As biotechnology advances, how do classical principles address unprecedented ethical challenges regarding genetic modification, artificial reproduction, and enhancement technologies? Divine transcendence provides frameworks requiring elaboration for specific bioethical questions. What does divine transcendence mean in an age of artificial intelligence potentially approaching or exceeding human cognitive capacities? How do classical concepts of consciousness, soul, and divine reality address technological challenges to traditional anthropology? In an interconnected world facing common challenges, how does Islamic understanding of transcendence contribute to global ethical frameworks? This requires both theoretical development showing Islam's universal dimensions and practical application addressing concrete international issues.

Future research could develop new methodological approaches advancing the field. Using computational analysis to identify patterns across vast textual corpora could reveal connections that human readers miss, with digital humanities tools enabling systematic study of enormous bodies of text impossible to analyze manually. How do contemporary Muslims across diverse contexts experience divine transcendence? Ethnographic studies would complement textual analysis by examining lived religion rather than only elite intellectual production, revealing how ordinary believers understand and experience transcendence. Studying neural correlates of mystical experience could illuminate classical descriptions of spiritual states while respecting their irreducibility to mere brain activity. Such interdisciplinary work requires careful methodology avoiding both reductionism and obscurantism. How can classical wisdom about transcendence be effectively taught in contemporary contexts? This requires educational research and pedagogical innovation developing methods that transmit traditional knowledge while addressing modern students' needs and assumptions.

As this study concludes, the enduring relevance of classical Islamic wisdom about divine transcendence becomes evident. In an age characterized by reductive materialism that denies transcendent reality entirely, fundamentalisms claiming to fully comprehend the divine and reducing mystery to dogmatic certainty, relativisms abandoning truth claims entirely in supposed tolerance, and technologies challenging traditional human self-understanding through artificial intelligence and biotechnology, the classical Islamic tradition offers profound resources. Its sophisticated balance—affirming transcendent truth while acknowledging human limitations, maintaining divine accessibility while preserving ultimate mystery—provides alternatives to contemporary extremes that prove equally unsatisfying intellectually and spiritually.

Perhaps the tradition's greatest wisdom lies in refusing premature resolution of creative tensions. Rather than forcing choice between divine transcendence and immanence, reason and revelation, law and spirituality, or tradition and innovation, classical Islamic thought maintains productive tensions that generate ongoing insight. This dialectical wisdom seems particularly relevant in our polarized age where binary thinking dominates public discourse. The tradition models how to hold apparently opposing truths simultaneously without either collapsing them into false unity or allowing them to fragment into irreconcilable opposition. Such thinking challenges contemporary habits while offering desperately needed alternatives.

The principle "laysa kamithlihi shay'un" ultimately calls for intellectual and spiritual humility. Recognizing that God transcends all human categories—including our best theological ones—prevents both fundamentalist certainty claiming to possess divine truth completely and relativist despair denying that any truth can be known. This humility enables confidence without arrogance, maintaining firm convictions without closed-mindedness that refuses to learn. It enables conviction without intellectual rigidity, holding truth claims firmly while acknowledging their inevitable inadequacy to the reality they attempt to express. It facilitates dialogue without compromise of principles, engaging others genuinely while maintaining distinctive commitments. It permits learning without loss of identity, remaining open to insights from unexpected sources without losing rootedness in tradition.

Classical Islamic wisdom insists that knowing about divine transcendence differs fundamentally from knowing divine transcendence. This challenges contemporary separation of academic knowledge from transformative wisdom, where universities study religion as object without encountering it as subject. The tradition calls for scholars who are also practitioners, whose intellectual work serves rather than replaces spiritual development. It calls for practitioners who think rigorously, refusing to oppose devotion and intellect or reduce religion to either emotionalism or rationalism. It demands knowledge that transforms the knower rather than remaining merely academic. It requires transformation guided by knowledge rather than enthusiastic but theologically uninformed experience. This integration of knowledge and being addresses contemporary fragmentation while modeling holistic religious life.

This study demonstrates that tradition lives through creative engagement with new challenges rather than mere repetition of inherited formulations. The patterns identified—preserving mystery within affirmation, maintaining creative tensions, integrating diverse approaches—provide not rigid rules requiring mechanical application but flexible frameworks for continued exploration. As contemporary Muslims face unprecedented challenges from globalization, scientific advance, ideological conflict, and rapid social change, classical wisdom about divine transcendence offers neither escape into an idealized past nor uncritical embrace of the present. Instead, it provides resources for authentic engagement that honors both inherited wisdom and contemporary reality. The One who is "naught is like unto Him" remains the same yesterday, today, and forever, providing unchanging anchor. Yet human understanding must constantly renew itself in approaching this eternal mystery, with each generation discovering fresh dimensions while remaining faithful to foundations.

In closing, we return to the Quranic verse that initiated this study: "laysa kamithlihi shay'un wa huwa al-samī' al-baṣīr"—"Naught is like unto Him, and He is the All-Hearing, the All-Seeing" (42:11). After exploring fourteen centuries of Islamic reflection on this principle, its depths appear even more profound than when we began. The verse establishes absolute divine transcendence through the negation that nothing resembles Him while simultaneously affirming real divine attributes through the declaration that He hears and sees. This sets the pattern for all authentic Islamic theology—neither sacrificing transcendence to maintain accessibility nor affirming transcendence in ways that render God utterly remote. Both poles must be held simultaneously in creative tension that defies simple resolution.

This study has attempted to trace how Muslim thinkers across centuries and contexts have wrestled with this creative tension, developing sophisticated approaches that honor both divine transcendence and accessibility. We have seen how each generation found new ways to express eternal truth, adapting language and frameworks while preserving essential commitments. We have observed how different schools emphasized complementary aspects, with diversity enriching rather than fragmenting the tradition. We have discovered how apparent contradictions often revealed deeper unities, with tensions proving productive rather than problematic when maintained rather than prematurely resolved.

Yet after all the analysis, careful textual examination, and pattern identification, the mystery remains. The One who is "naught is like unto Him" transcends not only our categories but our very attempts to show how He transcends categories. Every attempt to articulate transcendence, including this study's efforts, remains hopelessly inadequate to its object.

This is perhaps the ultimate lesson: authentic knowledge of divine transcendence culminates in recognition that such knowledge remains forever incomplete, forever opening onto greater mystery. The more we understand, the more we recognize how much exceeds understanding. The closer we approach, the more we perceive the infinite distance remaining. Progress in theology consists not in solving the mystery but in deepening appreciation of its inexhaustibility.

May this study serve those who seek to understand their tradition more deeply, providing access to classical wisdom that might otherwise remain inaccessible. May it serve those engaging contemporary challenges more wisely, showing how inherited resources address present concerns. May it serve those approaching the Divine more humbly, cultivating the reverent awe appropriate before the One who utterly transcends all creation. For in the end, all our patterns and analyses, all our careful distinctions and sophisticated frameworks, are but fingers pointing at the moon—useful for indicating direction but never to be mistaken for the luminous reality toward which they point. The greatest service scholarship can provide is directing attention beyond itself toward the Reality that exceeds all scholarly comprehension.

"Subḥāna rabbika rabbi al-'izzati 'ammā yaṣifūn, wa salāmun 'alā al-mursalīn, wa-l-ḥamdu li-llāhi rabbi al-'ālamīn"—"Glorified be your Lord, the Lord of Might, above what they describe. And peace be upon the messengers. And praise be to Allah, Lord of the worlds" (37:180-182).

Appendix A: Glossary of Technical Terms

This glossary provides definitions of key Arabic technical terms used throughout this study. Terms are listed alphabetically according to their transliteration. Related terms are cross-referenced to facilitate understanding of conceptual relationships.

'adam (عدم): Non-existence, non-being. In Islamic philosophy, the state of things before creation or the absence of existence. Often contrasted with wujūd (existence). See also: ma'dūm.

adab (أدب): Proper conduct, etiquette, courtesy. In Sufi contexts, the appropriate behavior and attitude toward God, one's shaykh, and fellow seekers. Encompasses both external behavior and internal spiritual courtesy.

'adl (عدل): Justice. One of the five principles of Mu'tazilite theology, asserting that God acts only according to justice and wisdom. See also: **ḥikma.**

af'āl (أفعال): Acts, actions (plural of fi'l). In theology, refers to divine acts or human actions. Ṣifāt al-af'āl are divine attributes of action (e.g., creating, providing).

aḥadiyya (أحدية): Absolute Oneness, Unity. The highest level of divine unity in Ibn 'Arabī's system, where even the divine names are undifferentiated. Contrasted with wāḥidiyya. See also: tawḥīd.

ahl al-ḥadīth (أهل الحديث): People of Hadith. Scholars who emphasize hadith and literal interpretation over rational speculation in theology.

ahl al-kitāb (أهل الكتاب): People of the Book. Quranic term for recipients of earlier revelations, particularly Jews and Christians.

aḥwāl (أحوال): Spiritual states (plural of ḥāl). Temporary spiritual conditions granted by God, as opposed to maqāmāt (stations) which are acquired through effort.

'aql (عقل): Intellect, reason. The faculty of rational thought and understanding. Central to philosophical and theological discourse about human capacity to know God.

'ārif (عارف): Gnostic, one who possesses experiential knowledge (ma'rifa) of God. Plural: 'ārifūn or 'urafā'.

'arsh (عرش): Throne. The divine throne mentioned in the Quran, often subject to theological interpretation regarding its nature and God's relationship to it.

aṣālat al-wujūd (أصالة الوجود): Primacy of existence. Mullā Ṣadrā's doctrine that existence is the fundamental reality, with quiddities being mental abstractions.

aṣl (أصل): Root, foundation, principle. Plural: uṣūl. In jurisprudence, the sources of law; in theology, fundamental principles.

asmā' al-ḥusnā (الأسماء الحسنى): The Beautiful Names. The divine names mentioned in the Quran, traditionally numbered at ninety-nine.

'ayn thābita (عين ثابتة): Fixed entity. In Ibn 'Arabī's system, the eternal archetypes of things in divine knowledge before their manifestation in existence. Plural: a'yān thābita.

baqā' (بقاء): Subsistence, permanence. The state of continuing in God after fanā' (annihilation). Also refers to divine eternity.

barzakh (برزخ): Isthmus, intermediate realm. A boundary that both separates and connects two things. In Ibn 'Arabī's thought, the imaginal realm between the spiritual and material worlds.

basṭ (بسط): Expansion. A spiritual state of joy and openness, often paired with qabḍ (contraction). Related to the divine name al-Bāsiṭ (the Expander).

bāṭin (باطن): Inner, hidden, esoteric. The inner meaning of scripture or reality. One of the divine names (al-Bāṭin, the Hidden). Contrasted with ẓāhir.

bid'a (بدعة): Innovation. In religious contexts, unauthorized changes to belief or practice. Can be classified as praiseworthy or blameworthy.

bilā kayf (بلا كيف): Without asking how, without modality. Theological principle for accepting divine attributes without speculating on their nature.

burhān (برهان): Demonstration, decisive proof. In logic and philosophy, a syllogistic argument yielding certain knowledge.

dhāt (ذات): Essence, self. The divine essence as distinguished from divine attributes (ṣifāt).

dhawq (ذوق): Taste, direct experience. In Sufism, immediate spiritual experience as opposed to theoretical knowledge.

dhikr (ذكر): Remembrance, invocation. The practice of remembering God through repetition of divine names or formulas.

fanā' (فناء): Annihilation, passing away. The mystical experience of ego dissolution in the divine presence. See also: baqā'.

faqr (فقر): Poverty, spiritual indigence. Recognition of one's absolute need for God. A central Sufi virtue.

farq (فرق): Separation, differentiation. Consciousness of the distinction between Creator and creation. Often contrasted with jam'.

fayḍ (فيض): Emanation, overflow. The process by which existence proceeds from God. Central to Neoplatonic-influenced Islamic philosophy.

fi'l (فعل): Act, action. See af'āl.

ghalaba (غلبة): Overwhelming, domination. State of being overcome by spiritual experience.

ghayb (غيب): Unseen, hidden. The realm of reality beyond sensory perception.

ḥadath (حدث): Temporal origination. The coming into being of something that did not exist. See also: ḥudūth.

ḥāl (حال): State, spiritual condition. See aḥwāl.

ḥaqīqa (حقيقة): Reality, truth. In Sufism, the inner reality as opposed to outer appearance. Often contrasted with sharī'a.

ḥaqq (حق): Truth, reality, right. Al-Ḥaqq is a divine name meaning "The Real" or "The Truth."

ḥaraka jawhariyya (حركة جوهرية): Substantial motion. Mullā Ṣadrā's doctrine that substance itself undergoes motion and change.

ḥayra (حيرة): Bewilderment, perplexity. A spiritual state of being overwhelmed by divine mystery.

ḥikma (حكمة): Wisdom. Divine wisdom or human philosophy. Al-ḥikma al-muta'āliya is Mullā Ṣadrā's "Transcendent Philosophy."

ḥudūth (حدوث): Temporal origination, coming into being. The state of being temporally created. See also: ḥadath.

ḥulūl (حلول): Incarnation, indwelling. The heretical belief that God enters into creation. Distinguished from orthodox understandings of divine presence.

ḥuḍūr (حضور): Presence. 'Ilm al-ḥuḍūrī is knowledge by presence, immediate non-conceptual awareness.

'ibāda (عبادة): Worship, service. Acts of devotion to God.

iḥdāth (إحداث): Bringing into existence, temporal origination. God's act of creating.

iḥsān (إحسان): Excellence, beauty, doing good. The highest level of religious practice: "to worship God as if you see Him."

ijmā' (إجماع): Consensus. In jurisprudence, the agreement of scholars on a religious matter.

ijtihād (اجتهاد): Independent reasoning, scholarly effort. The process of deriving legal or theological judgments from sources.

'ilm (علم): Knowledge, science. 'Ilm al-yaqīn is certain knowledge; 'ilm ḥuḍūrī is knowledge by presence; 'ilm ḥuṣūlī is acquired knowledge.

'ilm al-yaqīn (علم اليقين): Knowledge of certainty. The first level of certainty, based on proof and evidence. See also: 'ayn al-yaqīn, ḥaqq al-yaqīn.

imkān (إمكان): Possibility, contingency. The state of being possible rather than necessary.

'irfān (عرفان): Gnosis, mystical knowledge. Often used synonymously with taṣawwuf (Sufism).

'ishq (عشق): Passionate love. Sometimes used for intense divine love, though controversial due to its sensual connotations.

ishrāq (إشراق): Illumination. The philosophy of illumination associated with al-Suhrawardī.

ism (اسم): Name. Plural: asmā'. See asmā' al-ḥusnā.

istiḥsān (استحسان): Juristic preference. A principle in Islamic law allowing departure from strict analogy for the sake of equity.

istiwā' (استواء): Establishment. God's "establishment on the Throne," subject to various theological interpretations.

ittiḥād (اتحاد): Union, unification. Sometimes used for mystical union, though orthodox theology rejects any union of essences between God and creation.

i'tibārī (اعتباري): Conceptual, mentally constructed. Opposed to real (ḥaqīqī) existence.

jalāl (جلال): Majesty. Divine attributes of power and transcendence, often contrasted with jamāl (beauty).

jam' (جمع): Gathering, synthesis. Consciousness of divine unity. See also: farq.

jamāl (جمال): Beauty. Divine attributes of mercy and accessibility, often contrasted with jalāl (majesty).

jawhar (جوهر): Substance. In philosophy, that which subsists in itself, as opposed to 'araḍ (accident).

kalām (كلام): Speech; theology. 'Ilm al-kalām is Islamic systematic theology. Also refers to divine speech.

kashf (كشف): Unveiling, disclosure. Mystical illumination or direct spiritual perception.

kayfiyya (كيفية): Modality, quality, "how-ness." The specific mode of being, which in God's case transcends human comprehension.

khafḍ (خفض): Lowering, abasing. Related to the divine name al-Khāfiḍ (the Abaser).

khalq (خلق): Creation, creatures. Both the act of creating and the created things. Contrasted with al-Ḥaqq (the Real/God).

khalq jadīd (خلق جديد): New creation. The doctrine of perpetual divine creation at each moment.

khayāl (خيال): Imagination. The faculty between sense perception and intellect. 'Ālam al-khayāl or 'ālam al-mithāl is the imaginal world.

ma'ānī (معاني): Meanings (plural of ma'nā). The significations or realities behind words and forms.

maḥabba (محبة): Love. Divine love or human love for God. A central concept in Sufi thought.

māhiyya (ماهية): Quiddity, essence, "what-ness." What makes a thing what it is, as distinguished from its existence (wujūd).

ma'iyya (معية): With-ness, divine presence with creation. God's being "with" creation while remaining transcendent.

majāz (مجاز): Metaphor, figurative speech. Opposed to ḥaqīqa (literal meaning).

maqām (مقام): Station. A stable spiritual stage attained through effort. Plural: maqāmāt.

ma'rifa (معرفة): Gnosis, experiential knowledge. Distinguished from 'ilm (theoretical knowledge).

ma'ṣiya (معصية): Disobedience, sin. Acts contrary to divine command.

mithāl (مثال): Example, similitude, image. 'Ālam al-mithāl is the imaginal world. See also: khayāl.

muḥdath (محدث): Temporally originated, created. That which has a beginning in time.

mukāshafa (مكاشفة): Unveiling, spiritual disclosure. Direct mystical experience.

mulk (ملك): Dominion, sovereignty. God's absolute rule over creation.

mumkin (ممكن): Possible, contingent. That which can exist or not exist, requiring a cause for its existence.

munazzah (منزه): Transcendent, free from imperfection. Related to tanzīh.

murāqaba (مراقبة): Vigilance, contemplation. Spiritual practice of maintaining awareness of God's presence.

mushāhada (مشاهدة): Witnessing, vision. Direct spiritual perception of divine realities.

mutakallim (متكلم): Theologian. One who practices kalām. Plural: mutakallimūn.

nafs (نفس): Soul, self, ego. Has multiple levels from the lowest (nafs al-ammāra) to the highest (nafs al-muṭma'inna).

nafy (نفي): Negation. In theology, negating imperfections from God.

qabḍ (قبض): Contraction. A spiritual state of constraint, often paired with basṭ (expansion).

qaḍā' (قضاء): Divine decree. God's eternal decision regarding all events.

qadar (قدر): Divine predetermination, measure. God's determination of all things according to His knowledge and wisdom.

qadīm (قديم): Eternal, without beginning. An attribute of God alone in orthodox theology.

qahr (قهر): Subjugation, dominance. Related to the divine name al-Qāhir (the Subduer).

qalb (قلب): Heart. The spiritual center of the human being, organ of spiritual perception.

qiyās (قياس): Analogy. In jurisprudence, reasoning by analogy; in logic, syllogism.

qudra (قدرة): Power, capability. Divine omnipotence.

qurb (قرب): Nearness, proximity. Spiritual closeness to God.

raḥma (رحمة): Mercy, compassion. A central divine attribute.

rujū' (رجوع): Return. The soul's return to God; also the return to normal consciousness after mystical experience.

rūḥ (روح): Spirit. The subtle reality connecting body and soul to the divine.

ṣaḥw (صحو): Sobriety. Normal consciousness, especially after spiritual intoxication (sukr).

sharī'a (شريعة): The religious law, the outward path. Often contrasted with ḥaqīqa (inner reality).

shaṭḥ (شطح): Ecstatic utterance. Controversial statements made in states of spiritual overwhelming. Plural: shaṭaḥāt.

shirk (شرك): Associationism, polytheism. Attributing partners to God; the gravest sin in Islam.

shu'ūn (شؤون): Affairs, matters (plural of sha'n). Divine activities or concerns.

ṣifa (صفة): Attribute, quality. Divine attributes such as knowledge, power, mercy. Plural: ṣifāt.

silsila (سلسلة): Chain. The initiatic chain in Sufism connecting disciples to the Prophet through successive masters.

sirr (سر): Secret, mystery. The innermost consciousness; divine mysteries.

sukr (سكر): Intoxication. Spiritual overwhelming that may lead to ecstatic utterances.

ta'ayyun (تعين): Determination, entification. The process by which the Absolute becomes determined in particular forms.

tafwīḍ (تفويض): Delegation, entrustment. Entrusting the true meaning of ambiguous verses to God.

tajallī (تجلي): Self-disclosure, manifestation. God's revealing of Himself to creation. Plural: tajalliyāt.

tajdīd (تجديد): Renewal. The renewal of religion in each age; also the renewal of creation at each moment.

tajrīd (تجريد): Abstraction, stripping away. Removing anthropomorphic understandings from divine attributes.

tajsīm (تجسيم): Anthropomorphism, corporealism. The heretical attribution of bodily characteristics to God.

takhalluq (تخلق): Taking on divine qualities. The spiritual practice of embodying divine attributes within human limits.

takyīf (تكييف): Assigning modality. Attempting to describe how God's attributes subsist, which orthodoxy prohibits.

tanzīh (تنزيه): Transcendence, declaring God free from imperfection. Contrasted with tashbīh.

taqdīs (تقديس): Sanctification. Declaring God's absolute holiness and otherness.

taqwā (تقوى): God-consciousness, piety. Awareness of God that leads to righteous behavior.

tarīqa (طريقة): Path, way. The spiritual path; also a Sufi order. Plural:

ṭuruq.

tashbīh (تشبيه): Immanence, comparison, anthropomorphism. Likening God to creation. Must be balanced with tanzīh.

tashkīk (تشكيك): Gradation. The doctrine that reality admits of degrees of intensity.

taṣawwuf (تصوف): Sufism. The mystical dimension of Islam.

ta'ṭīl (تعطيل): Negation, stripping away. Denying divine attributes altogether; considered heretical.

tawakkul (توكل): Trust, reliance on God. Complete dependence on divine providence.

tawḥīd (توحيد): Divine unity, unification. The central doctrine of Islam affirming God's absolute oneness.

ta'wīl (تأويل): Interpretation, especially allegorical or esoteric. Going beyond the apparent meaning to deeper significance.

'ubūdiyya (عبودية): Servanthood. The state of being God's servant; the human side of the divine-human relationship.

'ulūm naqliyya (علوم نقلية): Transmitted sciences. Religious sciences based on revelation and tradition.

'ulūm 'aqliyya (علوم عقلية): Rational sciences. Sciences based on reason and observation.

uns (أنس): Intimacy. Spiritual intimacy with God, often contrasted with hayba (awe).

uṣūl (أصول): Foundations, principles (plural of aṣl). Uṣūl al-dīn are the principles of religion; uṣūl al-fiqh are the principles of jurisprudence.

waḥdat al-shuhūd (وحدة الشهود): Unity of witnessing. The mystical experience of seeing only God, associated with the Naqshbandī order.

waḥdat al-wujūd (وحدة الوجود): Unity of being/existence. The doctrine associated with Ibn 'Arabī that existence is one.

wāḥidiyya (واحدية): Unity in multiplicity. In Ibn 'Arabī's system, the level where divine names are differentiated while remaining one.

waḥy (وحي): Revelation. Divine communication to prophets.

wājib al-wujūd (واجب الوجود): Necessary Existent. That which must exist by its very nature; God alone.

walāya (ولاية): Sainthood, spiritual authority. The state of being God's friend (walī).

wārid (وارد): Divine influx. Spiritual experiences or insights that come to the seeker unbidden. Plural: wāridāt.

waṣl (وصل): Union, connection. Spiritual connection with God, though not union of essences.

wujūd (وجود): Existence, being. In philosophy, the act of existing as opposed to essence (māhiyya).

yaqīn (يقين): Certainty. Has three levels: 'ilm al-yaqīn (knowledge of certainty), 'ayn al-yaqīn (eye of certainty), and ḥaqq al-yaqīn (truth of certainty).

ẓāhir (ظاهر): Outward, manifest, exoteric. The outer meaning or appearance. One of divine names (al-Ẓāhir, the Manifest). Contrasted with bāṭin.

ẓann (ظن): Conjecture, opinion. Knowledge that is probable but not certain.

dhawq (ذوق): Taste, direct experience. Immediate spiritual perception as opposed to theoretical knowledge.

ẓuhūr (ظهور): Manifestation, appearance. The process by which the hidden becomes manifest.

zuhd (زهد): Asceticism, renunciation. Detachment from worldly concerns for the sake of the divine

Appendix B: Biographical Notes on Major Figures

This appendix provides biographical information on major figures discussed in this study, arranged chronologically. Each entry includes dates in both Islamic (AH) and Common Era (CE) calendars, geographical information, major works, and significance to the theme of divine transcendence.

Early Period (1st-3rd Century AH / 7th-9th Century CE)

Al-Ḥasan al-Baṣrī (21-110 AH / 642-728 CE)

Born in Medina, raised in Basra. One of the most influential figures of early Islam, bridging the gap between the Companions and later theological development. A renowned preacher, ascetic, and theologian who taught many of the founders of later schools.

Key Contributions: Emphasized divine transcendence through apophatic statements. His teachings on free will and divine justice influenced later Mu'tazilite thought. Famous for stating: "The root of all error is thinking you know Allah as you know created things."

Influence on Topic: Established early patterns of speaking about divine incomparability that would echo through Islamic thought.

Rābi'a al-'Adawiyya (95-185 AH / 714-801 CE)

From Basra, born into poverty, she later became the most famous female mystic in Islamic history. Revolutionary in making divine love central to spiritual life.

Key Contributions: Transformed Islamic spirituality by emphasizing pure, disinterested love of God. Her prayers rejecting Paradise and Hell in favor of God Himself became paradigmatic.

Major Sayings: "O God, if I worship You from fear of Hell, burn me in Hell. If I worship You from hope of Paradise, exclude me from Paradise. But if I worship You for Your own sake, do not withhold from me Your eternal beauty."

Influence on Topic: Demonstrated how divine transcendence could be approached through love rather than fear or philosophical speculation.

Ja'far al-Ṣādiq (80-148 AH / 699-765 CE)
Sixth Imam of Shi'i Islam, also recognized by Sunnis as a great scholar and mystic. Taught in Medina where students included Abū Ḥanīfa and Mālik ibn Anas.
Key Contributions: Developed sophisticated theological positions on divine attributes and human knowledge of God. Distinguished between levels of divine love and knowledge.
Influence on Topic: His teachings on the limits of human knowledge regarding divine essence influenced both Shi'i and Sunni thought.

Abū Ḥanīfa (80-150 AH / 699-767 CE)
Founder of the Hanafi school of law, also contributed to early theological development. Born in Kufa to a Persian family, became a successful merchant before devoting himself to scholarship.
Theological Contributions: His *al-Fiqh al-Akbar* contains important early statements on divine transcendence. Emphasized reason's role while maintaining its limits.
Key Position: "Allah has attributes subsisting in His essence. They are neither Him nor other than Him."

Mālik ibn Anas (93-179 AH / 711-795 CE)
Founder of the Maliki school of law, spent his entire life in Medina. His legal methodology emphasized practice of Medina alongside textual sources.
Famous Statement: Regarding divine "establishment on the Throne": "The establishment is known, the modality is unknown, belief in it is obligatory, and asking about it is innovation."
Influence on Topic: His "bilā kayf" (without asking how) became the paradigmatic Sunni approach to divine attributes.

Al-Muḥāsibī (165-243 AH / 781-857 CE)
From Baghdad, a foundational figure in Islamic psychology and spirituality. His rigorous self-examination influenced all later Sufi thought.
Major Works: *Ri'āyat Ḥuqūq Allah* (Observance of God's Rights), *al-Tawahhum* (Imagination)
Key Contributions: Developed sophisticated analysis of spiritual states and stages. Distinguished types of fanā' (annihilation) and their relationship to

divine attributes.

Dhū al-Nūn al-Miṣrī (180-245 AH / 796-859 CE)
Egyptian mystic and alchemist, considered one of the foundational figures of Sufism. Credited with formulating the distinction between ma'rifa (gnosis) and 'ilm (knowledge).
Key Teaching: "The gnostic knows God through God, while the scholar knows God through His creation."
Influence on Topic: Developed understanding of experiential knowledge of divine transcendence as distinct from theoretical knowledge.

Al-Kindī (185-256 AH / 801-873 CE)
First major Muslim philosopher, known as "Philosopher of the Arabs." From a noble Arab family, worked in Baghdad under Abbasid patronage.
Major Works: *On First Philosophy*, numerous treatises on logic, metaphysics, and mathematics
Philosophical Position: Attempted to harmonize Greek philosophy with Islamic theology. Argued for creation ex nihilo using philosophical arguments.
Key Contribution: "Truth is truth regardless of its source. We should not be ashamed to acknowledge truth wherever we find it."

Al-Bukhārī (194-256 AH / 810-870 CE)
From Bukhara, compiler of the most authoritative hadith collection. His *Ṣaḥīḥ* includes important traditions about divine attributes and transcendence.
Significance: Preserved prophetic traditions crucial for understanding divine transcendence, including the hadith of divine descent and the hadith of voluntary devotions.

Abū Yazīd al-Bisṭāmī (Bāyazīd) (188-261 AH / 804-875 CE)
Persian mystic from Bistam, famous for ecstatic utterances. Represented the "intoxicated" school of Sufism.
Famous Utterances: "Glory be to me! How great is my station!" "I am the Throne and the Footstool!"
Influence on Topic: His shaṭaḥāt (ecstatic utterances) forced Muslim

thinkers to develop frameworks for understanding mystical language about divine-human relationship.

Classical Period (4th-7th Century AH / 10th-13th Century CE)

Al-Junayd (215-298 AH / 830-910 CE)
From Baghdad, known as "Master of the Sufi Path." Student of al-Muḥāsibī and uncle of al-Shiblī. Represented the "sober" school of Sufism.
Key Teaching: "Tawḥīd is separating the eternal from the temporal."
Major Contribution: Developed sophisticated understanding of fanā' and baqā' that preserved orthodox distinction between Creator and creation.
Influence: His balanced approach became normative for mainstream Sufism.

Al-Ḥallāj (244-309 AH / 858-922 CE)
Persian mystic executed for his controversial teachings. His death marked a watershed in Islamic mysticism.
Famous Statement: "Anā al-Ḥaqq" (I am the Truth/Real)
Significance: His execution forced clearer articulation of boundaries in mystical expression and led to more careful formulations by later Sufis.

Al-Ash'arī (260-324 AH / 874-936 CE)
From Basra, founder of the Ash'arite school of theology. Originally a Mu'tazilite who then developed a middle position between rationalism and traditionalism.
Major Works: *Maqālāt al-Islāmiyyīn, al-Ibāna, al-Luma'*
Key Contribution: Developed the "bilā kayf" methodology systematically, using rational argumentation to defend traditional positions on divine attributes.

Al-Māturīdī (238-333 AH / 853-944 CE)
From Samarqand, founder of the Maturidite school of theology. Contemporary of al-Ash'arī but developed independently.
Major Works: *Kitāb al-Tawḥīd, Ta'wīlāt Ahl al-Sunna*
Distinctive Position: More optimistic about reason's capacity than Ash'arites while maintaining divine transcendence.

Al-Fārābī (257-339 AH / 870-950 CE)
From Farab (modern Kazakhstan), known as the "Second Teacher" after Aristotle. Major Muslim philosopher who influenced all later Islamic philosophy.
Major Works: *The Virtuous City, The Harmonization of the Opinions of Plato and Aristotle*
Key Contribution: Developed emanationist metaphysics attempting to reconcile divine transcendence with creation.

Ibn Masarra (269-319 AH / 883-931 CE)
From Córdoba, early Andalusian mystic and philosopher. His esoteric teachings influenced later Spanish Muslim thought including Ibn 'Arabī.
Significance: Developed early synthesis of philosophy and mysticism in the Western Islamic world.

Al-Sarrāj (d. 378 AH / 988 CE)
From Tus, author of one of the earliest Sufi manuals. His work preserved teachings of earlier masters.
Major Work: *Kitāb al-Luma' fi'l-Taṣawwuf*
Contribution: Systematized Sufi teachings on divine transcendence, providing orthodox framework for mystical experience.

Al-Kalābādhī (d. 380 AH / 990 CE)
From Bukhara, Hanafi jurist and theologian who defended Sufism's orthodoxy.
Major Work: *al-Ta'arruf li-Madhhab Ahl al-Taṣawwuf*
Significance: Demonstrated compatibility between Sufi teachings on transcendence and mainstream Sunni theology.

Al-Bāqillānī (338-403 AH / 950-1013 CE)
From Basra, major Ash'arite theologian who systematized the school's positions.
Major Works: *al-Tamhīd, al-Inṣāf, I'jāz al-Qur'ān*
Key Contributions: Refined Ash'arite positions on divine attributes and developed sophisticated responses to philosophical challenges.

Ibn Sīnā (Avicenna) (370-428 AH / 980-1037 CE)
From Bukhara, the most influential Muslim philosopher. His synthesis of Aristotelian and Neoplatonic thought shaped all later Islamic philosophy.
Major Works: *al-Shifā', al-Najāt, al-Ishārāt wa'l-Tanbīhāt*
Key Concept: The Necessary Existent (wājib al-wujūd) as philosophical articulation of divine transcendence.
Influence: His thought provoked both adoption and critique, especially from al-Ghazālī.

Al-Qushayrī (376-465 AH / 986-1074 CE)
From Nishapur, Ash'arite theologian and Sufi master. Student of al-Sulamī and teacher of al-Juwaynī.
Major Work: *al-Risāla al-Qushayriyya*, the most influential Sufi manual
Contribution: Provided definitive orthodox framework for understanding mystical experiences of divine transcendence.

Al-Hujwīrī (400-465 AH / 1009-1074 CE)
From Ghazni, settled in Lahore. Author of the first Persian treatise on Sufism.
Major Work: *Kashf al-Maḥjūb* (Unveiling of the Veiled)
Significance: Made Sufi teachings on divine transcendence accessible to Persian-speaking world.

Al-Juwaynī (419-478 AH / 1028-1085 CE)
From Nishapur, known as Imām al-Ḥaramayn. Teacher of al-Ghazālī and major Ash'arite theologian.
Major Works: *al-Irshād, al-Shāmil*
Key Contribution: Refined Ash'arite methodology and engaged seriously with philosophical challenges to traditional theology.

Al-Ghazālī (450-505 AH / 1058-1111 CE)
From Tus, perhaps the most influential post-formative Muslim thinker. Integrated philosophy, theology, law, and mysticism.
Major Works: *Iḥyā' 'Ulūm al-Dīn, Tahāfut al-Falāsifa, Mishkāt al-Anwār, al-Maqṣad al-Asnā*

Key Achievement: Synthesized rational and mystical approaches to divine transcendence while maintaining orthodox boundaries.

Al-Shahrastānī (479-548 AH / 1086-1153 CE)
From Shahristān, historian of religions and Ash'arite theologian.
Major Work: *al-Milal wa'l-Niḥal* (Book of Sects and Creeds)
Contribution: Provided comprehensive analysis of different approaches to divine transcendence across Islamic schools.
'Abd al-Qādir al-Jīlānī (470-561 AH / 1077-1166 CE)
From Gilan, settled in Baghdad. Founder of the Qadiriyya order and Ḥanbalī jurist.
Significance: Demonstrated integration of strict legal observance with profound mystical understanding of divine transcendence.

Al-Suhrawardī (549-587 AH / 1154-1191 CE)
From Suhraward, executed in Aleppo. Founder of Illuminationist philosophy.
Major Work: *Ḥikmat al-Ishrāq* (Philosophy of Illumination)
Key Contribution: Developed light metaphysics as alternative to Avicennan being metaphysics for understanding divine transcendence.

Ibn Rushd (Averroes) (520-595 AH / 1126-1198 CE)
From Córdoba, major philosopher and Mālikī judge. Defended philosophy against al-Ghazālī's critique.
Major Works: *Tahāfut al-Tahāfut*, *Faṣl al-Maqāl*, commentaries on Aristotle
Position: Argued for harmony between philosophy and revelation in understanding divine transcendence.

Fakhr al-Dīn al-Rāzī (544-606 AH / 1149-1210 CE)
From Rayy, major Ash'arite theologian and Quranic exegete who extensively used philosophy.
Major Works: *Mafātīḥ al-Ghayb* (Quranic commentary), *al-Maṭālib al-'Āliya*
Significance: Showed how philosophical sophistication could serve traditional theology of transcendence.

Ibn 'Arabī (560-638 AH / 1165-1240 CE)
From Murcia, settled in Damascus. Known as al-Shaykh al-Akbar, the most influential mystical thinker in Islamic history.
Major Works: *al-Futūḥāt al-Makkiyya, Fuṣūṣ al-Ḥikam*
Key Concepts: Waḥdat al-wujūd (Unity of Being), tajallī (divine self-disclosure), al-insān al-kāmil (Perfect Human)
Influence: His systematic mystical theology transformed understanding of divine transcendence and immanence.

Later Medieval Period (7th-10th Century AH / 13th-16th Century CE)

Ibn al-Fāriḍ (576-632 AH / 1181-1235 CE)
From Cairo, the greatest Arabic mystical poet. His poetry expressed profound experiences of divine transcendence.
Major Work: *Dīwān*, including the "Wine Ode" (al-Khamriyya) and "Poem of the Way" (Naẓm al-Sulūk)
Significance: Expressed mystical experience of transcendence in poetic form that influenced centuries of Sufi expression.
Ṣadr al-Dīn al-Qūnawī (d. 673 AH / 1274 CE)
From Konya, Ibn 'Arabī's stepson and chief disciple. Systematized and taught his master's doctrines.
Major Works: *Miftāḥ al-Ghayb, al-Fukūk*
Contribution: Provided philosophical precision to Ibn 'Arabī's mystical insights about divine transcendence.

Jalāl al-Dīn Rūmī (604-672 AH / 1207-1273 CE)
From Balkh, settled in Konya. Founder of the Mevlevi order and author of the most read mystical poetry in Islamic history.
Major Works: *Mathnawī, Dīwān-i Shams*
Approach: Used poetry and stories to convey experiences of divine transcendence that philosophical language could not capture.

Ibn Taymiyya (661-728 AH / 1263-1328 CE)
From Harran, settled in Damascus. Ḥanbalī theologian and reformer who critiqued both philosophers and many Sufis.

Major Works: *Dar' Ta'āruḍ al-'Aql wa'l-Naql*, numerous treatises and fatwas
Position: Maintained divine transcendence through strict adherence to scriptural descriptions while rejecting philosophical and mystical elaborations he saw as innovations.

Ibn 'Aṭā' Allah al-Iskandarī (658-709 AH / 1260-1309 CE)
From Alexandria, third master of the Shādhilī order. Integrated Akbarian metaphysics with sober Shādhilī practice.
Major Work: *al-Ḥikam al-'Aṭā'iyya* (Aphorisms)
Contribution: Expressed profound insights about divine transcendence in concise, memorable aphorisms.

'Abd al-Razzāq al-Qāshānī (d. 736 AH / 1335 CE)
Persian Sufi commentator on Ibn 'Arabī's works.
Major Work: Commentary on *Fuṣūṣ al-Ḥikam*
Significance: His interpretations shaped understanding of Akbarian doctrines about divine transcendence for later generations.

Al-Taftāzānī (722-792 AH / 1322-1390 CE)
From Taftazan, major theologian whose works became standard texts in madrasas.
Major Work: *Sharḥ al-'Aqā'id al-Nasafiyya*
Contribution: Provided clear, teaching-oriented presentations of orthodox positions on divine transcendence.

Ibn Khaldūn (732-808 AH / 1332-1406 CE)
From Tunis, historian and social philosopher. While known for historical work, also contributed to discussions of metaphysics.
Major Work: *al-Muqaddima*
Relevant Contribution: Analyzed the social and intellectual conditions affecting theological development, including concepts of transcendence.
Early Modern Period (10th-13th Century AH / 16th-19th Century CE)

Ibn Kamāl Pāshā (873-940 AH / 1468-1534 CE)
Ottoman Shaykh al-Islam and polymath scholar.
Contribution: Wrote treatises distinguishing orthodox from heterodox interpretations of divine transcendence, particularly regarding Ibn 'Arabī's

teachings.

Al-Sha'rānī (898-973 AH / 1493-1565 CE)
From Cairo, Sufi master and prolific author who defended Ibn 'Arabī while maintaining orthodox credentials.
Major Works: *al-Yawāqīt wa'l-Jawāhir*, *Laṭā'if al-Minan*
Significance: Showed how controversial mystical doctrines about transcendence could be understood within orthodox frameworks.

Mullā Ṣadrā (979-1050 AH / 1571-1640 CE)
From Shiraz, founder of Transcendent Philosophy school. Synthesized philosophy, theology, and mysticism.
Major Work: *al-Asfār al-Arba'a*
Key Concepts: Primacy of existence (aṣālat al-wujūd), substantial motion (al-ḥaraka al-jawhariyya)
Achievement: Created dynamic metaphysics preserving divine transcendence while explaining change.

Aḥmad Sirhindī (971-1034 AH / 1564-1624 CE)
From Sirhind, Naqshbandī master known as Mujaddid Alf-i Thānī (Renewer of the Second Millennium).
Key Concept: Waḥdat al-shuhūd (Unity of Witnessing) as alternative to waḥdat al-wujūd
Contribution: Provided framework for mystical experience of transcendence that emphasized Creator-creation distinction.

'Abd al-Ghanī al-Nābulusī (1050-1143 AH / 1641-1731 CE)
From Damascus, Sufi scholar who wrote extensively on Ibn 'Arabī's thought.
Contribution: Defended sophisticated understanding of divine transcendence in mystical thought against both anthropomorphists and those who denied divine attributes.

Shāh Walī Allah (1114-1176 AH / 1703-1762 CE)
From Delhi, major reformer who synthesized various Islamic sciences.
Major Work: *Ḥujjat Allah al-Bāligha*
Approach: Integrated traditional theology, philosophy, mysticism, and law in addressing divine transcendence.

Modern Period (13th-15th Century AH / 19th-21st Century CE)

Muhammad 'Abduh (1266-1323 AH / 1849-1905 CE)
From Egypt, Islamic modernist and reformer. Grand Mufti of Egypt.
Contribution: Reinterpreted classical theology for modern context, emphasizing reason while maintaining divine transcendence.

Muhammad Iqbal (1294-1357 AH / 1877-1938 CE)
From Sialkot, philosopher-poet of South Asia. Studied in Cambridge and Munich.
Major Work: *The Reconstruction of Religious Thought in Islam*
Key Contribution: Developed dynamic theology presenting God as Absolute Ego, creative and responsive rather than static.

Said Nursi (1294-1379 AH / 1877-1960 CE)
From Eastern Anatolia, Islamic scholar and revivalist.
Major Work: *Risale-i Nur*
Approach: Used "book of universe" to demonstrate divine attributes and transcendence for modern audience.

Seyyed Hossein Nasr (Born 1352 AH / 1933 CE)
From Tehran, philosopher and professor. Leading representative of perennial philosophy.
Major Works: *Knowledge and the Sacred, The Heart of Islam*
Position: Defends traditional metaphysics of transcendence against modern reductionism.

Fazlur Rahman (1337-1409 AH / 1919-1988 CE)
From Pakistan, Islamic modernist scholar. Taught at University of Chicago.
Major Work: *Major Themes of the Qur'an*
Contribution: Developed hermeneutical approach maintaining divine transcendence while ensuring contemporary relevance.

Mohamed Arkoun (1347-1431 AH / 1928-2010 CE)
From Algeria, professor at Sorbonne. Applied contemporary critical methods to Islamic thought.

Approach: Used modern philosophical tools to uncover "unthought" assumptions in classical approaches to transcendence.

Abdolkarim Soroush (Born 1364 AH / 1945 CE)
From Tehran, philosopher and reformist thinker.
Key Concept: Distinction between religion and religious knowledge
Contribution: Argues for epistemological humility regarding divine transcendence while maintaining religious commitment.

Timothy Winter (Abdal Hakim Murad) (Born 1379 AH / 1960 CE)
British Islamic scholar and Cambridge professor. Combines traditional learning with contemporary engagement.
Contribution: Articulates classical understanding of divine transcendence for contemporary Western audiences while maintaining scholarly rigor.

Appendix C: Chronological Overview of Developments

This chronological overview traces the major developments in Islamic thought regarding divine transcendence from the Quranic revelation through the contemporary period. Each era highlights key themes, figures, texts, and conceptual advances.

The Foundational Period (610-632 CE / Prophetic Era)

Quranic Revelation

610-632 CE: Progressive revelation establishing fundamental principles
Core verse: "Laysa kamithlihi shay'un" (42:11)
Divine names teaching transcendence with accessibility
Anthropomorphic expressions balanced with declarations of incomparability
Light Verse (24:35) providing metaphysical imagery

Prophetic Teaching

Hadith establishing interpretive principles
"Bilā kayf" approach in nascent form
Balance between transcendence (tanzīh) and accessibility
Prayers and supplications modeling theological language

The Era of the Companions and Successors (632-750 CE)

First Generation Responses (632-680)

Ibn 'Abbās (d. 687): Early exegetical principles for anthropomorphic verses
'Alī ibn Abī Ṭālib (d. 661): Sophisticated theological formulations
'Ā'isha (d. 678): Practical applications of transcendence principle

Second Generation Developments (680-750)

Al-Ḥasan al-Baṣrī (d. 728): First systematic theological reflections
Early Qadariyya: Debates about divine justice and human freedom
Proto-Murji'a: Questions about divine judgment and human actions

Key Developments
Establishment of interpretive principles for anthropomorphic texts
Beginning of theological schools
Integration of non-Arab converts bringing philosophical questions

The Classical Formative Period (750-950 CE)

Early Abbasid Era (750-850)
Translation Movement: Greek philosophical texts enter Islamic thought
Mu'tazilite Emergence:
Wāṣil ibn 'Aṭā' (d. 748): Systematic rational theology
Divine justice ('adl) and unity (tawḥīd) as organizing principles
Negation of divine attributes to preserve unity
The Miḥna Period (833-848)
Mu'tazilite doctrine becomes state orthodoxy
Debate over created vs. eternal Quran
Ahmad ibn Ḥanbal's resistance establishing traditionalist principles
Post-Miḥna Synthesis (850-950)
Al-Ash'arī (d. 936): Revolutionary synthesis
Rational defense of traditional positions
"Bilā kayf" methodology systematized
Attributes neither identical to nor separate from essence
Al-Māturīdī (d. 944): Parallel development in Central Asia
Greater confidence in reason
Emphasis on divine wisdom
Mediating positions on free will
Mystical Developments
Dhū al-Nūn (d. 859): Ma'rifa vs. 'ilm distinction
Al-Bisṭāmī (d. 875): Ecstatic utterances raising new questions
Al-Junayd (d. 910): "Sober" mysticism preserving orthodoxy

The Classical Period (950-1250 CE)

Philosophical Flourishing (950-1100)
Al-Fārābī (d. 950): Emanationist metaphysics

Ibn Sīnā (d. 1037):
Necessary Existent as philosophical articulation
Essence-existence distinction
Knowledge by presence
Al-Ghazālī (d. 1111):
Tahāfut al-Falāsifa critiquing philosophers
Integration of mysticism with orthodox theology
Sophisticated treatment of divine names

Theological Maturation (950-1150)
Al-Bāqillānī (d. 1013): Ash'arism systematized
Al-Juwaynī (d. 1085): Refined theological methodology
Al-Qushayrī (d. 1074): Orthodox Sufi manual
Development of theological curricula in madrasas

Andalusian Contributions (1000-1200)
Ibn Ḥazm (d. 1064): Ẓāhirī literalism with sophistication
Ibn Rushd (d. 1198): Defense of philosophy
Cross-cultural synthesis in Iberian context

Mystical Systematization (1100-1250)
Al-Ghazālī: Bridging theology and mysticism
'Abd al-Qādir al-Jīlānī (d. 1166): Mysticism within law
Al-Suhrawardī (d. 1191): Illuminationist philosophy
Ibn 'Arabī (d. 1240):
Waḥdat al-wujūd doctrine
Systematic mystical theology
Perfect Human (al-insān al-kāmil) concept

The Post-Classical Period (1250-1500 CE)

Consolidation and Commentary (1250-1350)
Ṣadr al-Dīn al-Qūnawī (d. 1274): Systematizing Ibn 'Arabī
Al-Rāzī's influence continues through commentaries
Madrasa curriculum standardization
Integration of philosophy into theology becomes standard

Responses and Reactions (1300-1400)
Ibn Taymiyya (d. 1328):
Critique of philosophy and mystical excess
Return to scripture and early authorities
Sophisticated theological argumentation
Ibn Qayyim al-Jawziyya (d. 1350): Elaborating teacher's positions
Debates over Ibn 'Arabī's orthodoxy

Regional Developments (1300-1500)
Ottoman lands: Integration of various schools
Persia: Continued philosophical development
India: Synthesis of local traditions
Africa: Distinctive theological emphases

The Early Modern Period (1500-1800 CE)

Ottoman Systematization (1500-1700)
Official adoption of Māturīdī-Ḥanafī theology
Ibn Kamāl Pāshā (d. 1534): Distinguishing orthodox from heterodox
Institutional support for particular interpretations
Commentary tradition flourishes

Safavid Philosophical Renaissance (1500-1700)
Mīr Dāmād (d. 1631): New philosophical synthesis
Mullā Ṣadrā (d. 1640):
Transcendent Philosophy (al-ḥikma al-muta'āliya)
Primacy of existence
Substantial motion
Dynamic metaphysics

Reform Movements (1600-1800)
Aḥmad Sirhindī (d. 1624): Waḥdat al-shuhūd vs. waḥdat al-wujūd
Shāh Walī Allah (d. 1762): Comprehensive synthesis
Muhammad ibn 'Abd al-Wahhāb (d. 1792): Purificationist approach
Responses to perceived innovations and foreign influences

The Modern Period (1800-1950 CE)

Early Modernist Responses (1850-1920)
Al-Afghānī (d. 1897): Pan-Islamic reform
Muhammad 'Abduh (d. 1905):
Rational interpretation for modern age
Maintaining transcendence while ensuring relevance
Rashīd Riḍā (d. 1935): Salafi modernism

Philosophical Reconstruction (1870-1940)
Muhammad Iqbal (d. 1938):
Dynamic conception of God
Critique of classical metaphysics
Integration with modern philosophy
God as Ultimate Ego
Traditional Responses (1880-1950)
Maḥmūd Shaltūt: Al-Azhar's modernization
Muṣṭafā al-Marāghī: Quranic exegesis for modern times
Preservation movements in traditional centers

The Contemporary Period (1950-Present)

Academic Engagement (1950-1980)
Fazlur Rahman (d. 1988): Hermeneutical approach
Seyyed Hossein Nasr: Perennialist philosophy
Toshihiko Izutsu: Semantic analysis of Quranic concepts
University-based Islamic studies

Diverse Approaches (1970-2000)
Mohamed Arkoun: Post-structuralist readings
Abdolkarim Soroush: Epistemological questions
Tariq Ramadan: European Muslim theology
Gender-inclusive interpretations emerging

Current Developments (2000-Present)
Digital revolution affecting transmission
Global accessibility of classical texts
New forms of teaching and community
Environmental theology incorporating transcendence
Neuroscience and consciousness studies engagement
Post-colonial theological reconstruction

Major Conceptual Developments Through Time

Divine Attributes

Early Period: Simple affirmation with "bilā kayf"
Classical: Sophisticated distinctions (essence/attributes)
Post-Classical: Integration with philosophy
Modern: Engagement with process thought

Mystical Experience

Early: Individual experiences and sayings
Classical: Systematic frameworks (fanā'/baqā')
Post-Classical: Metaphysical elaboration
Modern: Psychological and phenomenological analysis

Reason and Revelation

Early: Natural harmony assumed
Classical: Formal methodologies developed
Post-Classical: Synthesis achieved
Modern: New challenges from science and philosophy

Language and Transcendence

Early: Scriptural language accepted with qualification
Classical: Hermeneutical principles established
Post-Classical: Multiple interpretive levels recognized
Modern: Linguistic philosophy engagement

Patterns Across Periods

Consistent Themes

Preservation of "laysa kamithlihi shay'un" as fundamental
Balance between transcendence and immanence
Integration of diverse intellectual streams
Practical application alongside theoretical development

Recurring Challenges

Anthropomorphism vs. abstraction
Unity vs. attributes
Mystical experience vs. orthodox boundaries
Cultural translation of concepts

Methods of Resolution

Creative synthesis rather than simple choice
Levels of meaning and understanding
Institutional frameworks for transmission
Living tradition adapting to new contexts

Contemporary Trajectories

Emerging Themes

Global consciousness affecting theological expression
Scientific worldviews requiring response
Religious pluralism as lived reality
Gender justice within traditional frameworks
Environmental crisis demanding theological response

Continuing Traditions

Classical texts remain authoritative
Traditional institutions adapt rather than abandon
Mystical orders maintain experiential dimension
Legal frameworks provide practical grounding

Future Directions

Integration of contemporary philosophy
Neuroscience and consciousness studies
Global ethics and transcendence
Digital transformation of religious learning
Post-secular theological possibilities

Bibliography

Primary Sources (Organized by Period and Genre)

Early Period (1st-3rd Century AH / 7th-9th Century CE)

Quranic Exegesis

Al-Farrā', Abū Zakariyyā Yaḥyā ibn Ziyād. *Ma'ānī al-Qur'ān*. Ed. Aḥmad Yūsuf Najātī et al. 3 vols. Cairo: Dār al-Miṣriyya li'l-Ta'līf wa'l-Tarjama, 1955-1972.

Ibn Qutayba, Abū Muḥammad 'Abd Allāh ibn Muslim. *Ta'wīl Mushkil al-Qur'ān*. Ed. al-Sayyid Aḥmad Ṣaqr. Cairo: Dār al-Turāth, 1973.

Muqātil ibn Sulaymān. *Tafsīr Muqātil ibn Sulaymān*. Ed. 'Abd Allāh Maḥmūd Shiḥāta. 5 vols. Beirut: Mu'assasat al-Ta'rīkh al-'Arabī, 2002.

Al-Ṭabarī, Abū Ja'far Muḥammad ibn Jarīr. *Jāmi' al-Bayān 'an Ta'wīl Āy al-Qur'ān*. Ed. 'Abd Allāh ibn 'Abd al-Muḥsin al-Turkī. 26 vols. Cairo: Dār Hajar, 2001.

Hadith Collections

Al-Bukhārī, Muḥammad ibn Ismā'īl. *Ṣaḥīḥ al-Bukhārī*. Ed. Muḥammad Zuhayr ibn Nāṣir al-Nāṣir. 9 vols. Beirut: Dār Ṭawq al-Najāt, 2001.

Muslim ibn al-Ḥajjāj. *Ṣaḥīḥ Muslim*. Ed. Muḥammad Fu'ād 'Abd al-Bāqī. 5 vols. Beirut: Dār Iḥyā' al-Turāth al-'Arabī, n.d.

Al-Tirmidhī, Muḥammad ibn 'Īsā. *Sunan al-Tirmidhī*. Ed. Aḥmad Muḥammad Shākir et al. 5 vols. Cairo: Muṣṭafā al-Bābī al-Ḥalabī, 1975.

Early Theological Works

Abū Ḥanīfa, al-Nu'mān ibn Thābit. *Al-Fiqh al-Akbar*. In *al-'Ālim wa'l-Muta'allim*. Ed. Muḥammad Zāhid al-Kawtharī. Cairo: al-Maktaba al-Azhariyya li'l-Turāth, 2001.

Al-Ḥasan al-Baṣrī (attributed). *Risāla fi'l-Qadar*. Ed. Michael Schwarz in "The Letter of al-Ḥasan al-Baṣrī." Oriens 20 (1967): 15-30.

Ibn Abī Zayd al-Qayrawānī. *al-Risāla*. Ed. Abū al-Faḍl al-Dimyāṭī. Beirut: Dār Ibn Ḥazm, 2006.

Early Mystical Works

Al-Muḥāsibī, al-Ḥārith ibn Asad. *al-Ri'āya li-Ḥuqūq Allāh*. Ed. 'Abd al-Qādir Aḥmad 'Aṭā'. Beirut: Dār al-Kutub al-'Ilmiyya, 1985.

Al-Muḥāsibī. *al-Tawahhum*. Ed. 'Abd al-Qādir Aḥmad 'Aṭā'. Cairo: Dār al-I'tiṣām, 1980.

Classical Period (4th-7th Century AH / 10th-13th Century CE)

Theological Treatises

Al-Ash'arī, Abū'l-Ḥasan. *al-Ibāna 'an Uṣūl al-Diyāna*. Ed. Fawqiyya Ḥusayn Maḥmūd. Cairo: Dār al-Anṣār, 1977.

Al-Ash'arī. *al-Luma' fi'l-Radd 'alā Ahl al-Zaygh wa'l-Bida'*. Ed. Richard J. McCarthy. Beirut: Imprimerie Catholique, 1953.

Al-Ash'arī. *Maqālāt al-Islāmiyyīn wa-Ikhtilāf al-Muṣallīn*. Ed. Helmut Ritter. Wiesbaden: Franz Steiner, 1980.

Al-Bāqillānī, Abū Bakr Muḥammad. *al-Tamhīd*. Ed. Richard J. McCarthy. Beirut: al-Maktaba al-Sharqiyya, 1957.

Al-Bāqillānī. *al-Inṣāf fīmā Yajibu I'tiqāduhu wa-lā Yajūzu al-Jahl bihi*. Ed. Muḥammad Zāhid al-Kawtharī. Cairo: al-Maktaba al-Azhariyya li'l-Turāth, 2000.

Al-Bayhaqī, Abū Bakr Aḥmad. *al-Asmā' wa'l-Ṣifāt*. Ed. 'Abd Allāh ibn Muḥammad al-Ḥāshidī. 2 vols. Riyadh: Maktabat al-Sawādī, 1993.

Al-Ghazālī, Abū Ḥāmid. *al-Iqtiṣād fī'l-I'tiqād*. Ed. I. A. Çubukçu and H. Atay. Ankara: Nur Matbaasi, 1962.

Al-Ghazālī. *Tahāfut al-Falāsifa*. Ed. Michael E. Marmura. Provo: Brigham Young University Press, 2000.

Al-Juwaynī, Imām al-Ḥaramayn. *al-Irshād ilā Qawāṭi' al-Adilla fī Uṣūl al-I'tiqād*. Ed. Muḥammad Yūsuf Mūsā and 'Alī 'Abd al-Mun'im 'Abd al-Ḥamīd. Cairo: Maktabat al-Khānjī, 1950.

Al-Juwaynī. *al-Shāmil fī Uṣūl al-Dīn*. Ed. 'Alī Sāmī al-Nashshār et al. Alexandria: Mansha'at al-Ma'ārif, 1969.

Al-Māturīdī, Abū Manṣūr. *Kitāb al-Tawḥīd*. Ed. Fathalla Kholeif. Beirut: Dār al-Mashriq, 1970.

Al-Māturīdī. *Ta'wīlāt Ahl al-Sunna*. Ed. Majdī Bāsallūm. 10 vols. Beirut: Dār al-Kutub al-'Ilmiyya, 2005.

Al-Nasafī, Abū'l-Mu'īn Maymūn. *Tabṣirat al-Adilla fī Uṣūl al-Dīn*. Ed. Hüseyin Atay. 2 vols. Ankara: Diyanet İşleri Başkanlığı, 1993.

Al-Qāḍī 'Abd al-Jabbār. *al-Mughnī fī Abwāb al-Tawḥīd wa'l-'Adl*. Ed. various. 20 vols. Cairo: al-Dār al-Miṣriyya li'l-Ta'līf wa'l-Tarjama, 1960-1969.

Al-Rāzī, Fakhr al-Dīn. *al-Maṭālib al-'Āliya min al-'Ilm al-Ilāhī*. Ed. Aḥmad Ḥijāzī al-Saqqā. 9 vols. Beirut: Dār al-Kitāb al-'Arabī, 1987.

Al-Shahrastānī, Muḥammad ibn 'Abd al-Karīm. *al-Milal wa'l-Niḥal*. Ed. William Cureton. London: Society for the Publication of Oriental Texts, 1846.

Al-Ṭaḥāwī, Abū Ja'far. *Matn al-'Aqīda al-Ṭaḥāwiyya*. Various editions with commentaries.

Philosophical Works

Al-Fārābī, Abū Naṣr. *Ārā' Ahl al-Madīna al-Fāḍila*. Ed. Albert Naṣrī Nādir. Beirut: Dār al-Mashriq, 1985.

Al-Fārābī. *al-Jam' bayna Ra'yay al-Ḥakīmayn*. Ed. Albert Naṣrī Nādir. Beirut: Dār al-Mashriq, 1968.

Ibn Rushd (Averroes). *Tahāfut al-Tahāfut*. Ed. Maurice Bouyges. Beirut: Imprimerie Catholique, 1930.

Ibn Rushd. *Faṣl al-Maqāl fīmā bayna al-Ḥikma wa'l-Sharī'a min al-Ittiṣāl*. Ed. George F. Hourani. Leiden: Brill, 1959.

Ibn Sīnā (Avicenna). *al-Shifā': al-Ilāhiyyāt*. Ed. Georges C. Anawati et al. 2 vols. Cairo: Organisation Générale des Imprimeries Gouvernementales, 1960.

Ibn Sīnā. *al-Najāt min al-Gharq fī Baḥr al-Ḍalālāt*. Ed. Muḥammad Taqī Dānishpazhūh. Tehran: Dānishgāh-i Tihrān, 1985.

Ibn Sīnā. *al-Ishārāt wa'l-Tanbīhāt*. Ed. Sulaymān Dunyā. 4 vols. Cairo: Dār al-Ma'ārif, 1957-1960.

Al-Kindī, Abū Yūsuf Ya'qūb. *Rasā'il al-Kindī al-Falsafiyya*. Ed. Muḥammad 'Abd al-Hādī Abū Rīda. 2 vols. Cairo: Dār al-Fikr al-'Arabī, 1950-1953.

Al-Suhrawardī, Shihāb al-Dīn. *Ḥikmat al-Ishrāq*. Ed. Henry Corbin. Tehran: Institut Franco-Iranien, 1952.

Al-Suhrawardī. *al-Talwīḥāt al-Lawḥiyya wa'l-'Arshiyya*. Ed. Najafqulī Ḥabībī. Tehran: Imperial Iranian Academy of Philosophy, 1977.

Mystical Treatises

Al-Ghazālī, Abū Ḥāmid. *Iḥyā' 'Ulūm al-Dīn*. 4 vols. Beirut: Dār al-Ma'rifa, n.d.

Al-Ghazālī. *Mishkāt al-Anwār*. Ed. Abū'l-'Alā 'Afīfī. Cairo: al-Dār al-Qawmiyya, 1964.

Al-Ghazālī. *al-Maqṣad al-Asnā fī Sharḥ Ma'ānī Asmā' Allāh al-Ḥusnā*. Ed. Fadlou A. Shehadi. Beirut: Dār al-Mashriq, 1971.

Al-Hujwīrī, 'Alī ibn 'Uthmān. *Kashf al-Maḥjūb*. Ed. Valentin Zhukovsky. Leningrad: Dār al-Kutub al-'Ilmiyya, 1926.

Ibn 'Arabī, Muḥyī al-Dīn. *al-Futūḥāt al-Makkiyya*. Ed. 'Abd al-'Azīz Sulṭān al-Manṣūb. 12 vols. Cairo: al-Majlis al-A'lā li'l-Thaqāfa, 2017.

Ibn 'Arabī. *Fuṣūṣ al-Ḥikam*. Ed. Abū'l-'Alā 'Afīfī. Beirut: Dār al-Kitāb al-'Arabī, 1946.

Ibn 'Aṭā' Allāh al-Iskandarī. *al-Ḥikam al-'Aṭā'iyya*. Ed. Paul Nwyia. Beirut: Dār al-Mashriq, 1990.

Al-Kalābādhī, Abū Bakr. *al-Ta'arruf li-Madhhab Ahl al-Taṣawwuf*. Ed. Arthur John Arberry. Cairo: Maktabat al-Khānjī, 1934.

Al-Makkī, Abū Ṭālib. *Qūt al-Qulūb fī Mu'āmalat al-Maḥbūb*. Ed. 'Āṣim Ibrāhīm al-Kayyālī. 2 vols. Beirut: Dār al-Kutub al-'Ilmiyya, 2005.

Al-Niffarī, Muḥammad ibn 'Abd al-Jabbār. *al-Mawāqif wa'l-Mukhāṭabāt*. Ed. Arthur John Arberry. Cairo: Maktabat al-Khānjī, 1935.

Al-Qushayrī, 'Abd al-Karīm. *al-Risāla al-Qushayriyya*. Ed. 'Abd al-Ḥalīm Maḥmūd and Maḥmūd ibn al-Sharīf. Cairo: Dār al-Ma'ārif, 1995.

Al-Qushayrī. *Laṭā'if al-Ishārāt*. Ed. Ibrāhīm Basyūnī. 3 vols. Cairo: al-Hay'a al-Miṣriyya al-'Āmma li'l-Kitāb, 1981-1983.

Al-Sarrāj, Abū Naṣr. *Kitāb al-Luma' fi'l-Taṣawwuf*. Ed. Reynold A. Nicholson. Leiden: Brill, 1914.

Quranic Commentaries

Al-Qurṭubī, Muḥammad ibn Aḥmad. *al-Jāmi' li-Aḥkām al-Qur'ān*. Ed. Aḥmad al-Bardūnī and Ibrāhīm Aṭfīsh. 20 vols. Cairo: Dār al-Kutub al-Miṣriyya, 1964.

Al-Rāzī, Fakhr al-Dīn. *Mafātīḥ al-Ghayb (al-Tafsīr al-Kabīr)*. 32 vols. Beirut: Dār Iḥyā' al-Turāth al-'Arabī, 1420 AH.

Al-Zamakhsharī, Maḥmūd ibn 'Umar. *al-Kashshāf 'an Ḥaqā'iq Ghawāmiḍ al-Tanzīl*. 4 vols. Beirut: Dār al-Kitāb al-'Arabī, 1407 AH.

Post-Classical Period (8th-12th Century AH / 14th-18th Century CE)

Later Theological Works

Al-Ījī, 'Aḍud al-Dīn. *al-Mawāqif fī 'Ilm al-Kalām*. Ed. 'Abd al-Raḥmān 'Umayra. 3 vols. Beirut: Dār al-Jīl, 1997.

Ibn Taymiyya, Taqī al-Dīn. *Dar' Ta'āruḍ al-'Aql wa'l-Naql*. Ed. Muḥammad Rashād Sālim. 11 vols. Riyadh: Jāmi'at al-Imām Muḥammad ibn Sa'ūd, 1991.

Ibn Taymiyya. *Majmū' al-Fatāwā*. Ed. 'Abd al-Raḥmān ibn Muḥammad ibn Qāsim. 37 vols. Medina: Majma' al-Malik Fahd, 1995.

Al-Sanūsī, Muḥammad ibn Yūsuf. *Sharḥ al-'Aqīda al-Ṣughrā*. Various editions.

Al-Taftāzānī, Sa'd al-Dīn. *Sharḥ al-'Aqā'id al-Nasafiyya*. Ed. Claude Salamé. Damascus:

Ministry of Culture, 1974.

Philosophical Developments

Al-Dawwānī, Jalāl al-Dīn. *Sharḥ al-'Aqā'id al-'Aḍudiyya*. Various lithograph editions.

Ibn Kamāl Pāshā. *Rasā'il Ibn Kamāl*. Ed. Aḥmad Cevdet. Istanbul: Maṭba'a-i 'Āmire, 1316 AH.

Mullā Ṣadrā, Ṣadr al-Dīn al-Shīrāzī. *al-Ḥikma al-Muta'āliya fī'l-Asfār al-'Aqliyya al-Arba'a*. Ed. various. 9 vols. Beirut: Dār Iḥyā' al-Turāth al-'Arabī, 1981.

Mullā Ṣadrā. *al-Shawāhid al-Rubūbiyya*. Ed. Sayyid Jalāl al-Dīn Āshtiyānī. Mashhad: al-Markaz al-Jāmi'ī li'l-Nashr, 1981.

Later Mystical Works

'Abd al-Karīm al-Jīlī. *al-Insān al-Kāmil fī Ma'rifat al-Awākhir wa'l-Awā'il*. 2 vols. Cairo: Muṣṭafā al-Bābī al-Ḥalabī, 1956.

'Abd al-Ghanī al-Nābulusī. *Sharḥ Fuṣūṣ al-Ḥikam*. Various manuscript editions.

Al-Sha'rānī, 'Abd al-Wahhāb. *al-Yawāqīt wa'l-Jawāhir fī Bayān 'Aqā'id al-Akābir*. 2 vols. Cairo: Muṣṭafā al-Bābī al-Ḥalabī, 1959.

Aḥmad Sirhindī. *Maktūbāt-i Imām Rabbānī*. Ed. Nūr Aḥmad. Karachi: Educational Press, 1977.

Modern Period (13th-15th Century AH / 19th-21st Century CE)

Reformist Works

'Abduh, Muḥammad. *Risālat al-Tawḥīd*. Ed. Maḥmūd Abū Rayya. Cairo: Dār al-Ma'ārif, 1966.

Iqbal, Muhammad. *The Reconstruction of Religious Thought in Islam*. Ed. M. Saeed Sheikh. Lahore: Institute of Islamic Culture, 1989.

Nursi, Said. *Risale-i Nur Külliyatı*. Istanbul: Nesil, 2006.

Shaltūt, Maḥmūd. *al-Islām: 'Aqīda wa-Sharī'a*. Cairo: Dār al-Shurūq, 2001.

Contemporary Philosophical Works

Nasr, Seyyed Hossein. *Knowledge and the Sacred*. Edinburgh: Edinburgh University Press, 1981.

Rahman, Fazlur. *Major Themes of the Qur'an*. Minneapolis: Bibliotheca Islamica, 1980.

Soroush, Abdolkarim. *The Expansion of Prophetic Experience*. Trans. Nilou Mobasser. Leiden: Brill, 2009.

Secondary Sources (Organized by Topic)

General Studies on Islamic Theology

Abrahamov, Binyamin. *Islamic Theology: Traditionalism and Rationalism*. Edinburgh: Edinburgh University Press, 1998.

Gardet, Louis and M.-M. Anawati. *Introduction à la théologie musulmane*. Paris: Vrin, 1948.

Jackson, Sherman A. *On the Boundaries of Theological Tolerance in Islam: Abū Ḥāmid al-Ghazālī's Fayṣal al-Tafriqa*. Oxford: Oxford University Press, 2002.

Madelung, Wilferd. *Religious Schools and Sects in Medieval Islam*. London: Variorum Reprints, 1985.
Makdisi, George. *Ibn 'Aqil et la résurgence de l'Islam traditionaliste au XIe siècle*. Damascus: Institut Français de Damas, 1963.
Nagel, Tilman. *The History of Islamic Theology from Muhammad to the Present*. Trans. Thomas Thornton. Princeton: Markus Wiener, 2000.
Watt, W. Montgomery. *The Formative Period of Islamic Thought*. Edinburgh: Edinburgh University Press, 1973.
Wolfson, Harry Austryn. *The Philosophy of the Kalam*. Cambridge, MA: Harvard University Press, 1976.

Studies on Divine Transcendence and Attributes

Burrell, David B. *Knowing the Unknowable God: Ibn-Sina, Maimonides, Aquinas*. Notre Dame: University of Notre Dame Press, 1986.
El-Bizri, Nader. *The Phenomenological Quest between Avicenna and Heidegger*. Binghamton: Global Publications, 2000.
Frank, Richard M. *Beings and Their Attributes: The Teaching of the Basrian School of the Mu'tazila in the Classical Period*. Albany: State University of New York Press, 1978.
Gimaret, Daniel. *Les noms divins en Islam*. Paris: Cerf, 1988.
Netton, Ian Richard. *Allah Transcendent: Studies in the Structure and Semiotics of Islamic Philosophy, Theology and Cosmology*. London: Routledge, 1989.
Rahman, Fazlur. *The Philosophy of Mulla Sadra*. Albany: State University of New York Press, 1975.
Rudolph, Ulrich. *Al-Māturīdī and the Development of Sunnī Theology in Samarqand*. Trans. Rodrigo Adem. Leiden: Brill, 2015.
Williams, Wesley. *Aspects of the Creed of Imam Ahmad Ibn Hanbal: A Study of Anthropomorphism in Early Islamic Discourse*. International Journal of Middle East Studies 34.3 (2002): 441-463.

Ash'arite and Maturidite Studies

Allard, Michel. *Le problème des attributs divins dans la doctrine d'al-Aš'arī et de ses premiers grands disciples*. Beirut: Imprimerie Catholique, 1965.
Frank, Richard M. *Al-Ghazālī and the Ash'arite School*. Durham: Duke University Press, 1994.
McCarthy, Richard J. *The Theology of al-Ash'arī*. Beirut: Imprimerie Catholique, 1953.
Pessagno, J. Meric. *Imdād al-Fattāḥ and the Development of Maturidi Kalam*. Leiden: Brill, 2018.
Thiele, Jan. *Kausalität in der mu'tazilitischen Kosmologie*. Leiden: Brill, 2011.

Mu'tazilite Studies

Hourani, George F. *Islamic Rationalism: The Ethics of 'Abd al-Jabbār*. Oxford: Clarendon Press, 1971.
Martin, Richard C., Mark R. Woodward, and Dwi S. Atmaja. *Defenders of Reason in Islam: Mu'tazilism from Medieval School to Modern Symbol*. Oxford: Oneworld, 1997.
Peters, J. R. T. M. *God's Created Speech: A Study in the Speculative Theology of the Mu'tazilī Qāḍī l-Quḍāt Abū l-Ḥasan 'Abd al-Jabbār*. Leiden: Brill, 1976.

Van Ess, Josef. *Theologie und Gesellschaft im 2. und 3. Jahrhundert Hidschra*. 6 vols. Berlin: De Gruyter, 1991-1997.

Islamic Philosophy

Adamson, Peter. *Al-Kindī*. Oxford: Oxford University Press, 2007.
Corbin, Henry. *Avicenna and the Visionary Recital*. Trans. Willard R. Trask. Princeton: Princeton University Press, 1960.
Davidson, Herbert A. *Alfarabi, Avicenna, and Averroes on Intellect*. Oxford: Oxford University Press, 1992.
Fakhry, Majid. *A History of Islamic Philosophy*. 3rd ed. New York: Columbia University Press, 2004.
Gutas, Dimitri. *Avicenna and the Aristotelian Tradition*. 2nd ed. Leiden: Brill, 2014.
Kalin, Ibrahim. *Knowledge in Later Islamic Philosophy: Mullā Ṣadrā on Existence, Intellect, and Intuition*. Oxford: Oxford University Press, 2010.
Leaman, Oliver. *An Introduction to Classical Islamic Philosophy*. Cambridge: Cambridge University Press, 2002.
McGinnis, Jon. *Avicenna*. Oxford: Oxford University Press, 2010.
Nasr, Seyyed Hossein. *Three Muslim Sages: Avicenna, Suhrawardī, Ibn 'Arabī*. Cambridge, MA: Harvard University Press, 1964.
Rizvi, Sajjad H. *Mullā Ṣadrā and Metaphysics: Modulation of Being*. London: Routledge, 2009.
Wisnovsky, Robert. *Avicenna's Metaphysics in Context*. Ithaca: Cornell University Press, 2003.
Ziai, Hossein. *Knowledge and Illumination: A Study of Suhrawardī's Ḥikmat al-Ishrāq*. Atlanta: Scholars Press, 1990.

Sufism and Mystical Theology

Addas, Claude. *Quest for the Red Sulphur: The Life of Ibn 'Arabī*. Trans. Peter Kingsley. Cambridge: Islamic Texts Society, 1993.
Arberry, Arthur J. *Sufism: An Account of the Mystics of Islam*. London: Allen & Unwin, 1950.
Böwering, Gerhard. *The Mystical Vision of Existence in Classical Islam: The Qur'ānic Hermeneutics of the Ṣūfī Sahl At-Tustarī*. Berlin: De Gruyter, 1980.
Chittick, William C. *The Sufi Path of Knowledge: Ibn al-'Arabī's Metaphysics of Imagination*. Albany: State University of New York Press, 1989.
Chittick, William C. *The Self-Disclosure of God: Principles of Ibn al-'Arabī's Cosmology*. Albany: State University of New York Press, 1998.
Chodkiewicz, Michel. *An Ocean Without Shore: Ibn Arabî, the Book, and the Law*. Trans. David Streight. Albany: State University of New York Press, 1993.
Cornell, Vincent J. *Realm of the Saint: Power and Authority in Moroccan Sufism*. Austin: University of Texas Press, 1998.
Ernst, Carl W. *Words of Ecstasy in Sufism*. Albany: State University of New York Press, 1985.
Izutsu, Toshihiko. *Sufism and Taoism: A Comparative Study of Key Philosophical Concepts*. Berkeley: University of California Press, 1983.
Karamustafa, Ahmet T. *Sufism: The Formative Period*. Edinburgh: Edinburgh University Press, 2007.
Knysh, Alexander. *Ibn 'Arabi in the Later Islamic Tradition: The Making of a Polemical

Image in Medieval Islam*. Albany: State University of New York Press, 1999.
Massignon, Louis. *The Passion of al-Hallāj: Mystic and Martyr of Islam*. Trans. Herbert Mason. 4 vols. Princeton: Princeton University Press, 1982.
Meier, Fritz. *Essays on Islamic Piety and Mysticism*. Trans. John O'Kane. Leiden: Brill, 1999.
Morris, James Winston. *The Reflective Heart: Discovering Spiritual Intelligence in Ibn 'Arabī's Meccan Illuminations*. Louisville: Fons Vitae, 2005.
Nwyia, Paul. *Exégèse coranique et langage mystique*. Beirut: Dar el-Machreq, 1970.
Radtke, Bernd and John O'Kane. *The Concept of Sainthood in Early Islamic Mysticism*. London: Curzon Press, 1996.
Schimmel, Annemarie. *Mystical Dimensions of Islam*. Chapel Hill: University of North Carolina Press, 1975.
Sells, Michael A. *Early Islamic Mysticism: Sufi, Qur'an, Mi'raj, Poetic and Theological Writings*. New York: Paulist Press, 1996.

Quranic Studies and Hermeneutics

Ayoub, Mahmoud. *The Qur'an and Its Interpreters*. 2 vols. Albany: State University of New York Press, 1984-1992.
Boullata, Issa J. *Literary Structures of Religious Meaning in the Qur'an*. Richmond: Curzon, 2000.
Gätje, Helmut. *The Qur'ān and Its Exegesis*. Trans. Alford T. Welch. Berkeley: University of California Press, 1976.
Goldziher, Ignaz. *Die Richtungen der islamischen Koranauslegung*. Leiden: Brill, 1920.
Heath, Peter. *Allegory and Philosophy in Avicenna (Ibn Sînâ)*. Philadelphia: University of Pennsylvania Press, 1992.
Izutsu, Toshihiko. *God and Man in the Koran: Semantics of the Koranic Weltanschauung*. Tokyo: Keio Institute of Cultural and Linguistic Studies, 1964.
Izutsu, Toshihiko. *Ethico-Religious Concepts in the Qur'ān*. Montreal: McGill University Press, 1966.
McAuliffe, Jane Dammen, ed. *Encyclopaedia of the Qur'ān*. 6 vols. Leiden: Brill, 2001-2006.
Rahman, Fazlur. *Major Themes of the Qur'an*. 2nd ed. Chicago: University of Chicago Press, 2009.
Saleh, Walid A. *The Formation of the Classical Tafsīr Tradition: The Qur'ān Commentary of al-Tha'labī*. Leiden: Brill, 2004.
Wild, Stefan, ed. *The Qur'an as Text*. Leiden: Brill, 1996.

Modern Islamic Thought

Abu-Rabi', Ibrahim M. *Contemporary Arab Thought: Studies in Post-1967 Arab Intellectual History*. London: Pluto Press, 2004.
Adams, Charles C. *Islam and Modernism in Egypt*. London: Oxford University Press, 1933.
Arkoun, Mohammed. *The Unthought in Contemporary Islamic Thought*. London: Saqi Books, 2002.
Esposito, John L. and John O. Voll. *Makers of Contemporary Islam*. Oxford: Oxford University Press, 2001.
Hourani, Albert. *Arabic Thought in the Liberal Age, 1798-1939*. Cambridge: Cambridge University Press, 1983.

Keddie, Nikki R. *An Islamic Response to Imperialism: Political and Religious Writings of Sayyid Jamāl ad-Dīn "al-Afghānī"*. Berkeley: University of California Press, 1983.

Kerr, Malcolm H. *Islamic Reform: The Political and Legal Theories of Muḥammad 'Abduh and Rashīd Riḍā*. Berkeley: University of California Press, 1966.

Kurzman, Charles, ed. *Liberal Islam: A Sourcebook*. Oxford: Oxford University Press, 1998.

Moaddel, Mansoor and Kamran Talattof, eds. *Contemporary Debates in Islam: An Anthology of Modernist and Fundamentalist Thought*. New York: St. Martin's Press, 2000.

Rahman, Fazlur. *Islam and Modernity: Transformation of an Intellectual Tradition*. Chicago: University of Chicago Press, 1982.

Taji-Farouki, Suha. *Modern Muslim Intellectuals and the Qur'an*. Oxford: Oxford University Press, 2004.

Vahdat, Farzin. *God and Juggernaut: Iran's Intellectual Encounter with Modernity*. Syracuse: Syracuse University Press, 2002.

Comparative and Methodological Studies

Burrell, David B. *Freedom and Creation in Three Traditions*. Notre Dame: University of Notre Dame Press, 1993.

Chittick, William C. *In Search of the Lost Heart: Explorations in Islamic Thought*. Albany: State University of New York Press, 2012.

Corbin, Henry. *History of Islamic Philosophy*. Trans. Liadain Sherrard. London: Kegan Paul International, 1993.

Hodgson, Marshall G. S. *The Venture of Islam*. 3 vols. Chicago: University of Chicago Press, 1974.

Hourani, George F. *Reason and Tradition in Islamic Ethics*. Cambridge: Cambridge University Press, 1985.

Kraemer, Joel L. *Humanism in the Renaissance of Islam*. Leiden: Brill, 1992.

Makdisi, George. *The Rise of Colleges: Institutions of Learning in Islam and the West*. Edinburgh: Edinburgh University Press, 1981.

Rosenthal, Franz. *Knowledge Triumphant: The Concept of Knowledge in Medieval Islam*. Leiden: Brill, 1970.

Sabra, A. I. *The Optics of Ibn al-Haytham*. 2 vols. London: Warburg Institute, 1989.

Winter, Tim, ed. *The Cambridge Companion to Classical Islamic Theology*. Cambridge: Cambridge University Press, 2008.

Specialized Monographs on Divine Transcendence

Abrahamov, Binyamin. *Anthropomorphism and Interpretation of the Qur'ān in the Theology of al-Qāsim ibn Ibrāhīm*. Leiden: Brill, 1996.

Adamson, Peter. *The Arabic Plotinus: A Philosophical Study of the "Theology of Aristotle"*. London: Duckworth, 2002.

Arnaldez, Roger. *Grammaire et théologie chez Ibn Hazm de Cordoue*. Paris: Vrin, 1956.

Bello, Iysa A. *The Medieval Islamic Controversy Between Philosophy and Orthodoxy: Ijmā' and Ta'wīl in the Conflict Between al-Ghazālī and Ibn Rushd*. Leiden: Brill, 1989.

Black, Deborah L. *Logic and Aristotle's Rhetoric and Poetics in Medieval Arabic Philosophy*. Leiden: Brill, 1990.

Böwering, Gerhard. *The Mystical Vision of Existence in Classical Islam*. Berlin: De Gruyter,

1980.
Brockopp, Jonathan E., ed. *Islamic Ethics of Life: Abortion, War, and Euthanasia*. Columbia: University of South Carolina Press, 2003.
Daiber, Hans. *The Islamic Concept of Belief in the 4th/10th Century*. Tokyo: Institute for the Study of Languages and Cultures of Asia and Africa, 1995.
El-Bizri, Nader, ed. *The Ikhwān al-Ṣafā' and their Rasā'il: An Introduction*. Oxford: Oxford University Press, 2008.
Fadel, Mohammad. *Adjudication in the Mālikī Madhhab: A Study of Legal Process in Medieval Islamic Law*. PhD diss., University of Chicago, 1995.
Frank, Richard M. *Creation and the Cosmic System: Al-Ghazālī and Avicenna*. Heidelberg: Carl Winter, 1992.
Gardet, Louis. *La pensée religieuse d'Avicenne*. Paris: Vrin, 1951.
Gimaret, Daniel. *La doctrine d'al-Ash'arī*. Paris: Cerf, 1990.
Griffel, Frank. *Al-Ghazālī's Philosophical Theology*. Oxford: Oxford University Press, 2009.
Hallaq, Wael B. *Ibn Taymiyya Against the Greek Logicians*. Oxford: Clarendon Press, 1993.
Hourani, George F. *Averroes on the Harmony of Religion and Philosophy*. London: Luzac, 1961.
Ibrahim, Lutpi. *The Concept of Iḥsān in al-Ghazālī*. PhD diss., University of Edinburgh, 1986.
Inati, Shams. *The Problem of Evil: Ibn Sînâ's Theodicy*. Binghamton: Global Publications, 2000.
Jackson, Sherman A. *Islam and the Problem of Black Suffering*. Oxford: Oxford University Press, 2009.
Janssens, Jules. *An Annotated Bibliography on Ibn Sînâ*. Leuven: University Press, 1991.
Khalil, Atif. *Repentance and the Return to God: Tawba in Early Sufism*. Albany: State University of New York Press, 2018.
Langermann, Y. Tzvi. *The Jews and the Sciences in the Middle Ages*. Aldershot: Ashgate, 1999.
Lizzini, Olga. *Fluxus (fayd): Indagine sui fondamenti della metafisica e della fisica di Avicenna*. Bari: Pagina, 2011.
Marmura, Michael E. *Probing in Islamic Philosophy: Studies in the Philosophies of Ibn Sina, al-Ghazali and Other Major Muslim Thinkers*. Binghamton: Global Academic Publishing, 2005.
Morris, James W. *Ibn 'Arabi and His Interpreters*. Journal of the American Oriental Society 106-107 (1986-1987).
Murata, Sachiko. *The Tao of Islam: A Sourcebook on Gender Relationships in Islamic Thought*. Albany: State University of New York Press, 1992.
Ormsby, Eric L. *Theodicy in Islamic Thought: The Dispute Over al-Ghazālī's "Best of All Possible Worlds"*. Princeton: Princeton University Press, 1984.
Picken, Gavin. *Spiritual Purification in Islam: The Life and Works of al-Muḥāsibī*. London: Routledge, 2011.
Renard, John. *Knowledge of God in Classical Sufism*. New York: Paulist Press, 2004.
Shihadeh, Ayman. *The Teleological Ethics of Fakhr al-Dīn al-Rāzī*. Leiden: Brill, 2006.
Street, Tony. *Avicenna and the Principle of Sufficient Reason*. London: The Warburg Institute, 2000.
Treiger, Alexander. *Inspired Knowledge in Islamic Thought: Al-Ghazālī's Theory of Mystical Cognition and Its Avicennian Foundation*. London: Routledge, 2012.

Van Ess, Josef. *The Flowering of Muslim Theology*. Cambridge, MA: Harvard University Press, 2006.
Vasalou, Sophia. *Moral Agents and Their Deserts: The Character of Mu'tazilite Ethics*. Princeton: Princeton University Press, 2008.
Watt, W. Montgomery. *The Faith and Practice of al-Ghazālī*. London: Allen and Unwin, 1953.
Williams, Wesley. *Aspects of the Creed of Imam Ahmad Ibn Hanbal*. International Journal of Middle East Studies 34 (2002): 441-463.
Winter, Tim. *The Last Trump Card: Islam and the Supersession of Other Faiths*. Studies in Interreligious Dialogue 9.2 (1999): 133-155.
Wolfson, Harry A. *Avicenna, Algazali, and Averroes on Divine Attributes*. In *Studies in the History of Philosophy and Religion*, vol. 2. Cambridge, MA: Harvard University Press, 1977.
Yahya, Osman. *Histoire et classification de l'œuvre d'Ibn 'Arabī*. 2 vols. Damascus: Institut Français de Damas, 1964.
Zaehner, R. C. *Hindu and Muslim Mysticism*. London: Athlone Press, 1960.

Contemporary Studies and Articles

Abrahamov, Binyamin. "Al-Ghazālī's Theory of Causality." Studia Islamica 67 (1988): 75-98.
Adamson, Peter. "Al-Kindī and the Mu'tazila: Divine Attributes, Creation and Freedom." Arabic Sciences and Philosophy 13 (2003): 45-77.
Algar, Hamid. "Imām Mūsā al-Kāẓim and Ṣūfī Tradition." Islamic Studies 42.3 (2003): 431-454.
Amir-Moezzi, Mohammad Ali. "Theology and Ideology: The Shi'i Dimension." In *The Study of Shi'i Islam*, edited by Farhad Daftary and Gurdofarid Miskinzoda. London: I.B. Tauris, 2014.
Anjum, Ovamir. "Sufism without Mysticism: Ibn Qayyim al-Ǧawziyyah's Objectives in Madāriǧ al-Sālikīn." Oriens 49 (2021): 211-267.
Ansari, Zafar Ishaq. "Islamic Juristic Terminology before Šāfi'ī: A Semantic Analysis with Special Reference to Kūfa." Arabica 19.3 (1972): 255-300.
Arberry, A. J. "Avicenna: His Life and Times." In *Avicenna: Scientist and Philosopher*, edited by G. M. Wickens. London: Luzac, 1952.
Baffioni, Carmela. "Al-Nasafī, Maymūn b. Muḥammad." In *Encyclopaedia of Islam*, Second Edition. Leiden: Brill.
Brown, Jonathan A. C. "Scripture in the Modern Muslim World: Qur'an and Hadith." In *Islam in the Modern World*, edited by Jeffrey T. Kenney and Ebrahim Moosa. London: Routledge, 2013.
Calder, Norman. "Tafsīr from Ṭabarī to Ibn Kathīr: Problems in the Description of a Genre." In *Approaches to the Qur'ān*, edited by G. R. Hawting and Abdul-Kader A. Shareef. London: Routledge, 1993.
Cook, Michael. "The Origins of Kalām." Bulletin of the School of Oriental and African Studies 43 (1980): 32-43.
Crone, Patricia. "Excursus II: Ungodly Cosmologies." In *The Oxford Handbook of Islamic Theology*, edited by Sabine Schmidtke. Oxford: Oxford University Press, 2016.
Daiber, Hans. "God versus Causality: Al-Ghazālī's Solution and its Historical Background." In *Islam and Rationality: The Impact of al-Ghazālī*, edited by Georges Tamer. Leiden: Brill, 2015.

El-Rouayheb, Khaled. "From Ibn Ḥajar al-Haytamī to Khayr al-Dīn al-Ālūsī: Changing Views of Ibn Taymiyya among Sunni Islamic Scholars." In *Ibn Taymiyya and His Times*, edited by Yossef Rapoport and Shahab Ahmed. Oxford: Oxford University Press, 2010.

Endress, Gerhard. "The Defense of Reason: The Plea for Philosophy in the Religious Community." Zeitschrift für Geschichte der Arabisch-Islamischen Wissenschaften 6 (1990): 1-49.

Fakhry, Majid. "The Classical Islamic Arguments for the Existence of God." The Muslim World 47 (1957): 133-145.

Frank, Richard M. "Moral Obligation in Classical Muslim Theology." Journal of Religious Ethics 11 (1983): 204-223.

Gilliot, Claude. "Exegesis of the Qur᾽ān: Classical and Medieval." In *Encyclopaedia of the Qur'ān*, edited by Jane Dammen McAuliffe. Leiden: Brill, 2002.

Gimaret, Daniel. "Un problème de théologie musulmane: Dieu veut-il les actes mauvais?" Studia Islamica 40 (1974): 5-73; 41 (1975): 63-92.

Gleave, Robert. "Maḳāṣid al-Sharīʿa." In *Encyclopaedia of Islam*, Second Edition. Leiden: Brill.

Griffel, Frank. "Al-Ghazālī's Concept of Prophecy: The Introduction of Avicennan Psychology into Ašʿarite Theology." Arabic Sciences and Philosophy 14 (2004): 101-144.

Gutas, Dimitri. "Avicenna's Eastern ('Oriental') Philosophy: Nature, Contents, Transmission." Arabic Sciences and Philosophy 10 (2000): 159-180.

Hallaq, Wael B. "Was the Gate of Ijtihad Closed?" International Journal of Middle East Studies 16 (1984): 3-41.

Harvey, Ramon. "Transcendent God, Rational World: Muʿtazilī Theology and Natural Philosophy." In *The Oxford Handbook of Islamic Theology*, edited by Sabine Schmidtke. Oxford: Oxford University Press, 2016.

Heath, Peter. "Creative Hermeneutics: A Comparative Analysis of Three Islamic Approaches." Arabica 36 (1989): 173-210.

Hoover, Jon. "Ibn Taymiyya's Use of Ibn Rushd to Refute the Incorporealism of Fakhr al-Dīn al-Rāzī." In *Islamic Philosophy from the 12th to the 14th Century*, edited by Abdelkader Al Ghouz. Göttingen: V&R Unipress, 2018.

Ibrahim, Bilal. "Faḫr ad-Dīn ar-Rāzī, Ibn al-Hayṯam and Aristotelian Science: Essentialism versus Phenomenalism in Post-Classical Islamic Thought." Oriens 41 (2013): 379-431.

Inati, Shams. "Ibn Sīnā on Single Expressions." In *Medieval Islamic Philosophical Writings*, edited by Muhammad Ali Khalidi. Cambridge: Cambridge University Press, 2005.

Izutsu, Toshihiko. "The Paradox of Light and Darkness in the Garden of Mystery of Shabastarī." In *Anagogic Qualities of Literature*, edited by Joseph Strelka. University Park: Pennsylvania State University Press, 1971.

Jackson, Sherman A. "The Alchemy of Domination? Some Ashʿarite Responses to Muʿtazilite Ethics." International Journal of Middle East Studies 31 (1999): 185-201.

Janssens, Jules. "Al-Ghazzālī's Tahāfut: Is it Really a Rejection of Ibn Sīnā's Philosophy?" Journal of Islamic Studies 12 (2001): 1-17.

Karamustafa, Ahmet T. "Early Sufism in Eastern Anatolia." In *Classical Persian Sufism: From Its Origins to Rumi*, edited by Leonard Lewisohn. London: Khaniqahi Nimatullahi Publications, 1993.

Kars, Aydogan. "Unsaying God: Negative Theology in Medieval Islam." PhD diss., University of California, Berkeley, 2011.

Khalidi, Muhammad Ali. "Al-Ghazālī on Causality." In *Medieval Islamic Philosophical Writings*, edited by Muhammad Ali Khalidi. Cambridge: Cambridge University Press, 2005.

Knysh, Alexander. "'Orthodoxy' and 'Heresy' in Medieval Islam: An Essay in Reassessment." The Muslim World 83 (1993): 48-67.

Kukkonen, Taneli. "Possible Worlds in the Tahâfut al-Falâsifa: Al-Ghazâlî on Creation and Contingency." Journal of the History of Philosophy 38 (2000): 479-502.

Laoust, Henri. "La pensée et l'action politiques d'al-Māwardī." Revue des études islamiques 36 (1968): 11-92.

Leaman, Oliver. "Ibn Rushd on Happiness and Philosophy." Studia Islamica 52 (1980): 167-181.

Lizzini, Olga. "Ibn Sina's Metaphysics." In *The Stanford Encyclopedia of Philosophy*, edited by Edward N. Zalta. Stanford: Stanford University, 2016.

Madelung, Wilferd. "Al-Māturīdī." In *Encyclopaedia of Islam*, Second Edition. Leiden: Brill.

Makdisi, George. "Ash'arī and the Ash'arites in Islamic Religious History." Studia Islamica 17 (1962): 37-80; 18 (1963): 19-39.

Marmura, Michael E. "Al-Ghazālī's Attitude to the Secular Sciences and Logic." In *Essays on Islamic Philosophy and Science*, edited by George F. Hourani. Albany: State University of New York Press, 1975.

McGinnis, Jon. "Avicenna's Natural Philosophy." In *The Stanford Encyclopedia of Philosophy*, edited by Edward N. Zalta. Stanford: Stanford University, 2016.

Melchert, Christopher. "The Transition from Asceticism to Mysticism at the Middle of the Ninth Century C.E." Studia Islamica 83 (1996): 51-70.

Michot, Jean R. "La pandémie avicennienne au VIe/XIIe siècle." Arabica 40 (1993): 287-344.

Moosa, Ebrahim. "The Debts and Burdens of Critical Islam." In *Progressive Muslims: On Justice, Gender, and Pluralism*, edited by Omid Safi. Oxford: Oneworld, 2003.

Morris, James W. "The Spiritual Ascension: Ibn 'Arabī and the Mi'rāj." Journal of the American Oriental Society 107-108 (1987-1988).

Nagel, Tilman. "Das Problem der Orthodoxie im frühen Islam." Studien zum Minderheitenproblem im Islam 1 (1973): 7-44.

Nasr, Seyyed Hossein. "Existence (wujūd) and Quiddity (māhiyyah) in Islamic Philosophy." International Philosophical Quarterly 29 (1989): 409-428.

Netton, Ian Richard. "Basic Structures and Signs of Alienation in the 'Risālat Ḥayy ibn Yaqẓān' of Ibn Ṭufayl." Journal of Arabic Literature 9 (1978): 21-33.

Ormsby, Eric. "Creation in Time in Islamic Thought with Special Reference to al-Ghazālī." In *God and Creation*, edited by David B. Burrell and Bernard McGinn. Notre Dame: University of Notre Dame Press, 1990.

Pavlin, James. "Sunni Kalām and Theological Controversies." In *History of Islamic Philosophy*, edited by Seyyed Hossein Nasr and Oliver Leaman. London: Routledge, 1996.

Rahman, Fazlur. "The Eternity of the World and the Heavenly Bodies in Post-Avicennan Philosophy." In *Essays on Islamic Philosophy and Science*, edited by George F. Hourani. Albany: State University of New York Press, 1975.

Reinhart, A. Kevin. "Transcendence and Social Practice: Muftīs and Qāḍīs as Religious Interpreters." Annales Islamologiques 27 (1993): 5-25.

Renard, John. "Al-Jihād al-Akbar: Notes on a Theme in Islamic Spirituality." The Muslim World 78 (1988): 225-242.

Rizvi, Sajjad H. "Mysticism and Philosophy: Ibn 'Arabī and Mullā Ṣadrā." In *The Cambridge Companion to Arabic Philosophy*, edited by Peter Adamson and Richard C. Taylor. Cambridge: Cambridge University Press, 2005.

Rosenthal, Franz. "Ibn 'Arabī between 'Philosophy' and 'Mysticism'." Oriens 31 (1988): 1-35.

Sabra, A. I. "The Appropriation and Subsequent Naturalization of Greek Science in Medieval Islam: A Preliminary Statement." History of Science 25 (1987): 223-243.

Schimmel, Annemarie. "Some Aspects of Mystical Prayer in Islam." Die Welt des Islams 2 (1952): 112-125.

Schmidtke, Sabine. "The Theology of al-'Allāma al-Ḥillī." PhD diss., University of Oxford, 1991.

Shihadeh, Ayman. "From al-Ghazālī to al-Rāzī: 6th/12th Century Developments in Muslim Philosophical Theology." Arabic Sciences and Philosophy 15 (2005): 141-179.

Street, Tony. "An Outline of Avicenna's Syllogistic." Archiv für Geschichte der Philosophie 84 (2002): 129-160.

Taylor, Richard C. "Averroes on Psychology and the Principles of Metaphysics." Journal of the History of Philosophy 36 (1998): 507-523.

Treiger, Alexander. "Monism and Monotheism in al-Ghazālī's Mishkāt al-anwār." Journal of Qur'anic Studies 9 (2007): 1-27.

Van Ess, Josef. "The Logical Structure of Islamic Theology." In *Logic in Classical Islamic Culture*, edited by Gustave E. von Grunebaum. Wiesbaden: Otto Harrassowitz, 1970.

Walbridge, John. "Suhrawardī and Illuminationism." In *The Cambridge Companion to Arabic Philosophy*, edited by Peter Adamson and Richard C. Taylor. Cambridge: Cambridge University Press, 2005.

Walker, Paul E. "The Ismaili Vocabulary of Creation." Studia Islamica 40 (1974): 75-85.

Watt, W. Montgomery. "The Origin of the Islamic Doctrine of Acquisition." Journal of the Royal Asiatic Society (1943): 234-247.

Weiss, Bernard. "Knowledge of the Past: The Theory of Tawātur According to Ghazālī." Studia Islamica 61 (1985): 81-105.

Wisnovsky, Robert. "One Aspect of the Avicennian Turn in Sunnī Theology." Arabic Sciences and Philosophy 14 (2004): 65-100.

Wolfson, Harry A. "The Twice-Revealed Averroes." Speculum 36 (1961): 373-392.

Yahya, Osman. "L'œuvre de Ṣadr al-Dīn al-Qūnawī." In *Histoire de la philosophie islamique*, edited by Henry Corbin. Paris: Gallimard, 1986.

Zaehner, R. C. "Abū Yazīd of Bisṭām: A Turning Point in Islamic Mysticism." Indo-Iranian Journal 1 (1957): 286-301.

www.ingramcontent.com/pod-product-compliance
Lightning Source LLC
Chambersburg PA
CBHW061601120626
46550CB00004B/1570
* 9 7 8 1 9 9 9 0 6 5 6 5 2 *